ART: TSUBASA HADUKI
ORIGINAL STORY: REKI KAWAHARA
CHARACTER DESIGN: abec

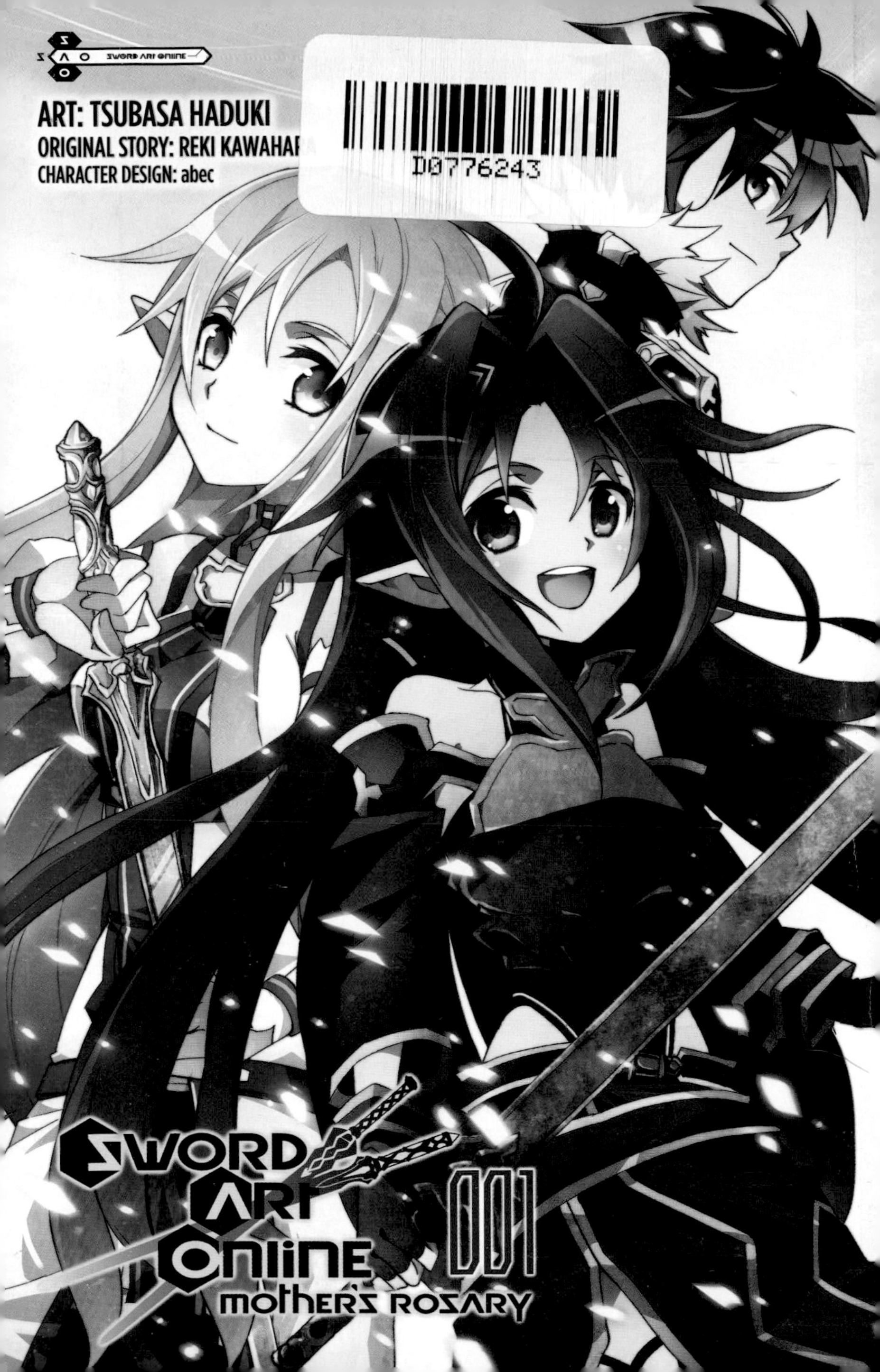
SWORD ART ONLINE
001
mother's rosary

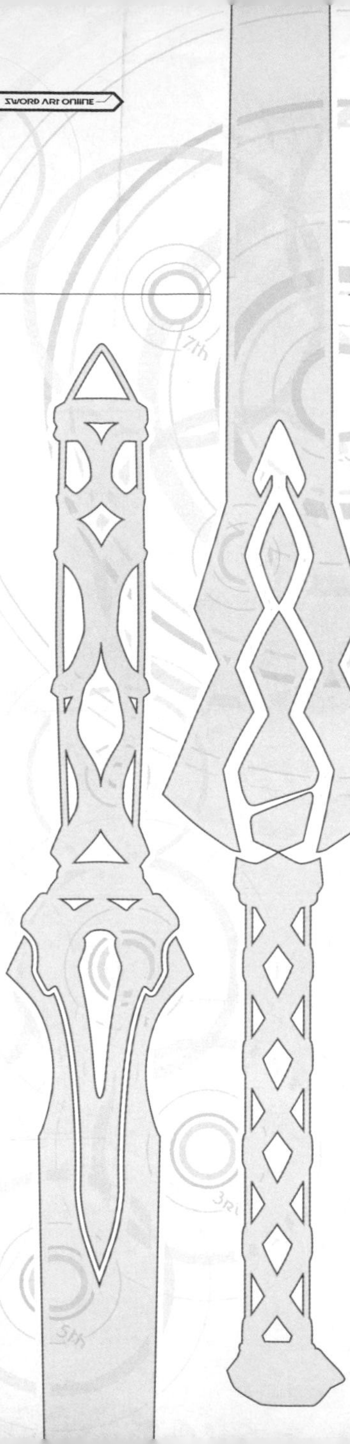

001

SWORD ART ONLINE mother's rosary

art : tsubasa haduki
original story : reki kawahara
character design : abec

contents

date : 7 jan 2026 wed 14:56

ymir alfheim online

SWORD ART ONLINE
mother's ROSARY

001

SWORD ART ONLINE mother's ROSARY

art : tsubasa haduki
original story : reki kawahara
character design : abec

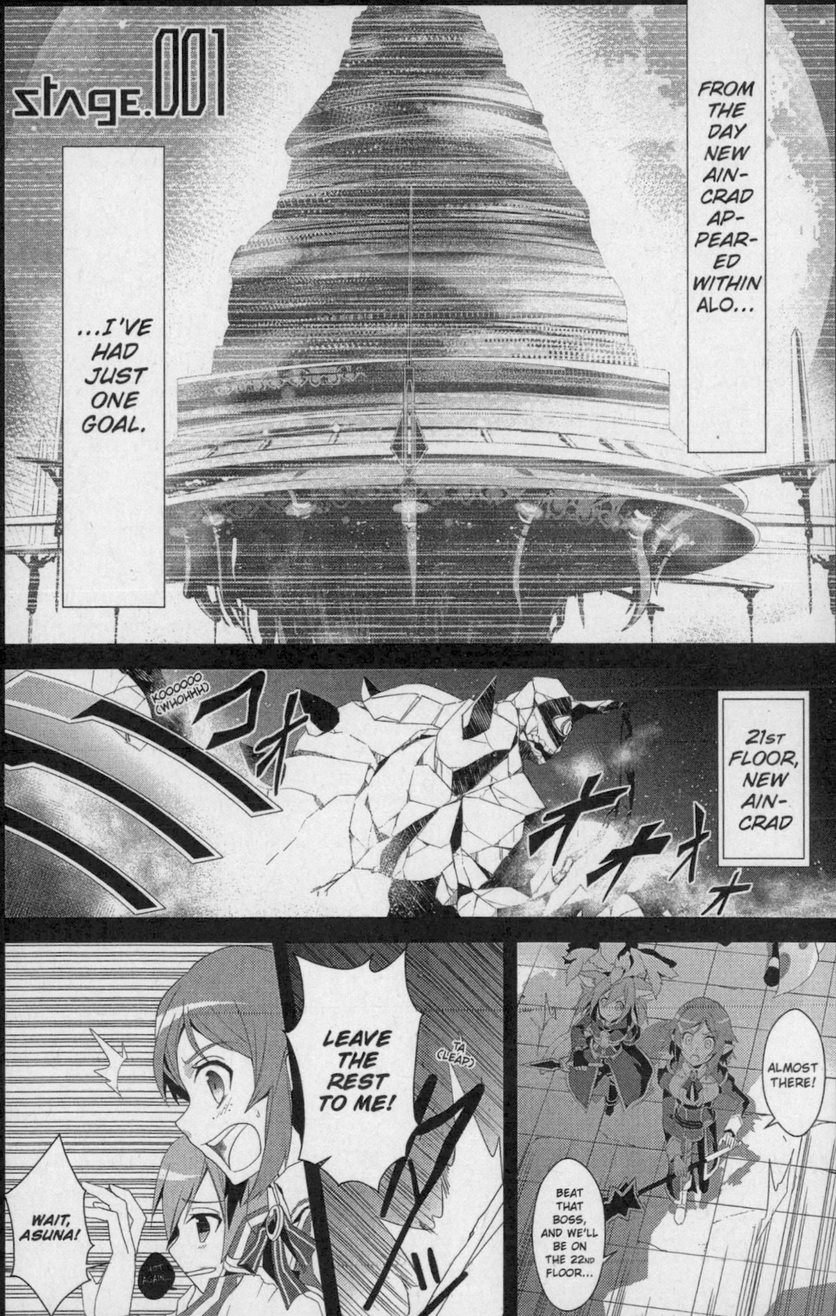
stage.001
FROM THE DAY NEW AINCRAD APPEARED WITHIN ALO...
...I'VE HAD JUST ONE GOAL.
21st FLOOR, NEW AINCRAD
KOOOOOO (WHOHHH)
ALMOST THERE!
BEAT THAT BOSS, AND WE'LL BE ON THE 22nd FLOOR...
TA (LEAP)
LEAVE THE REST TO ME!
WAIT, ASUNA!
NOT AGAIN...

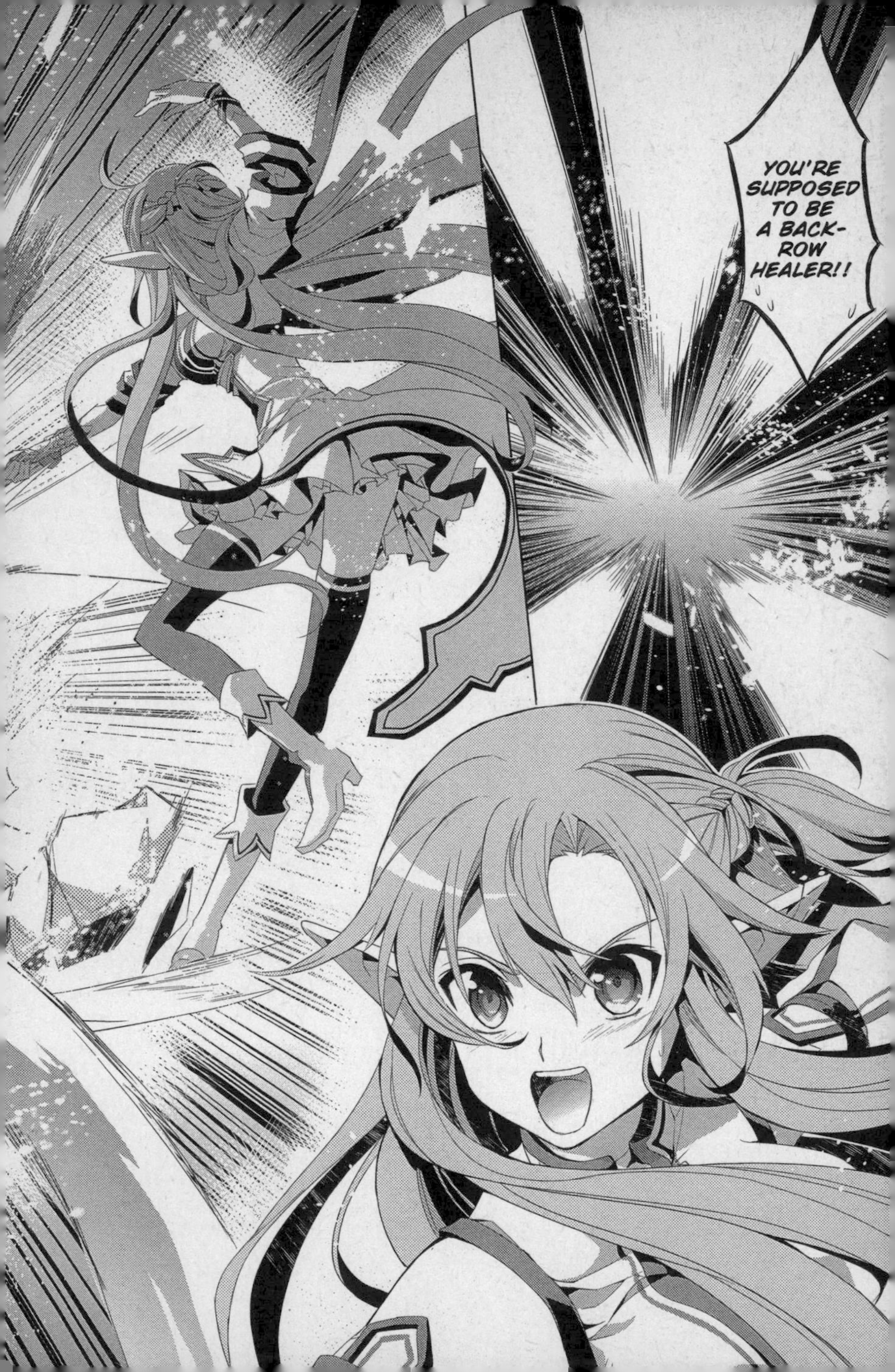
YOU'RE SUPPOSED TO BE A BACK-ROW HEALER!!

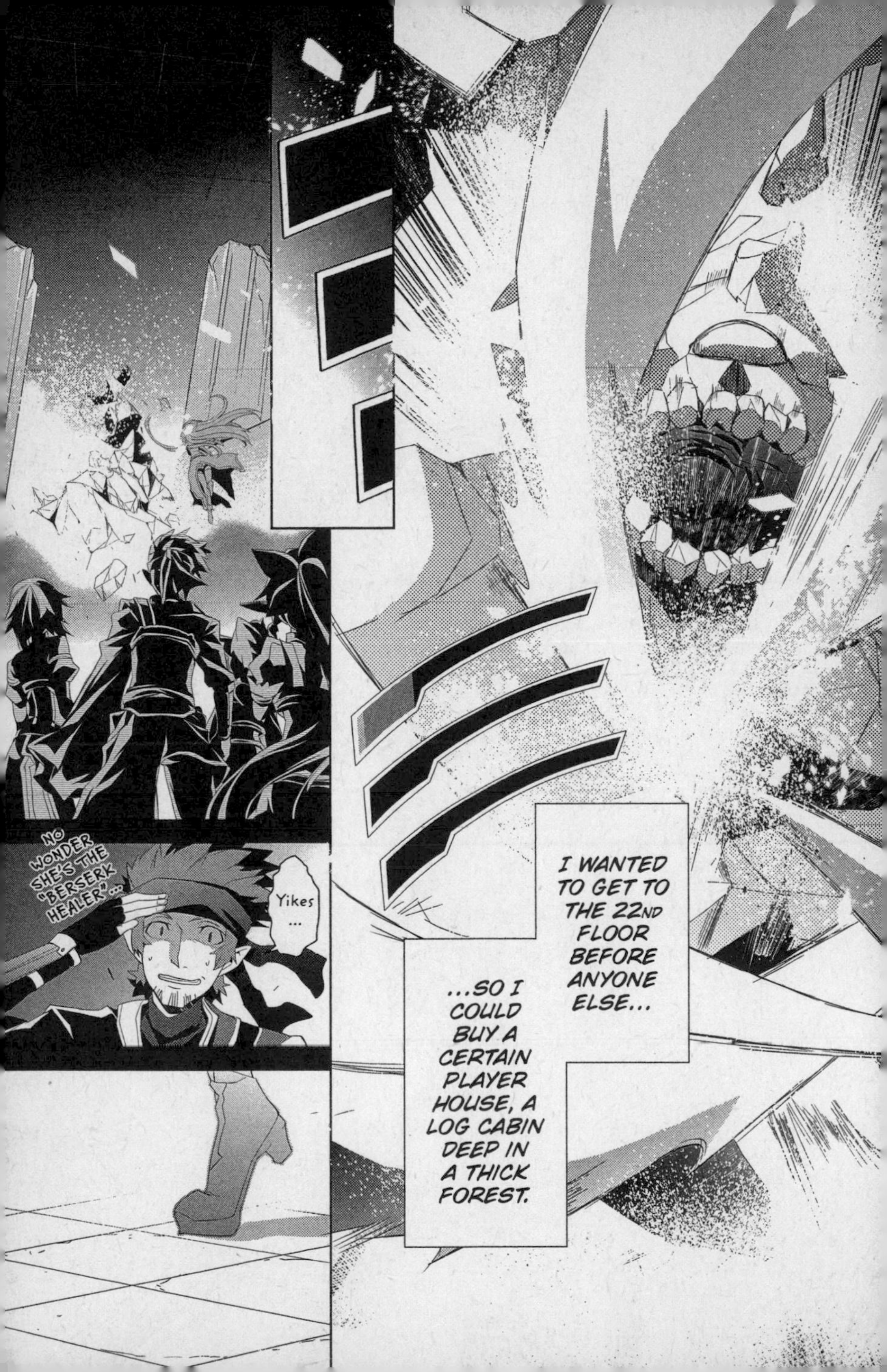
I WANTED TO GET TO THE 22ND FLOOR BEFORE ANYONE ELSE...
...SO I COULD BUY A CERTAIN PLAYER HOUSE, A LOG CABIN DEEP IN A THICK FOREST.
Yikes ...
NO WONDER SHE'S THE "BERSERK HEALER"...

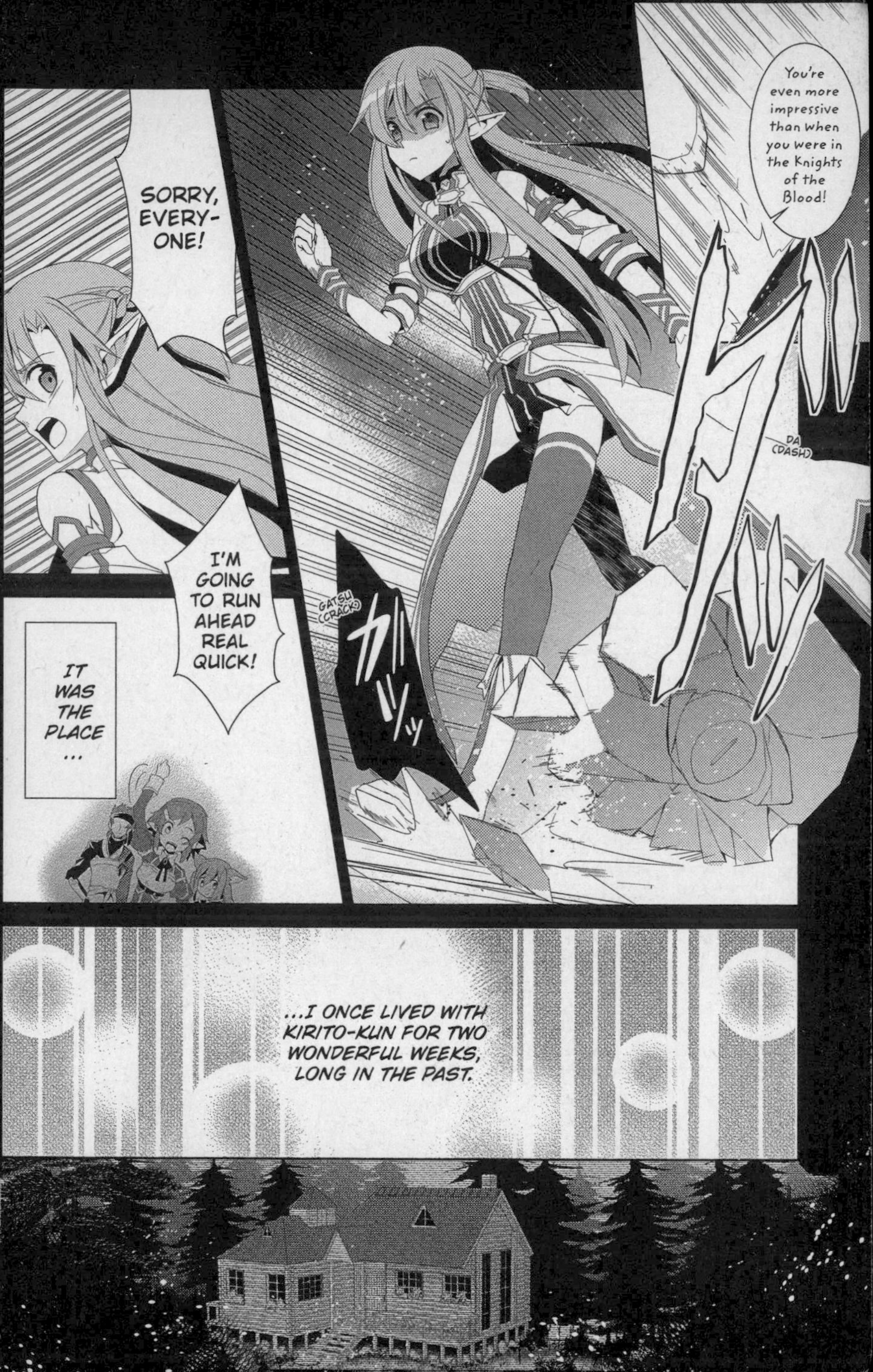
You're even more impressive than when you were in the Knights of the Blood!
DA (DASH)
GATSU (CRACK)
SORRY, EVERY-ONE!
I'M GOING TO RUN AHEAD REAL QUICK!
IT WAS THE PLACE...
...I ONCE LIVED WITH KIRITO-KUN FOR TWO WONDERFUL WEEKS, LONG IN THE PAST.

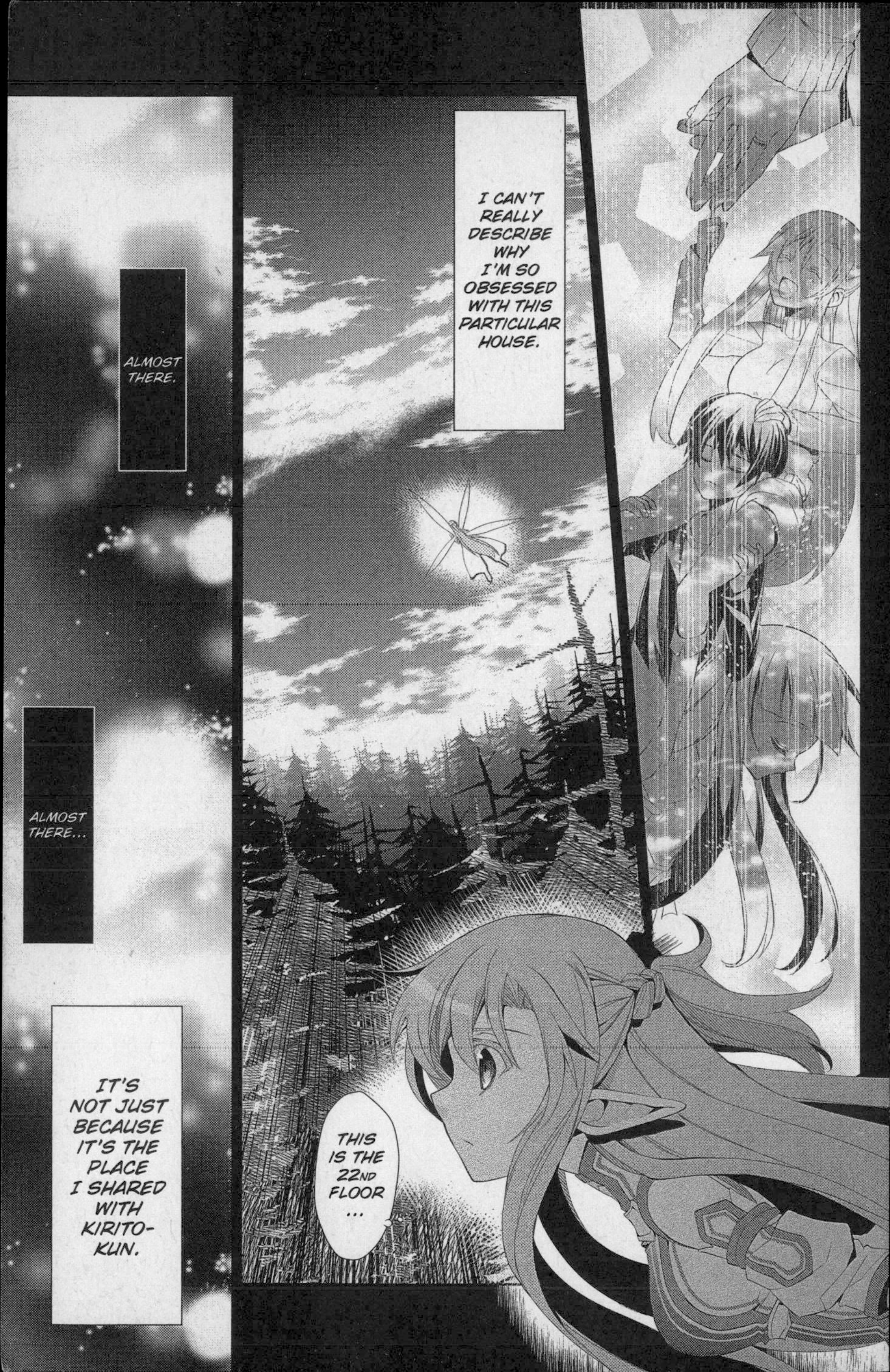
I CAN'T REALLY DESCRIBE WHY I'M SO OBSESSED WITH THIS PARTICULAR HOUSE.
THIS IS THE 22ND FLOOR...
ALMOST THERE.
ALMOST THERE...
IT'S NOT JUST BECAUSE IT'S THE PLACE I SHARED WITH KIRITO-KUN.

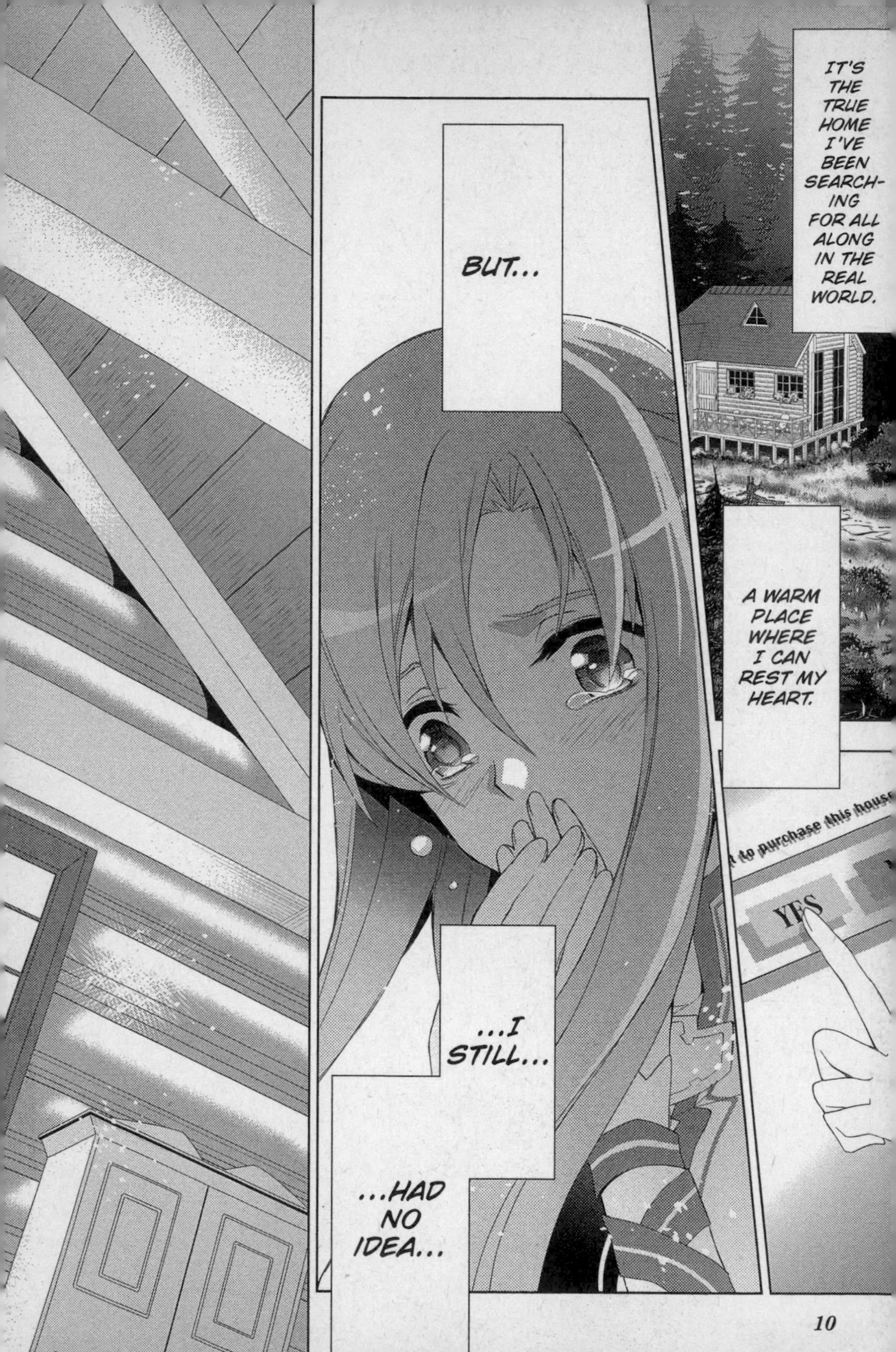
IT'S THE TRUE HOME I'VE BEEN SEARCHING FOR ALL ALONG IN THE REAL WORLD.
A WARM PLACE WHERE I CAN REST MY HEART.
to purchase this house
YES
BUT...
...I STILL...
...HAD NO IDEA...

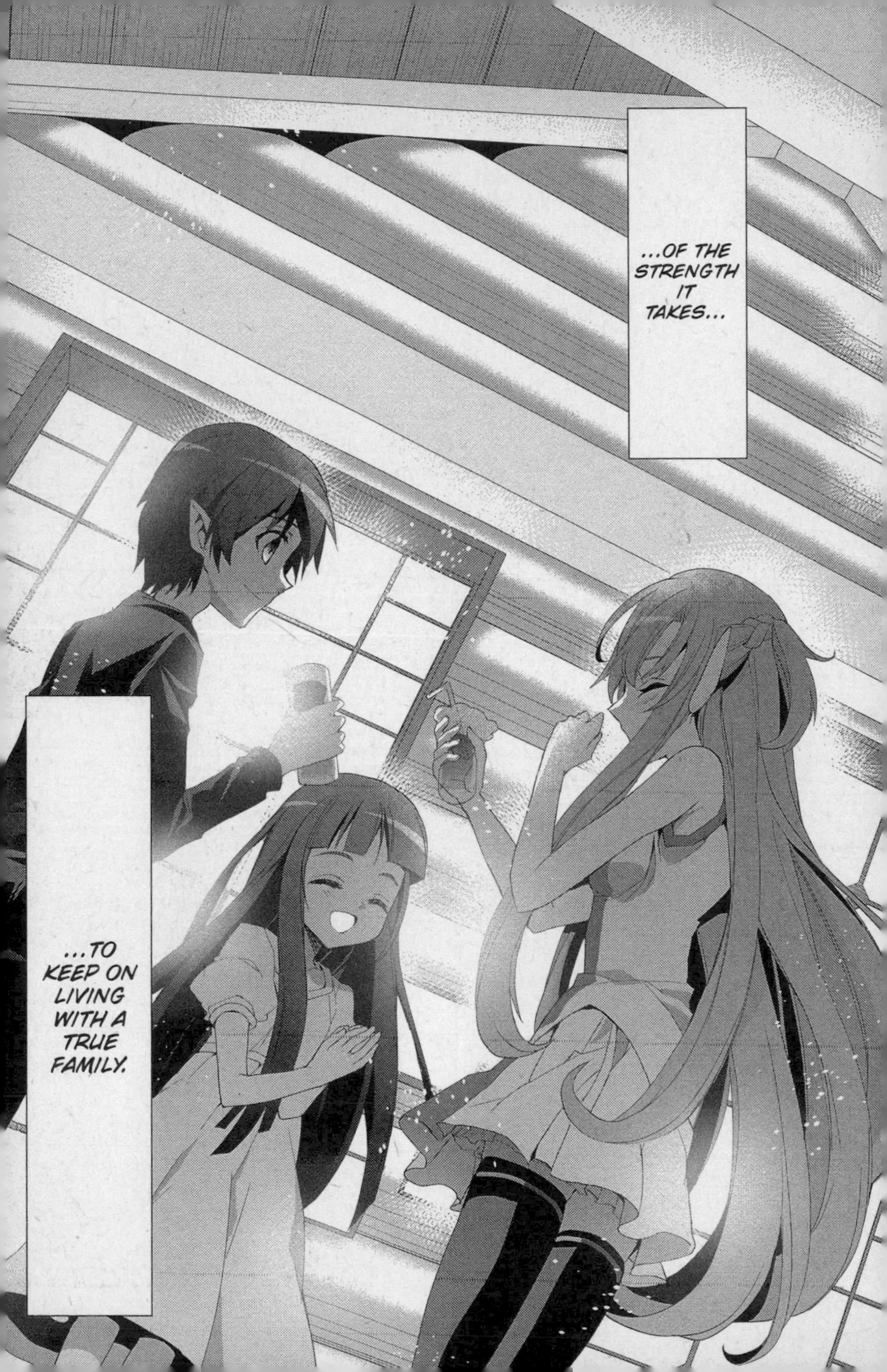
...OF THE STRENGTH IT TAKES...
...TO KEEP ON LIVING WITH A TRUE FAMILY.

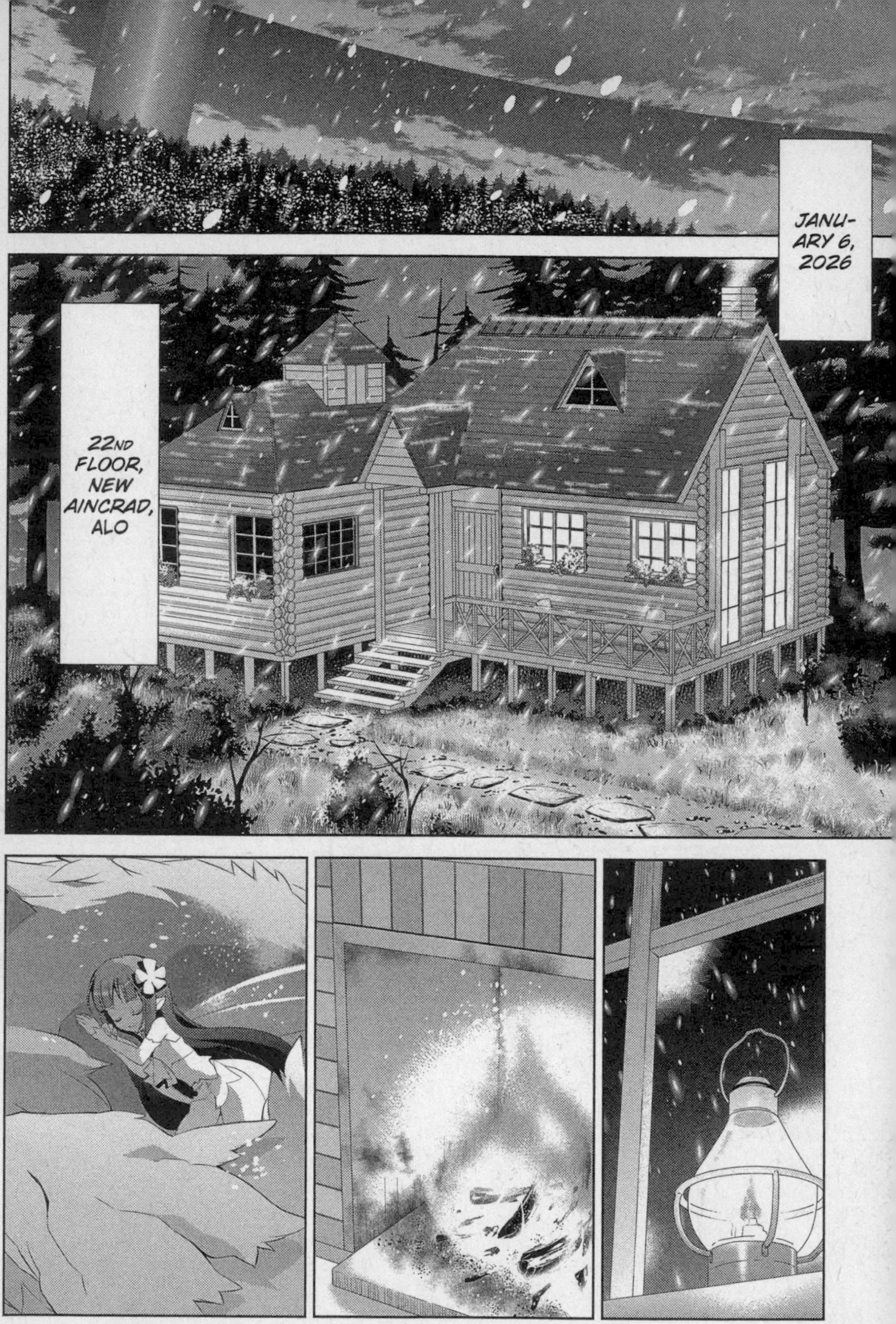
JANU-
ARY 6,
2026
22nd
FLOOR,
NEW
AINCRAD,
ALO

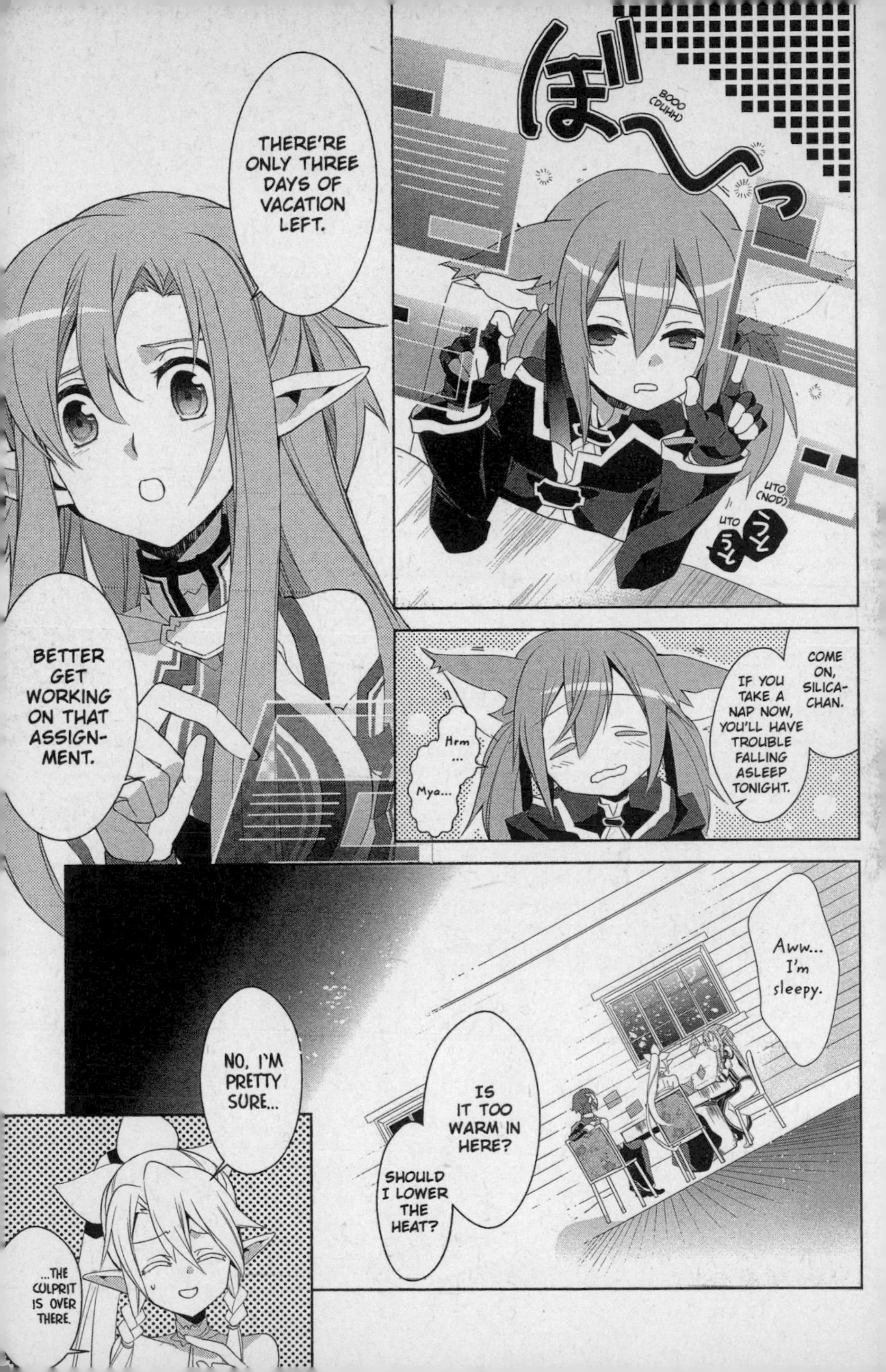
ぼ〜っ
BOOO (DUHH)
うと
うと
UTO (NOD)
UTO
THERE'RE ONLY THREE DAYS OF VACATION LEFT.
BETTER GET WORKING ON THAT ASSIGNMENT.
COME ON, SILICA-CHAN.
IF YOU TAKE A NAP NOW, YOU'LL HAVE TROUBLE FALLING ASLEEP TONIGHT.
Hrm... Mya...
Aww... I'm sleepy.
IS IT TOO WARM IN HERE?
SHOULD I LOWER THE HEAT?
NO, I'M PRETTY SURE...
...THE CULPRIT IS OVER THERE.

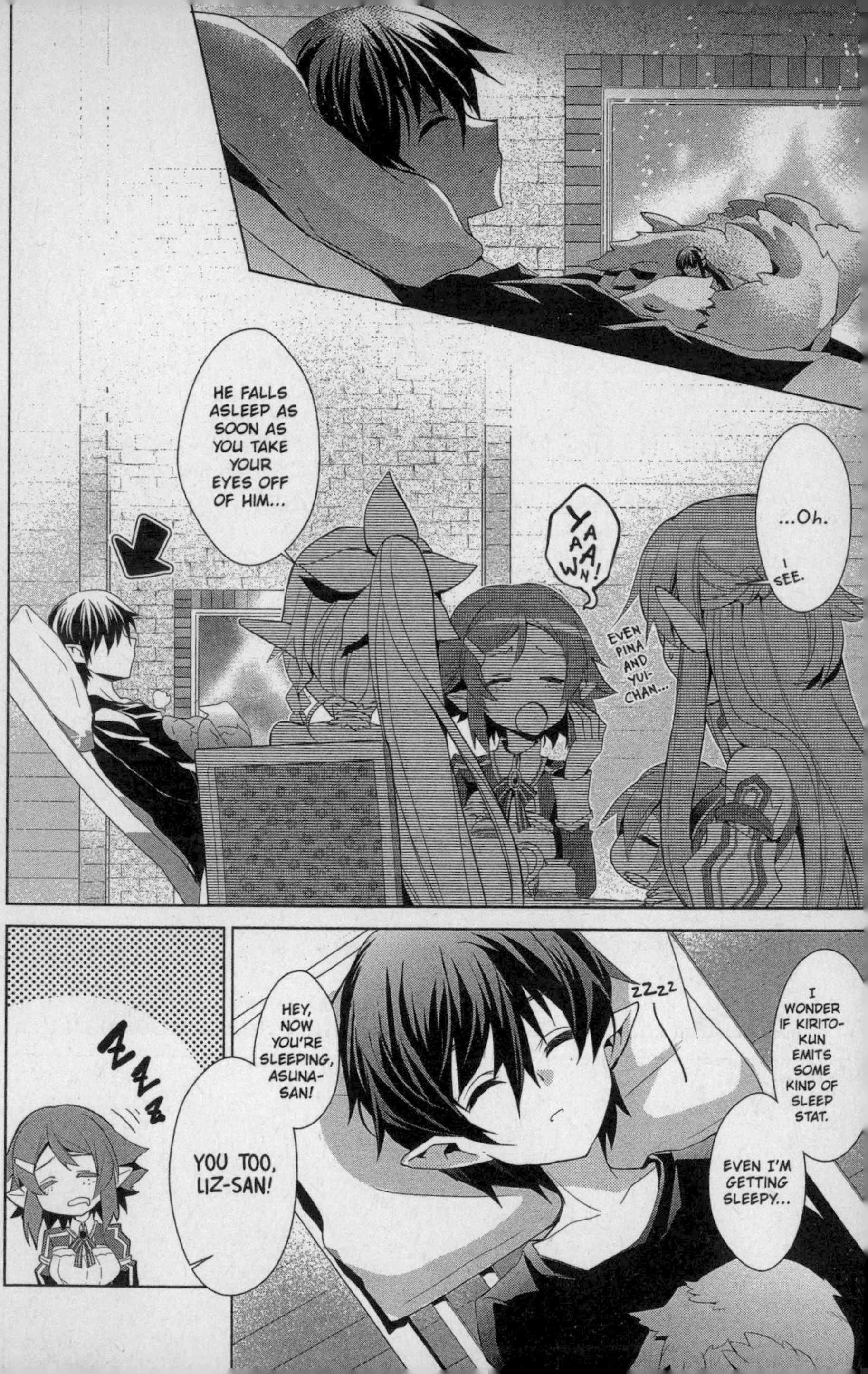
...Oh.
I SEE.
YAAAWN!
EVEN PINA AND YUI-CHAN...
HE FALLS ASLEEP AS SOON AS YOU TAKE YOUR EYES OFF OF HIM...
I WONDER IF KIRITO-KUN EMITS SOME KIND OF SLEEP STAT.
EVEN I'M GETTING SLEEPY...
ZZZZ
HEY, NOW YOU'RE SLEEPING, ASUNA-SAN!
YOU TOO, LIZ-SAN!
ZZZ

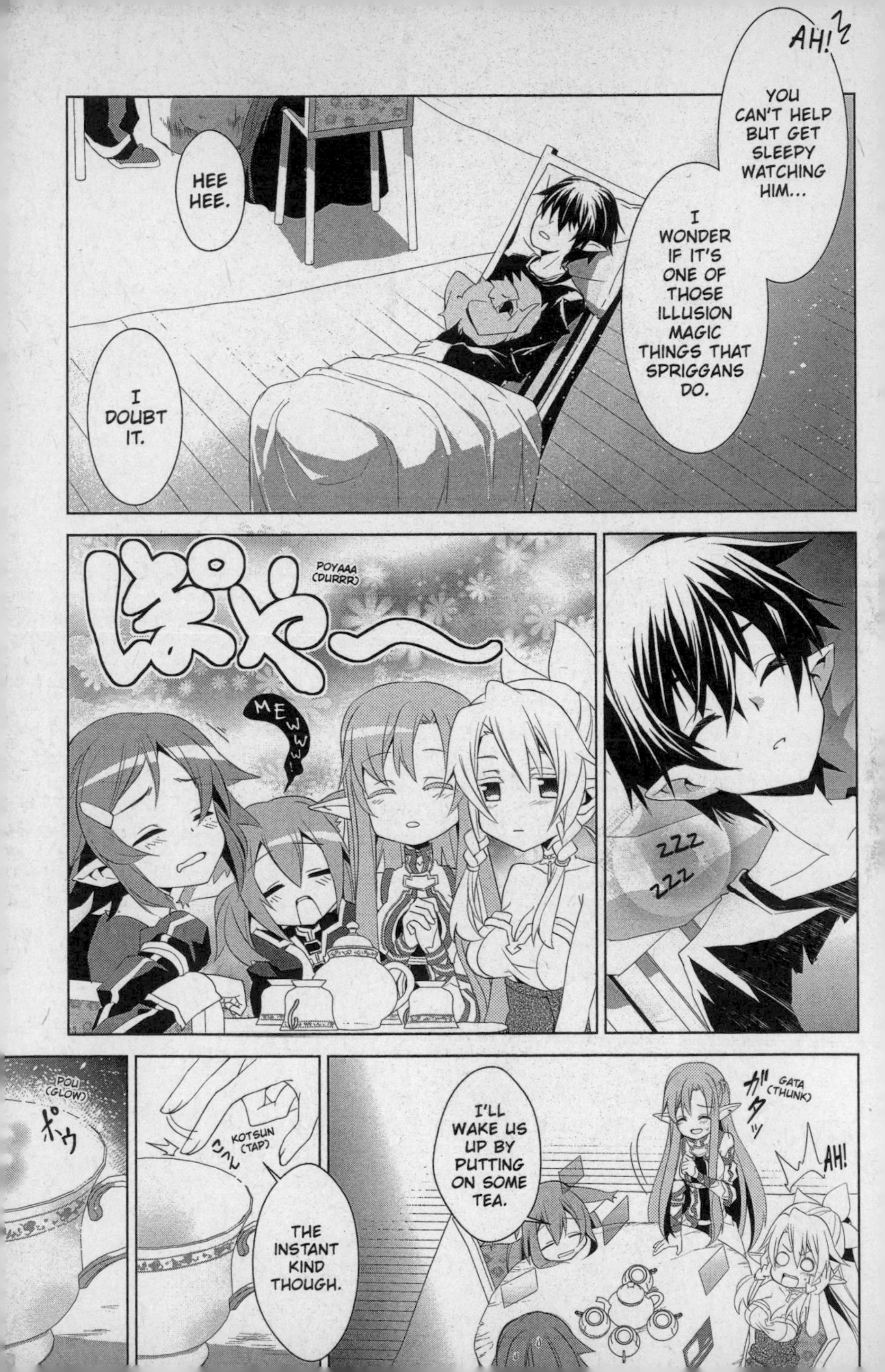

AH!
YOU CAN'T HELP BUT GET SLEEPY WATCHING HIM...
I WONDER IF IT'S ONE OF THOSE ILLUSION MAGIC THINGS THAT SPRIGGANS DO.
HEE HEE.
I DOUBT IT.
ZZZ ZZZ
ぽや〜
POYAAA (DURRR)
MEWWW!
ガタッ
GATA (THUNK)
AH!
I'LL WAKE US UP BY PUTTING ON SOME TEA.
コツン
KOTSUN (TAP)
THE INSTANT KIND THOUGH.
ポウ
POU (GLOW)

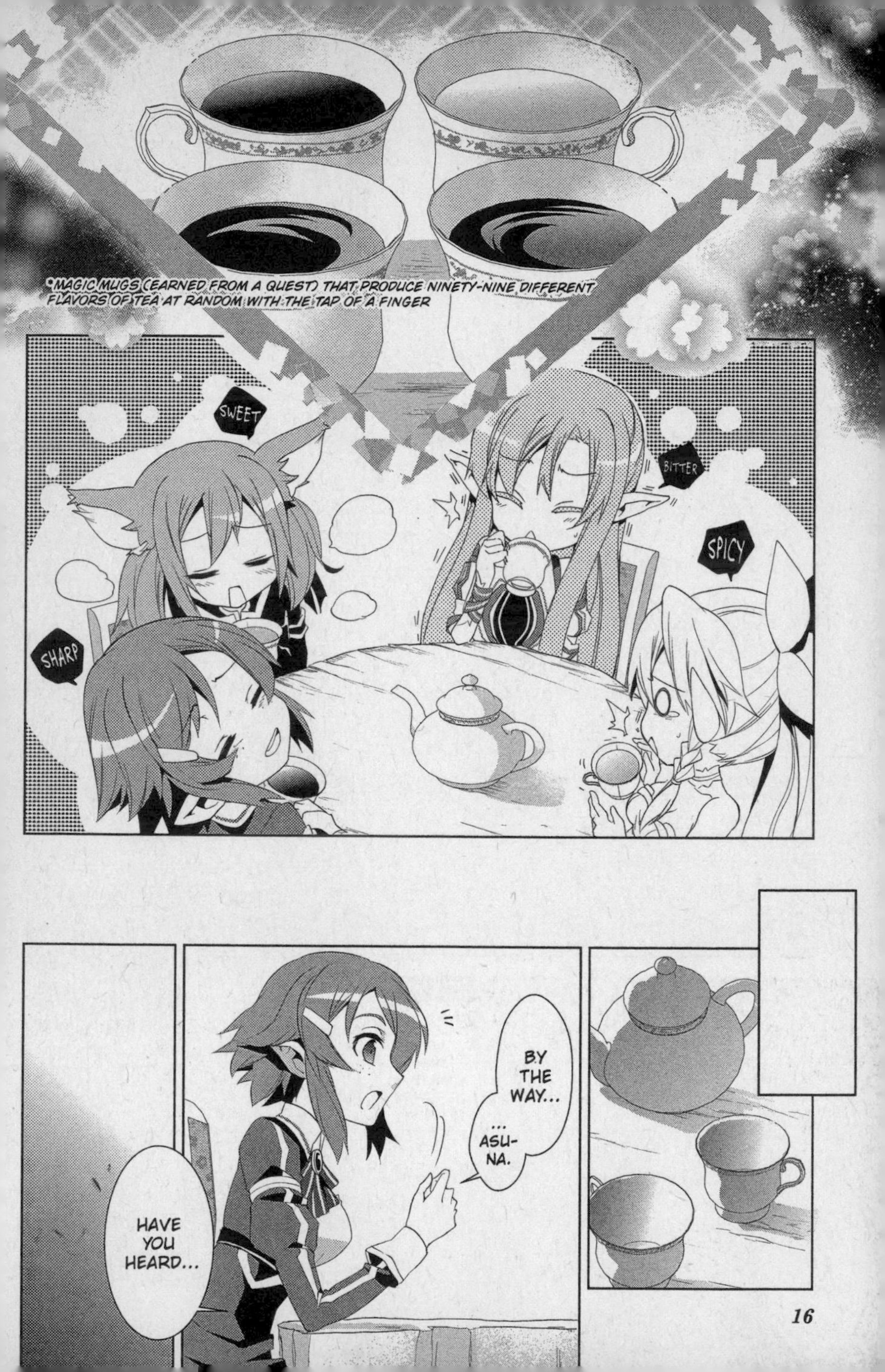
*MAGIC MUGS (EARNED FROM A QUEST) THAT PRODUCE NINETY-NINE DIFFERENT FLAVORS OF TEA AT RANDOM WITH THE TAP OF A FINGER
SPICY
BITTER
SWEET
SHARP
BY THE WAY...
...ASUNA.
HAVE YOU HEARD...

...ABOUT ABSOLUTE SWORD?

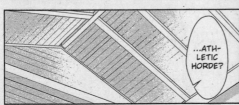

...ATH-LETIC HORDE?

ARE THEY STARTING A RACE OR SOME-THING?

NO, NO, NO.

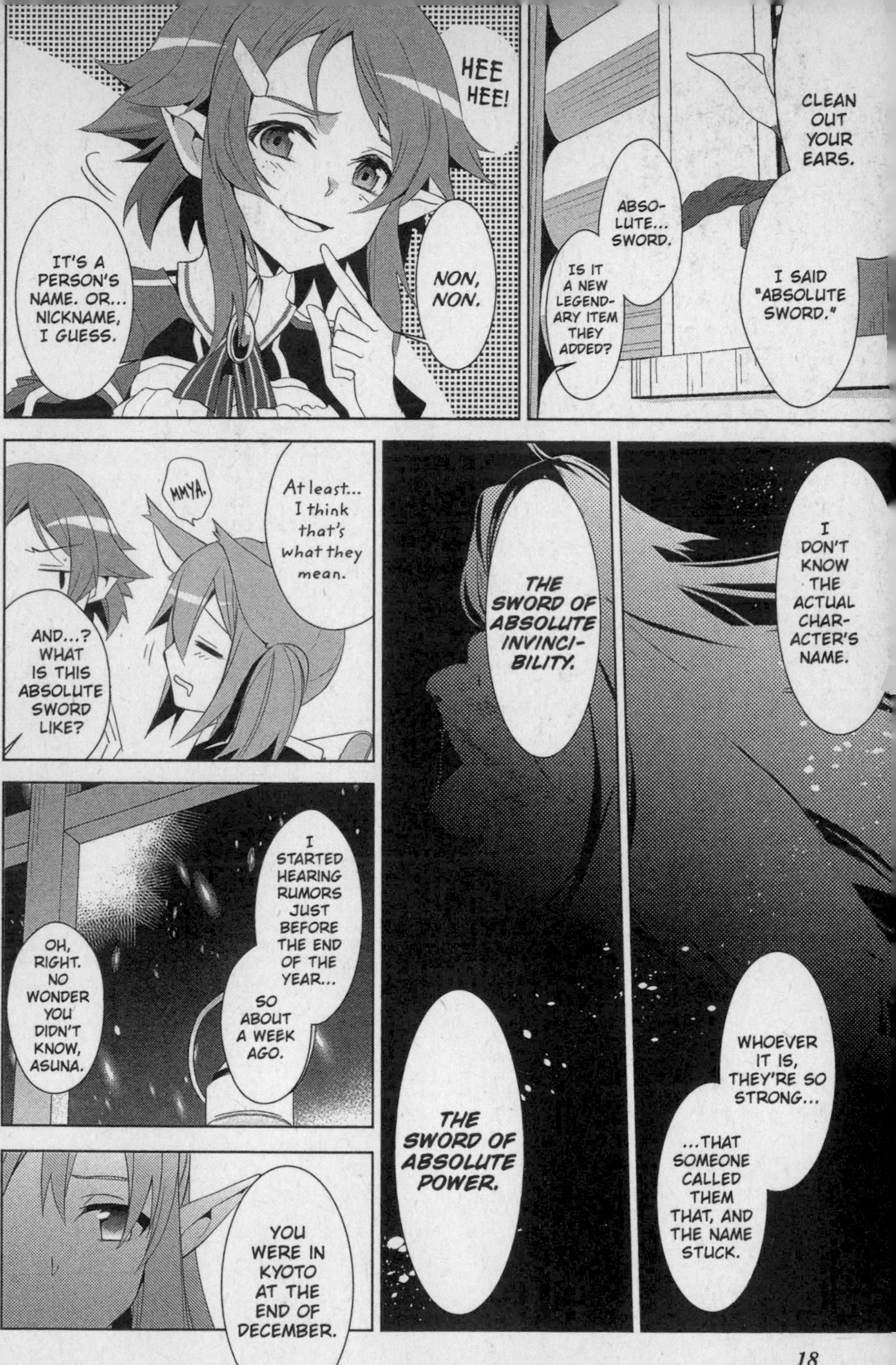
CLEAN OUT YOUR EARS.
I SAID "ABSOLUTE SWORD."
ABSO-LUTE... SWORD.
IS IT A NEW LEGEND-ARY ITEM THEY ADDED?
HEE HEE!
NON, NON.
IT'S A PERSON'S NAME. OR... NICKNAME, I GUESS.
I DON'T KNOW THE ACTUAL CHAR-ACTER'S NAME.
WHOEVER IT IS, THEY'RE SO STRONG...
...THAT SOMEONE CALLED THEM THAT, AND THE NAME STUCK.
THE SWORD OF ABSOLUTE INVINCI-BILITY.
THE SWORD OF ABSOLUTE POWER.
At least... I think that's what they mean.
MMYA.
AND...? WHAT IS THIS ABSOLUTE SWORD LIKE?
I STARTED HEARING RUMORS JUST BEFORE THE END OF THE YEAR...
SO ABOUT A WEEK AGO.
OH, RIGHT. NO WONDER YOU DIDN'T KNOW, ASUNA.
YOU WERE IN KYOTO AT THE END OF DECEMBER.

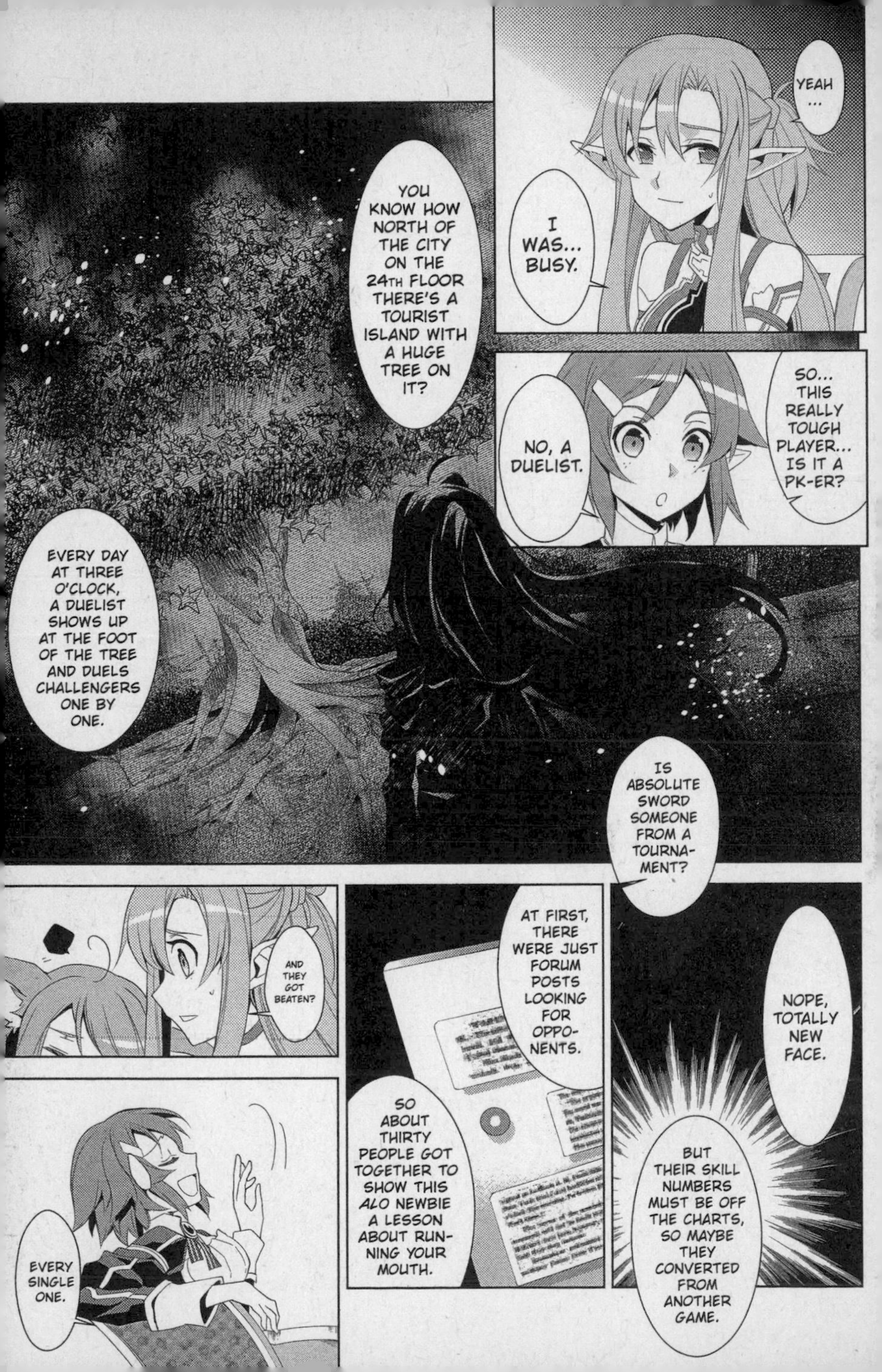
YEAH...
I WAS... BUSY.
SO... THIS REALLY TOUGH PLAYER... IS IT A PK-ER?
NO, A DUELIST.
YOU KNOW HOW NORTH OF THE CITY ON THE 24TH FLOOR THERE'S A TOURIST ISLAND WITH A HUGE TREE ON IT?
EVERY DAY AT THREE O'CLOCK, A DUELIST SHOWS UP AT THE FOOT OF THE TREE AND DUELS CHALLENGERS ONE BY ONE.
IS ABSOLUTE SWORD SOMEONE FROM A TOURNA-MENT?
NOPE, TOTALLY NEW FACE.
BUT THEIR SKILL NUMBERS MUST BE OFF THE CHARTS, SO MAYBE THEY CONVERTED FROM ANOTHER GAME.
AT FIRST, THERE WERE JUST FORUM POSTS LOOKING FOR OPPO-NENTS.
SO ABOUT THIRTY PEOPLE GOT TOGETHER TO SHOW THIS ALO NEWBIE A LESSON ABOUT RUN-NING YOUR MOUTH.
AND THEY GOT BEATEN?
EVERY SINGLE ONE.

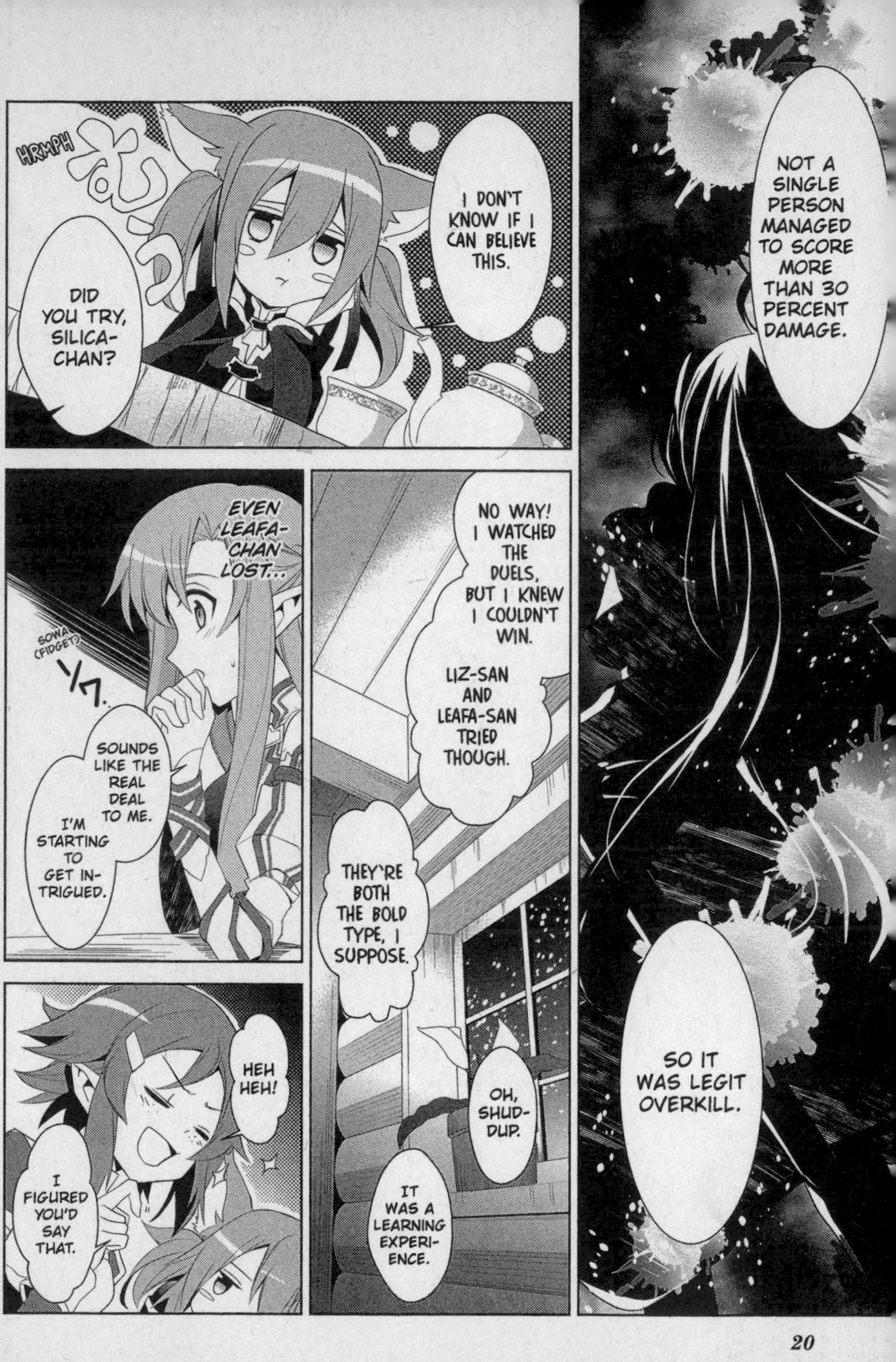
NOT A SINGLE PERSON MANAGED TO SCORE MORE THAN 30 PERCENT DAMAGE.
SO IT WAS LEGIT OVERKILL.
I DON'T KNOW IF I CAN BELIEVE THIS.
HRMPH
DID YOU TRY, SILICA-CHAN?
NO WAY! I WATCHED THE DUELS, BUT I KNEW I COULDN'T WIN.
LIZ-SAN AND LEAFA-SAN TRIED THOUGH.
THEY'RE BOTH THE BOLD TYPE, I SUPPOSE.
OH, SHUD-DUP.
IT WAS A LEARNING EXPERI-ENCE.
EVEN LEAFA-CHAN LOST...
SOWA (FIDGET)
SOUNDS LIKE THE REAL DEAL TO ME.
I'M STARTING TO GET IN-TRIGUED.
HEH HEH!
I FIGURED YOU'D SAY THAT.

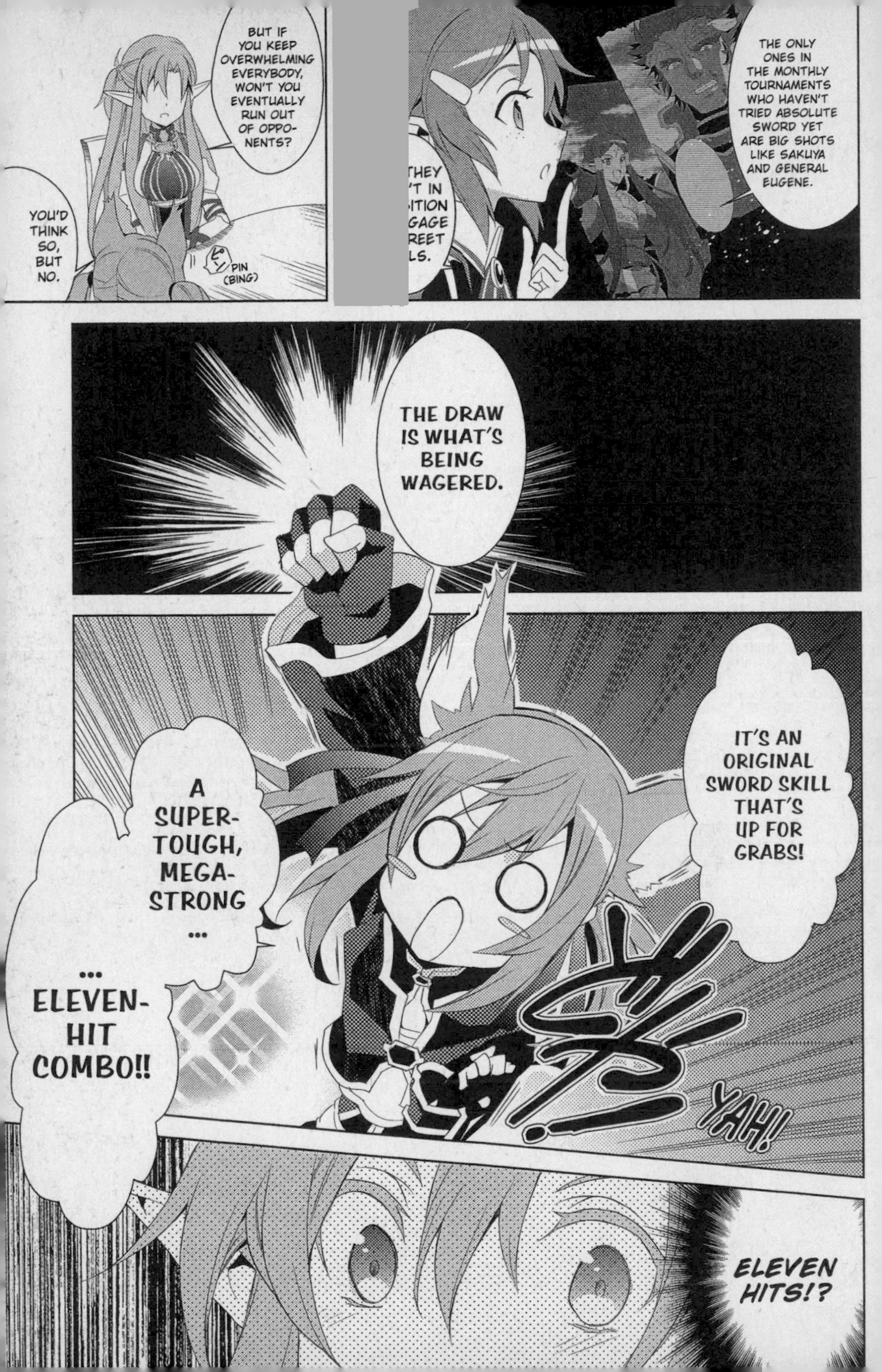
THE ONLY ONES IN THE MONTHLY TOURNAMENTS WHO HAVEN'T TRIED ABSOLUTE SWORD YET ARE BIG SHOTS LIKE SAKUYA AND GENERAL EUGENE.
THEY 'T IN SITION GAGE REET LS.
BUT IF YOU KEEP OVERWHELMING EVERYBODY, WON'T YOU EVENTUALLY RUN OUT OF OPPO-NENTS?
YOU'D THINK SO, BUT NO.
PIN (BING)
THE DRAW IS WHAT'S BEING WAGERED.
IT'S AN ORIGINAL SWORD SKILL THAT'S UP FOR GRABS!
A SUPER-TOUGH, MEGA-STRONG ...
... ELEVEN-HIT COMBO!!
YAH!
ELEVEN HITS!?

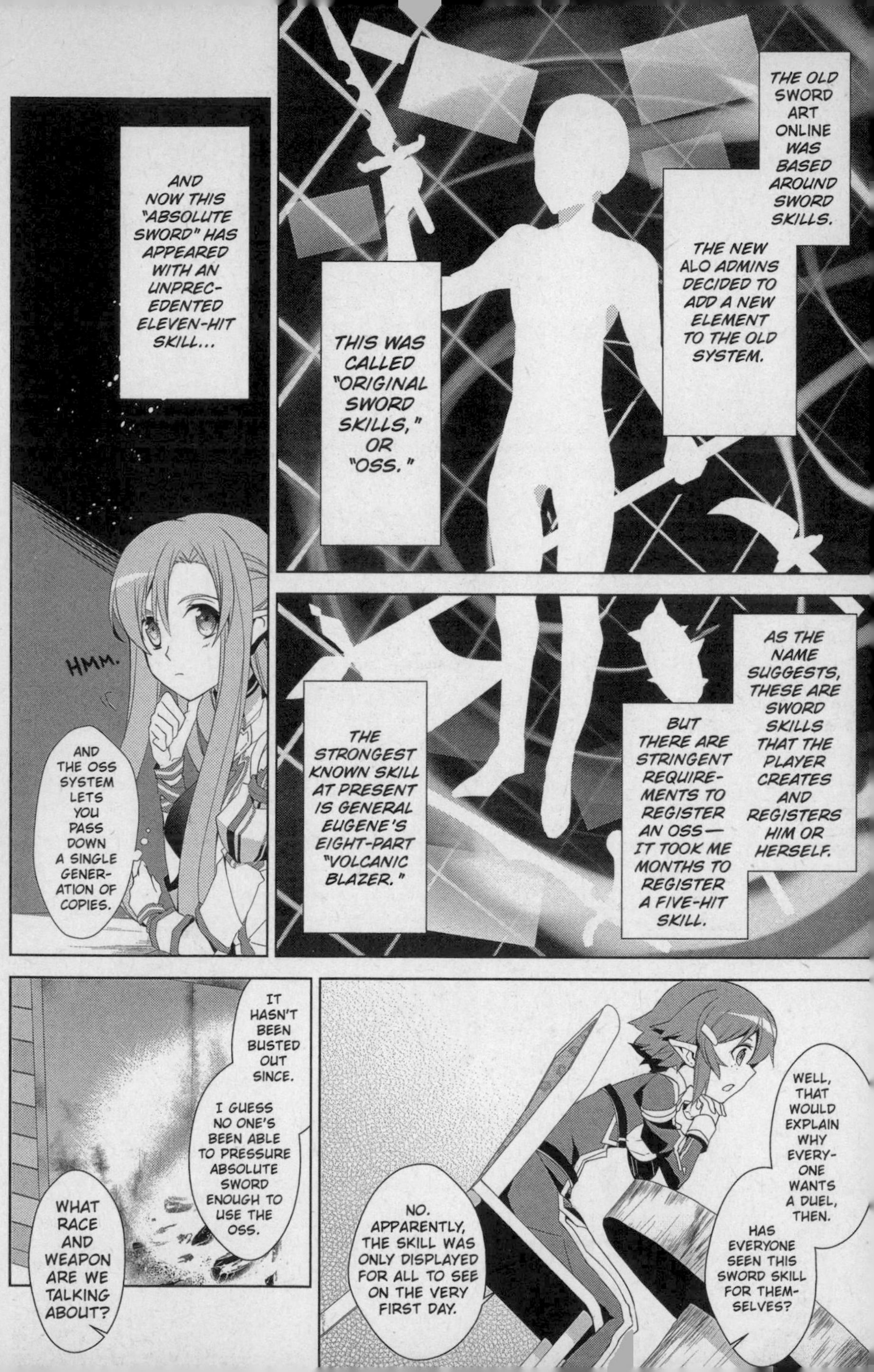
THE OLD SWORD ART ONLINE WAS BASED AROUND SWORD SKILLS.
THE NEW ALO ADMINS DECIDED TO ADD A NEW ELEMENT TO THE OLD SYSTEM.
THIS WAS CALLED "ORIGINAL SWORD SKILLS," OR "OSS."
AS THE NAME SUGGESTS, THESE ARE SWORD SKILLS THAT THE PLAYER CREATES AND REGISTERS HIM OR HERSELF.
BUT THERE ARE STRINGENT REQUIRE-MENTS TO REGISTER AN OSS— IT TOOK ME MONTHS TO REGISTER A FIVE-HIT SKILL.
THE STRONGEST KNOWN SKILL AT PRESENT IS GENERAL EUGENE'S EIGHT-PART "VOLCANIC BLAZER."
AND NOW THIS "ABSOLUTE SWORD" HAS APPEARED WITH AN UNPREC-EDENTED ELEVEN-HIT SKILL...
HMM.
AND THE OSS SYSTEM LETS YOU PASS DOWN A SINGLE GENER-ATION OF COPIES.
WELL, THAT WOULD EXPLAIN WHY EVERY-ONE WANTS A DUEL, THEN.
HAS EVERYONE SEEN THIS SWORD SKILL FOR THEM-SELVES?
NO. APPARENTLY, THE SKILL WAS ONLY DISPLAYED FOR ALL TO SEE ON THE VERY FIRST DAY.
IT HASN'T BEEN BUSTED OUT SINCE.
I GUESS NO ONE'S BEEN ABLE TO PRESSURE ABSOLUTE SWORD ENOUGH TO USE THE OSS.
WHAT RACE AND WEAPON ARE WE TALKING ABOUT?

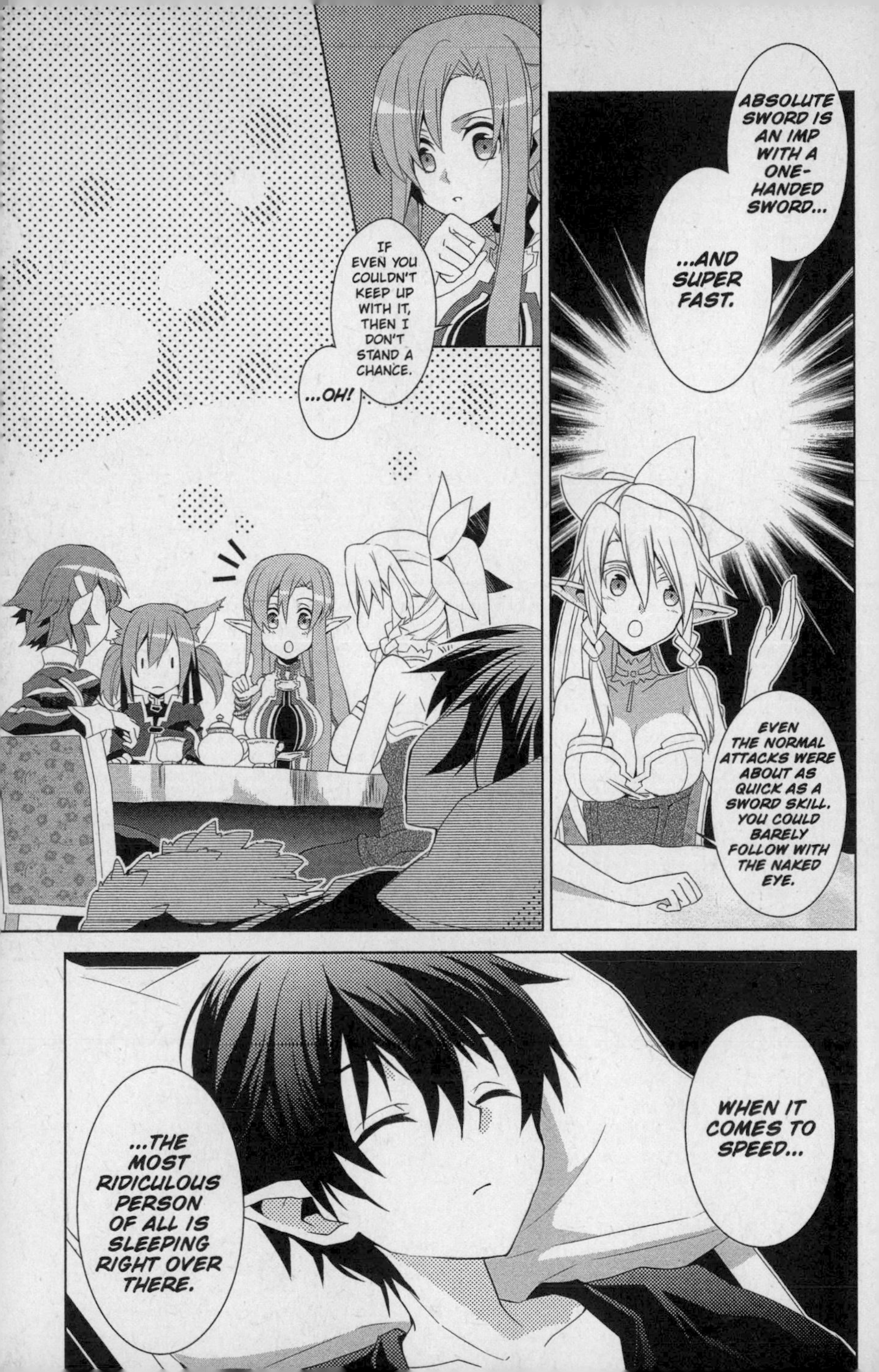
ABSOLUTE SWORD IS AN IMP WITH A ONE-HANDED SWORD...
...AND SUPER FAST.
EVEN THE NORMAL ATTACKS WERE ABOUT AS QUICK AS A SWORD SKILL. YOU COULD BARELY FOLLOW WITH THE NAKED EYE.
IF EVEN YOU COULDN'T KEEP UP WITH IT, THEN I DON'T STAND A CHANCE.
...OH!
WHEN IT COMES TO SPEED...
...THE MOST RIDICULOUS PERSON OF ALL IS SLEEPING RIGHT OVER THERE.

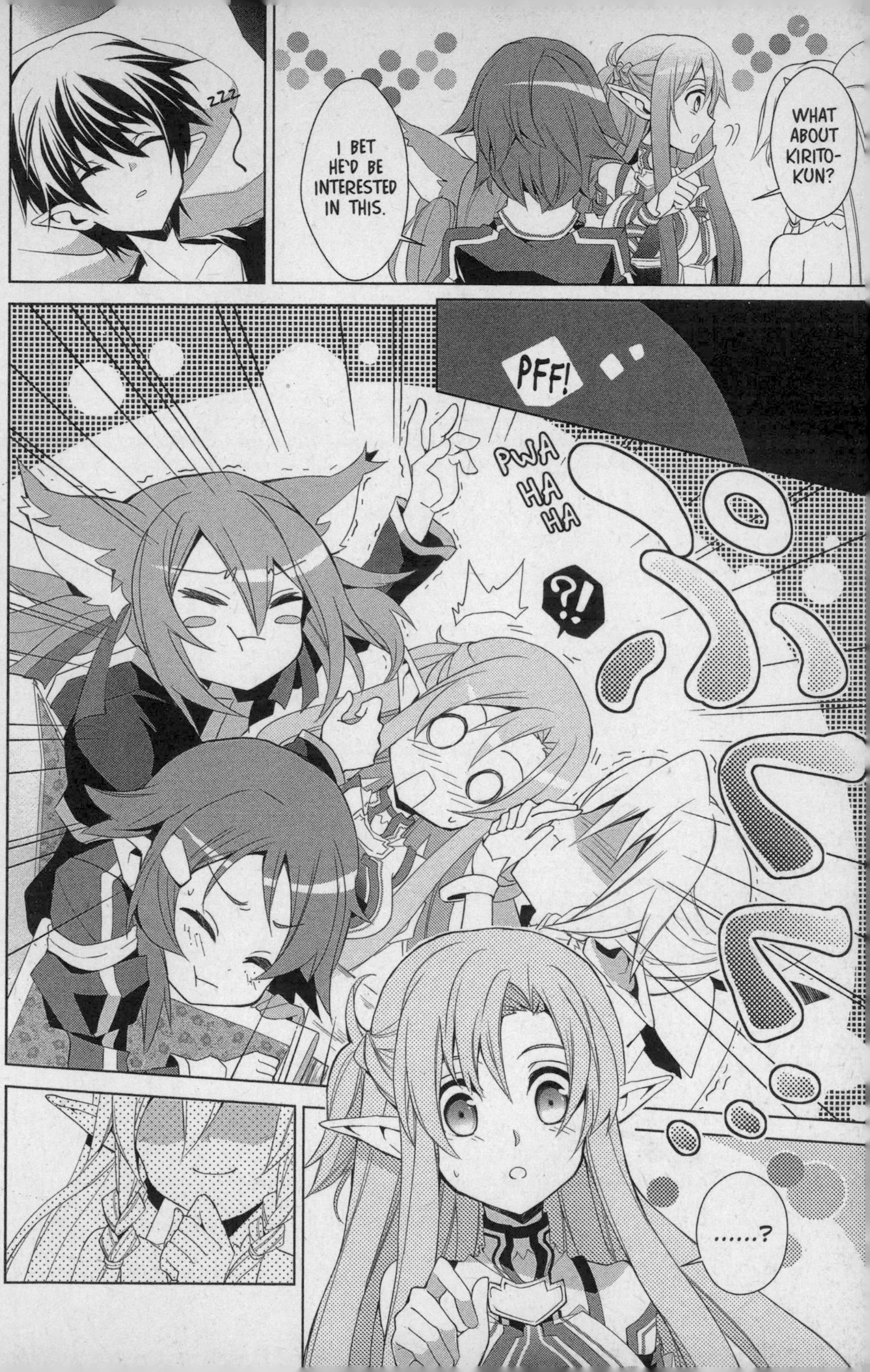
WHAT ABOUT KIRITO-KUN?
I BET HE'D BE INTERESTED IN THIS.
ZZZ
PFF!
PWA HA HA HA
?!
......?

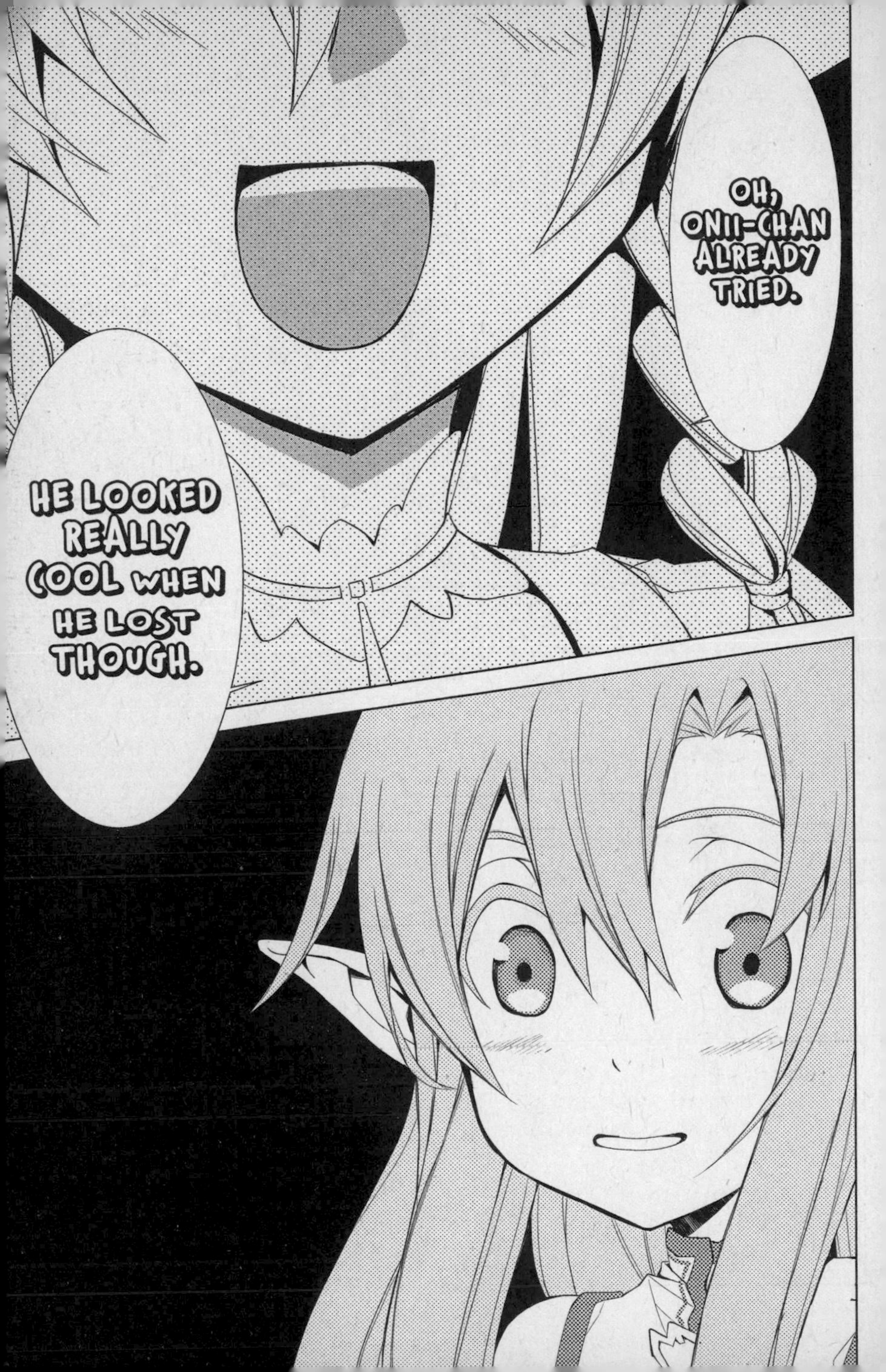
OH, ONII-CHAN ALREADY TRIED.
HE LOOKED REALLY COOL WHEN HE LOST THOUGH.

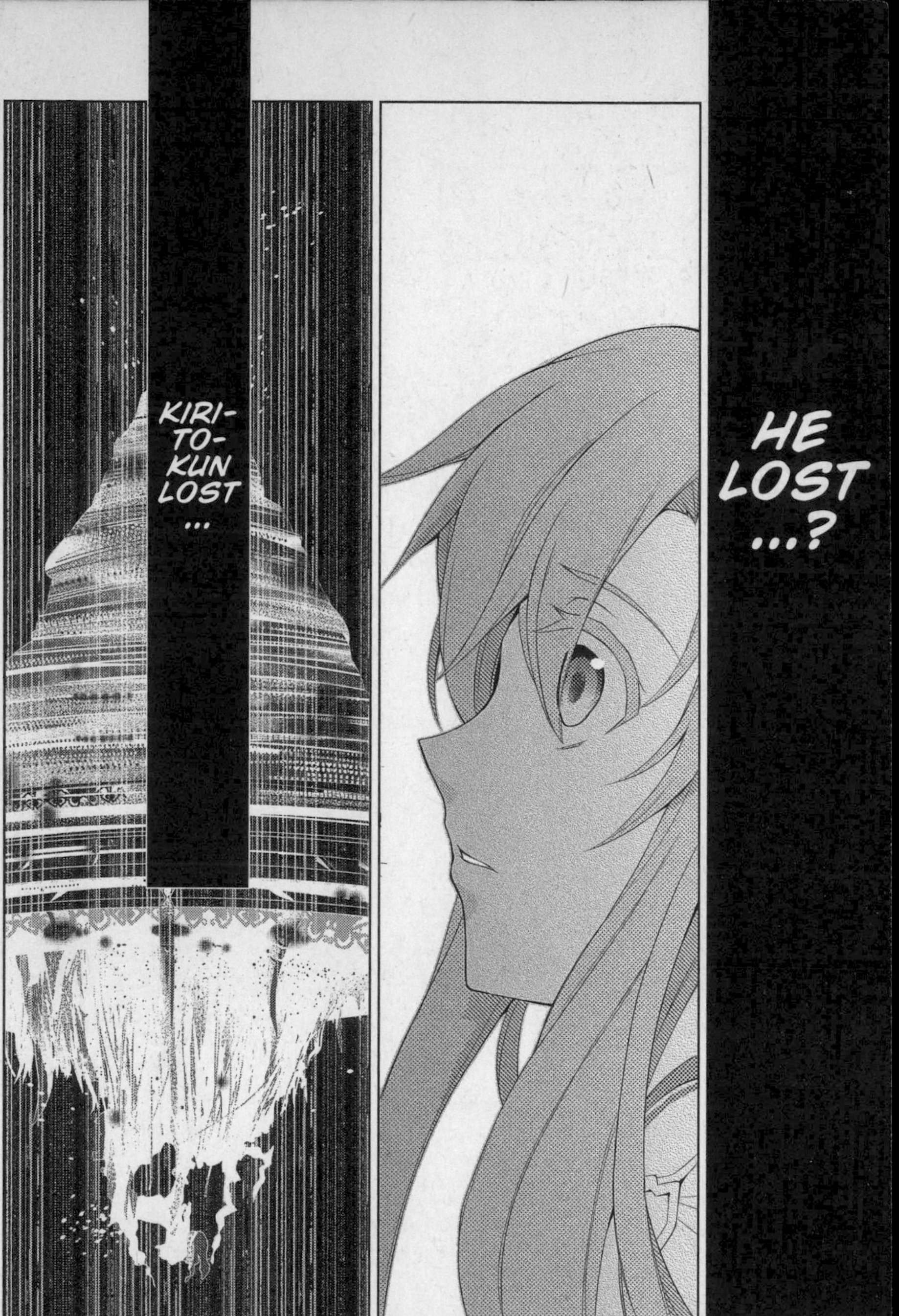
HE LOST ...?
KIRI-TO-KUN LOST ...

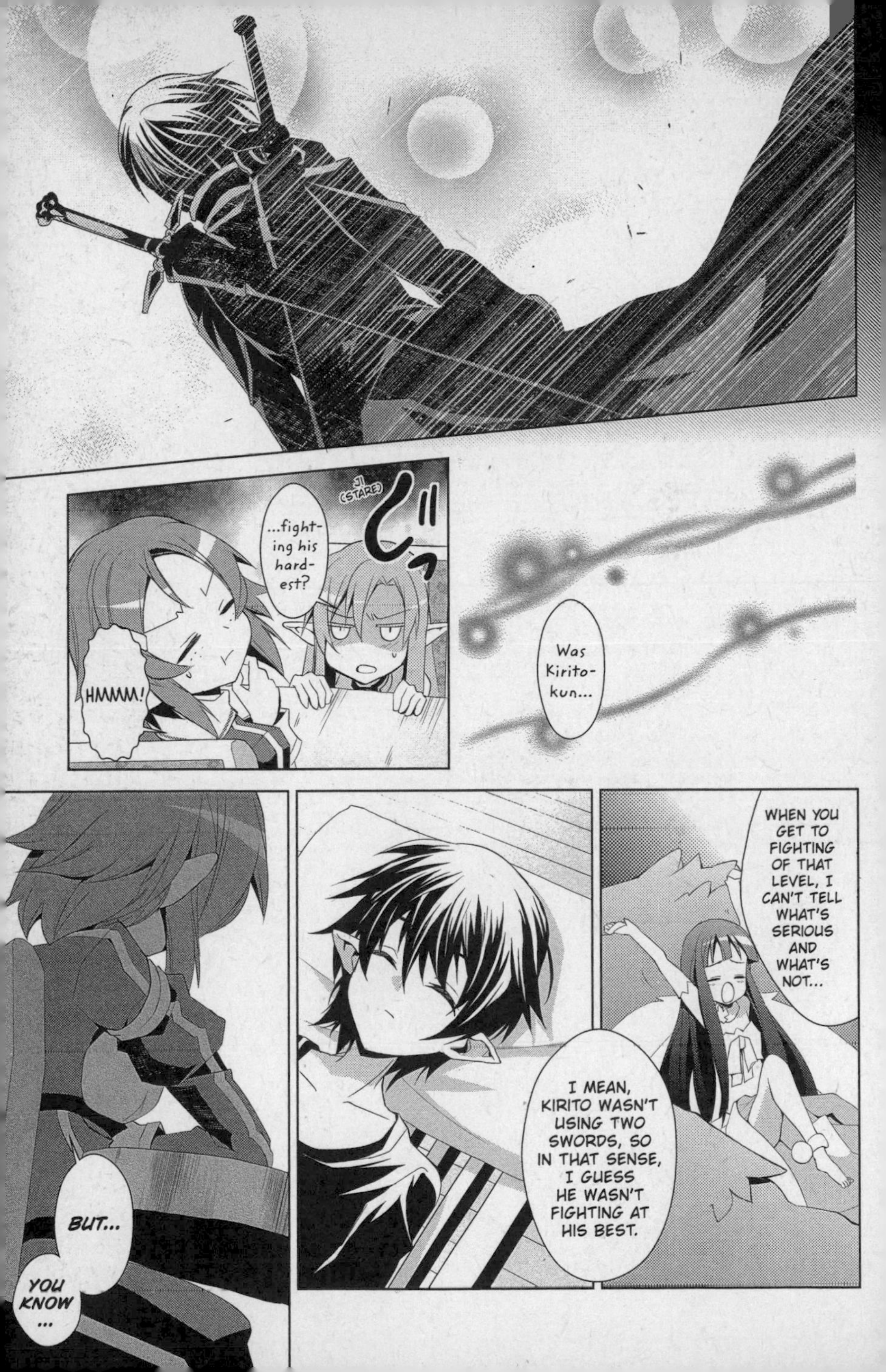
Was Kirito-kun...
...fighting his hardest?
JI (STARE)
じっ
HMMM!
WHEN YOU GET TO FIGHTING OF THAT LEVEL, I CAN'T TELL WHAT'S SERIOUS AND WHAT'S NOT...
I MEAN, KIRITO WASN'T USING TWO SWORDS, SO IN THAT SENSE, I GUESS HE WASN'T FIGHTING AT HIS BEST.
BUT...
YOU KNOW ...

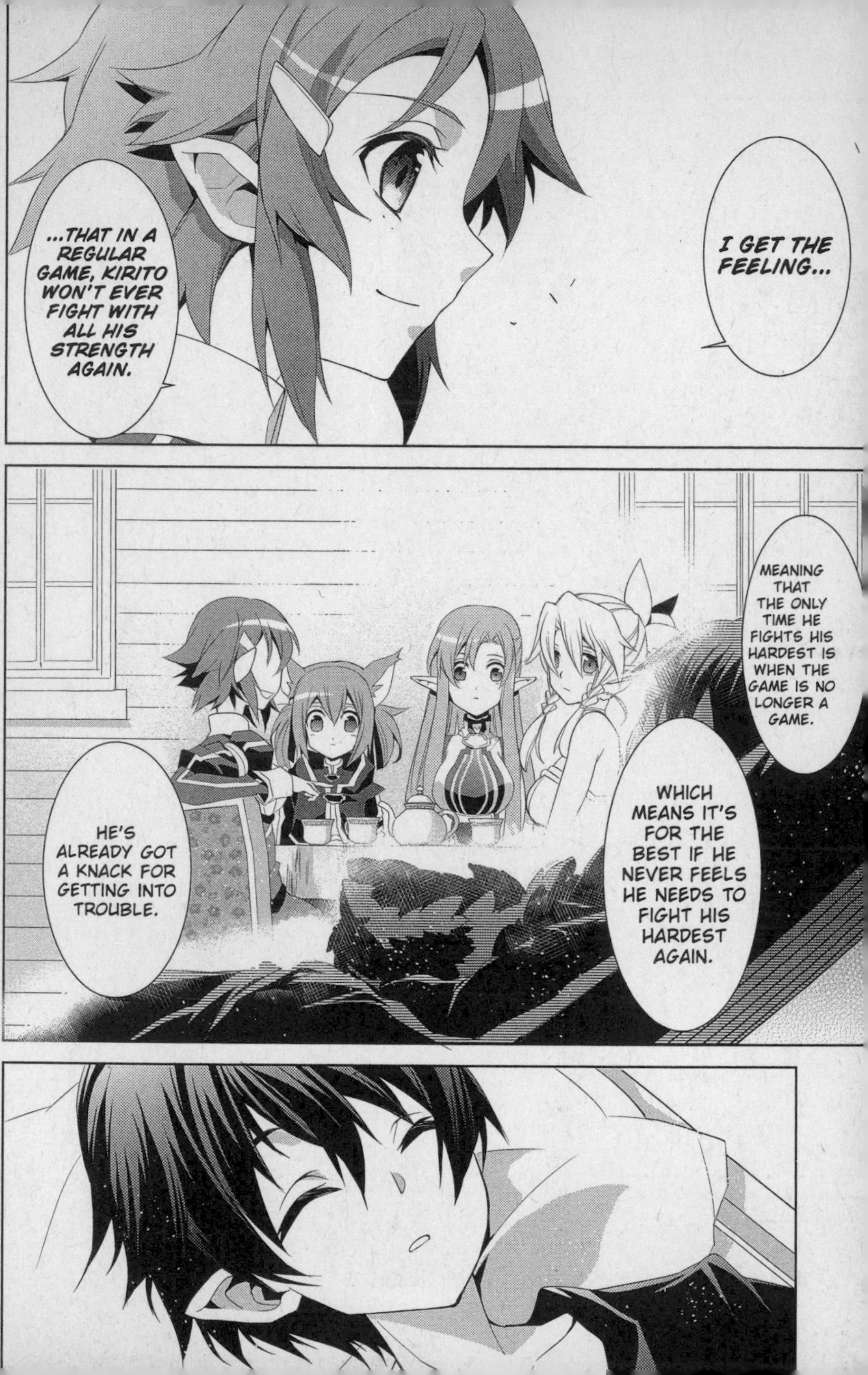
I GET THE FEELING...
...THAT IN A REGULAR GAME, KIRITO WON'T EVER FIGHT WITH ALL HIS STRENGTH AGAIN.
MEANING THAT THE ONLY TIME HE FIGHTS HIS HARDEST IS WHEN THE GAME IS NO LONGER A GAME.
WHICH MEANS IT'S FOR THE BEST IF HE NEVER FEELS HE NEEDS TO FIGHT HIS HARDEST AGAIN.
HE'S ALREADY GOT A KNACK FOR GETTING INTO TROUBLE.

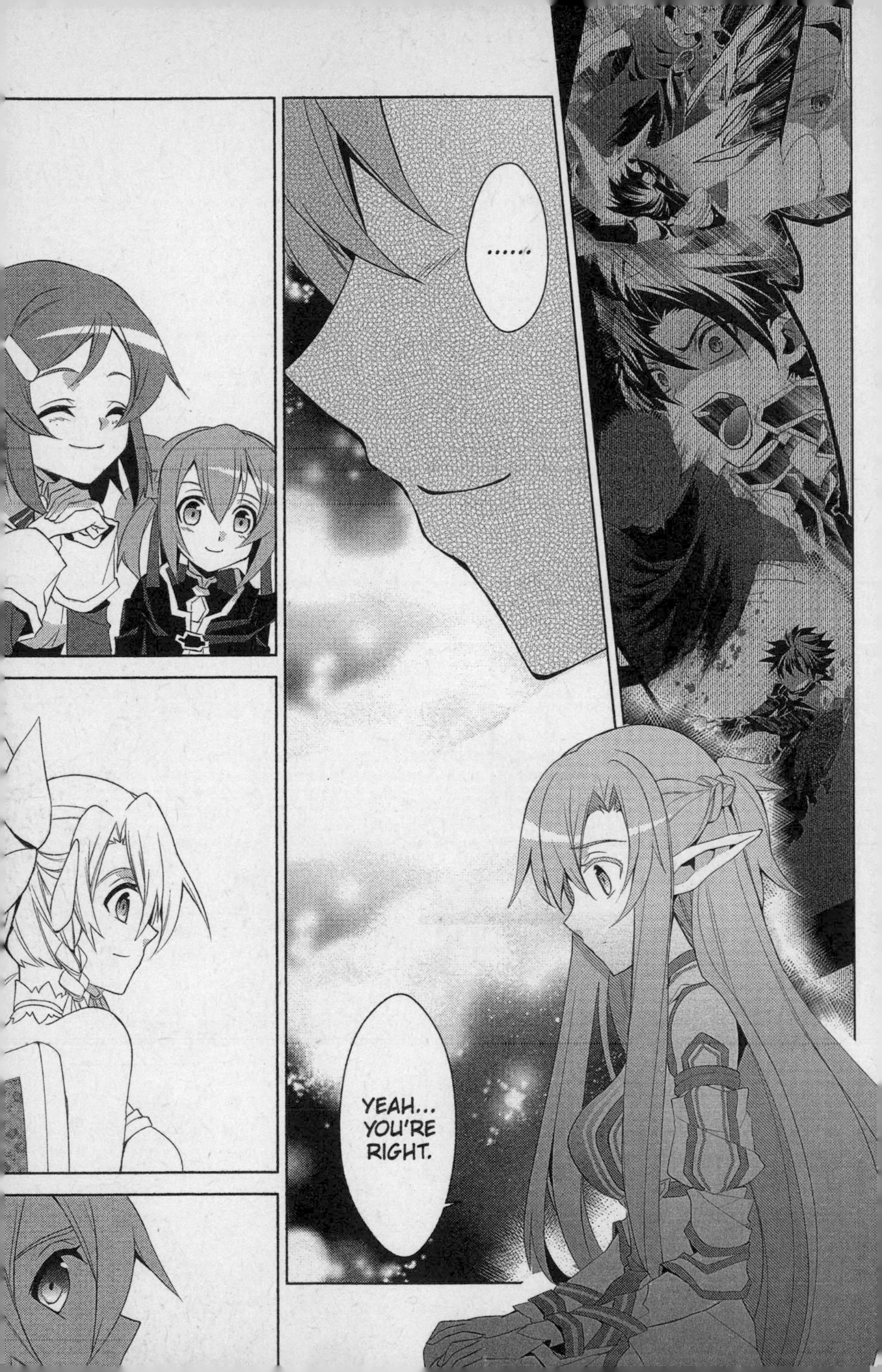
......
YEAH... YOU'RE RIGHT.

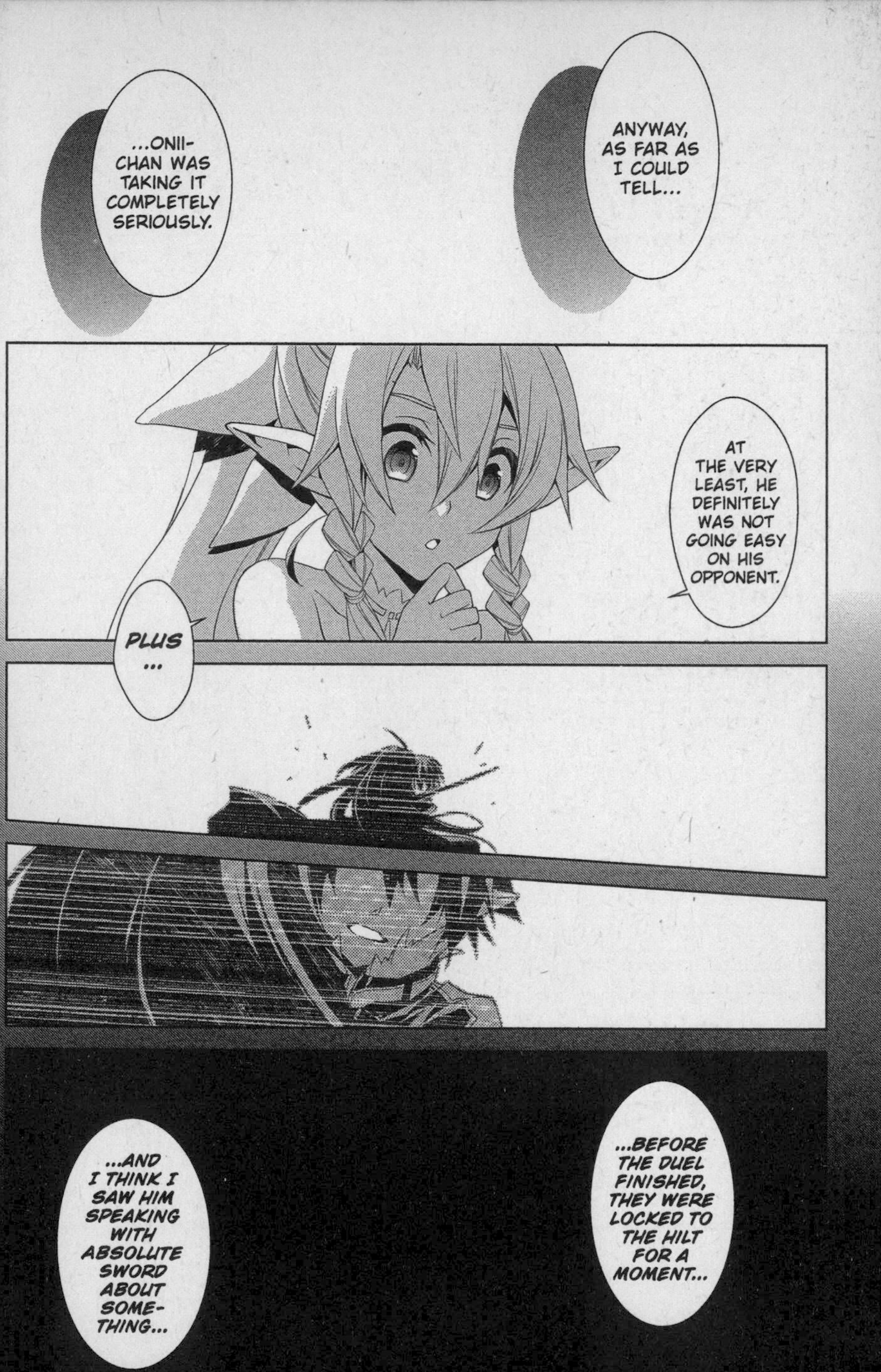
ANYWAY, AS FAR AS I COULD TELL...
...ONII-CHAN WAS TAKING IT COMPLETELY SERIOUSLY.
AT THE VERY LEAST, HE DEFINITELY WAS NOT GOING EASY ON HIS OPPONENT.
PLUS ...
...BEFORE THE DUEL FINISHED, THEY WERE LOCKED TO THE HILT FOR A MOMENT...
...AND I THINK I SAW HIM SPEAKING WITH ABSOLUTE SWORD ABOUT SOME-THING...

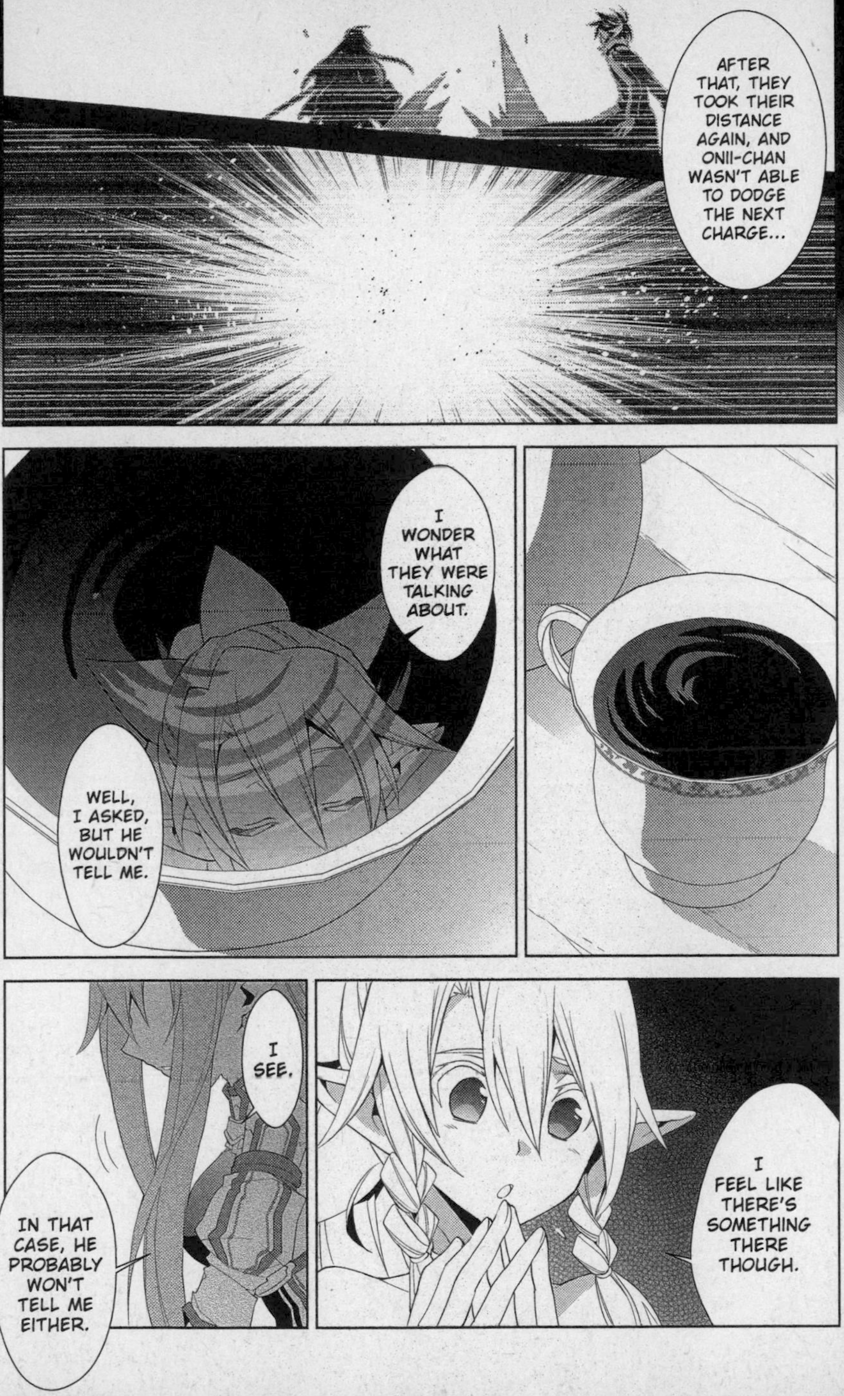
AFTER THAT, THEY TOOK THEIR DISTANCE AGAIN, AND ONII-CHAN WASN'T ABLE TO DODGE THE NEXT CHARGE...
I WONDER WHAT THEY WERE TALKING ABOUT.
WELL, I ASKED, BUT HE WOULDN'T TELL ME.
I FEEL LIKE THERE'S SOMETHING THERE THOUGH.
I SEE.
IN THAT CASE, HE PROBABLY WON'T TELL ME EITHER.

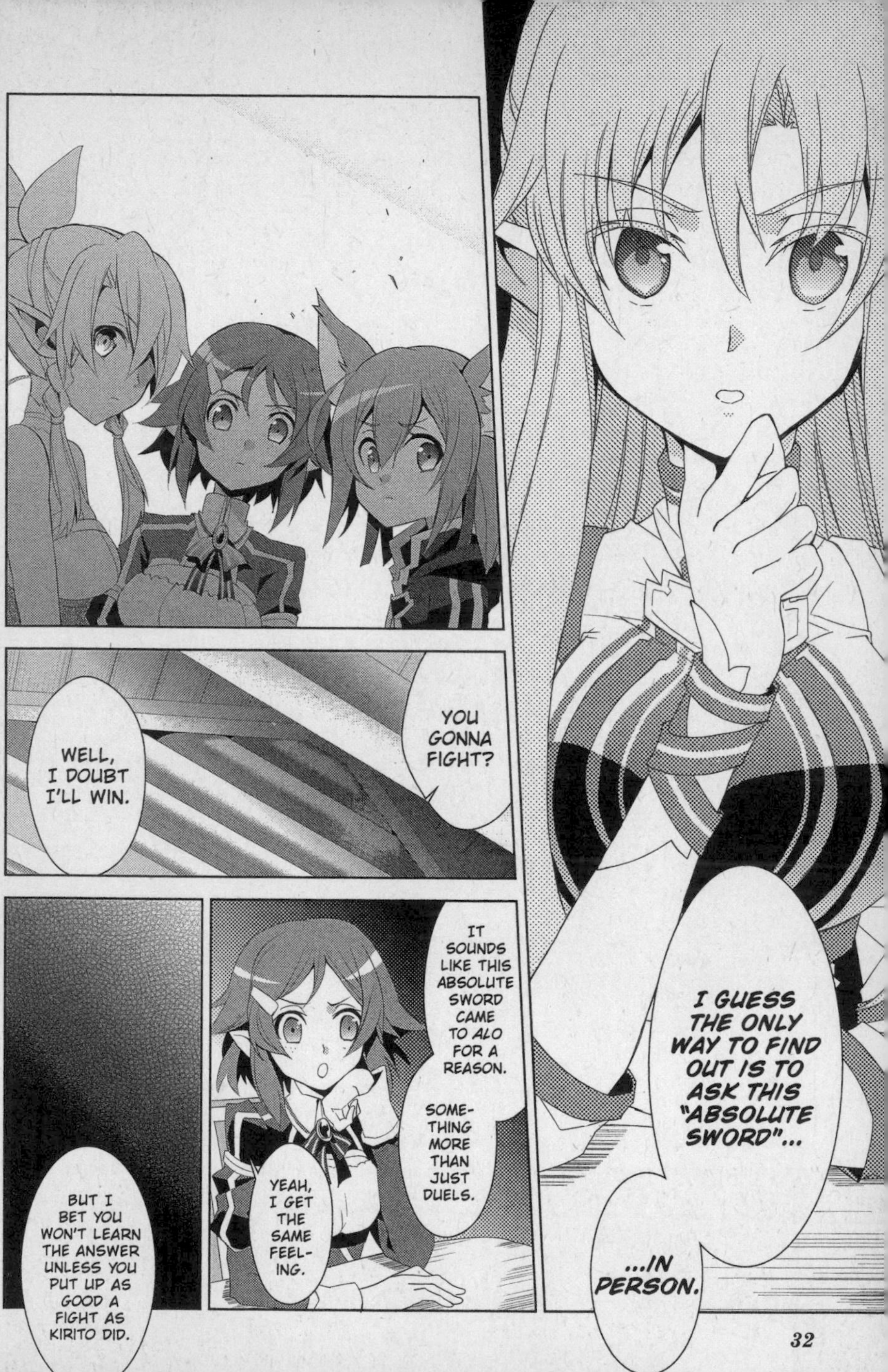
I GUESS THE ONLY WAY TO FIND OUT IS TO ASK THIS "ABSOLUTE SWORD"...
...IN PERSON.
YOU GONNA FIGHT?
WELL, I DOUBT I'LL WIN.
IT SOUNDS LIKE THIS ABSOLUTE SWORD CAME TO ALO FOR A REASON.
SOME-THING MORE THAN JUST DUELS.
YEAH, I GET THE SAME FEEL-ING.
BUT I BET YOU WON'T LEARN THE ANSWER UNLESS YOU PUT UP AS GOOD A FIGHT AS KIRITO DID.

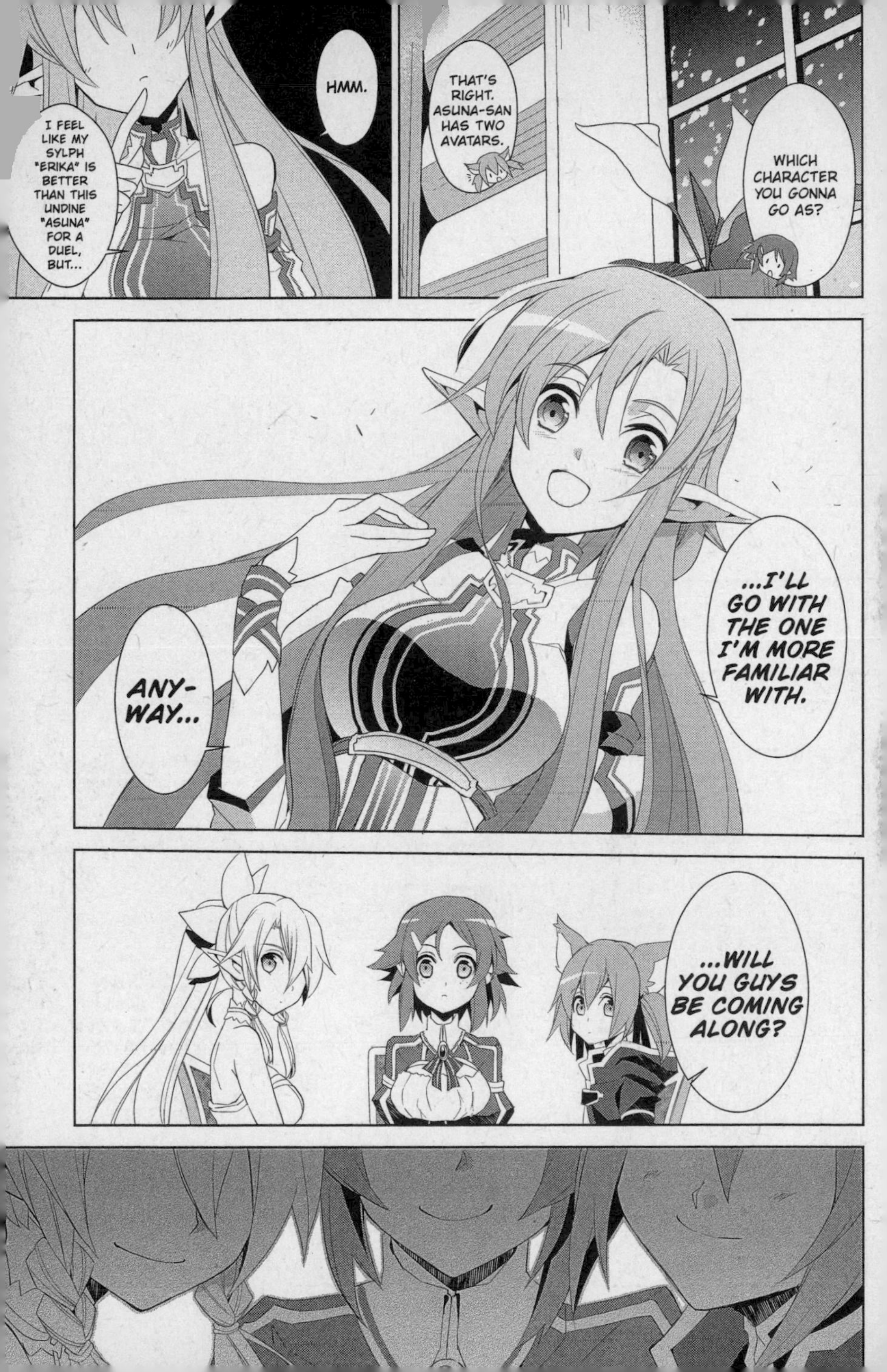
WHICH CHARACTER YOU GONNA GO AS?
THAT'S RIGHT. ASUNA-SAN HAS TWO AVATARS.
HMM.
I FEEL LIKE MY SYLPH "ERIKA" IS BETTER THAN THIS UNDINE "ASUNA" FOR A DUEL, BUT...
...I'LL GO WITH THE ONE I'M MORE FAMILIAR WITH.
ANY-WAY...
...WILL YOU GUYS BE COMING ALONG?

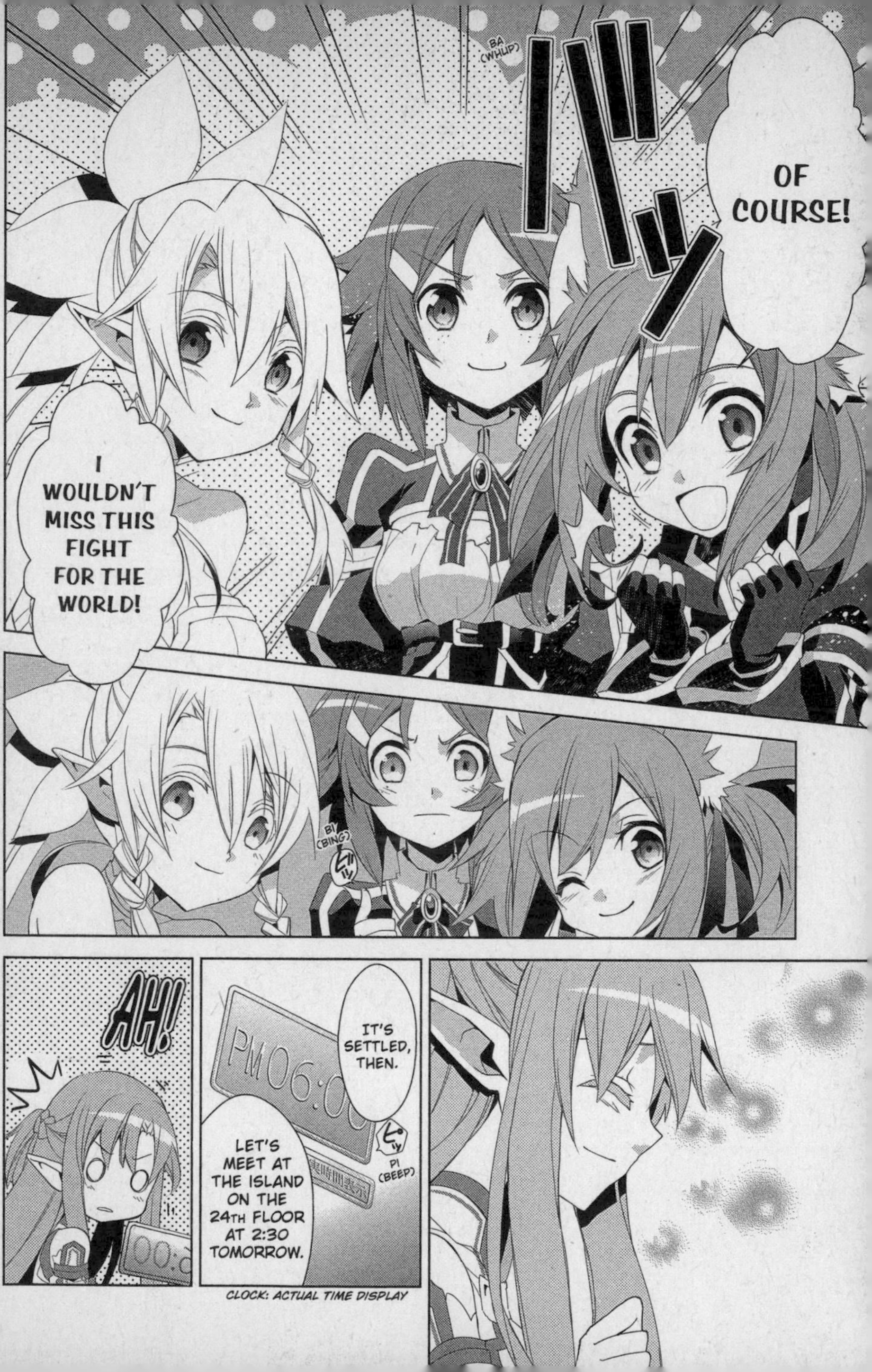
BA (WHUP)
OF COURSE!
I WOULDN'T MISS THIS FIGHT FOR THE WORLD!
BI (BING)
IT'S SETTLED, THEN.
PI (BEEP)
LET'S MEET AT THE ISLAND ON THE 24TH FLOOR AT 2:30 TOMORROW.
CLOCK: ACTUAL TIME DISPLAY
AH!

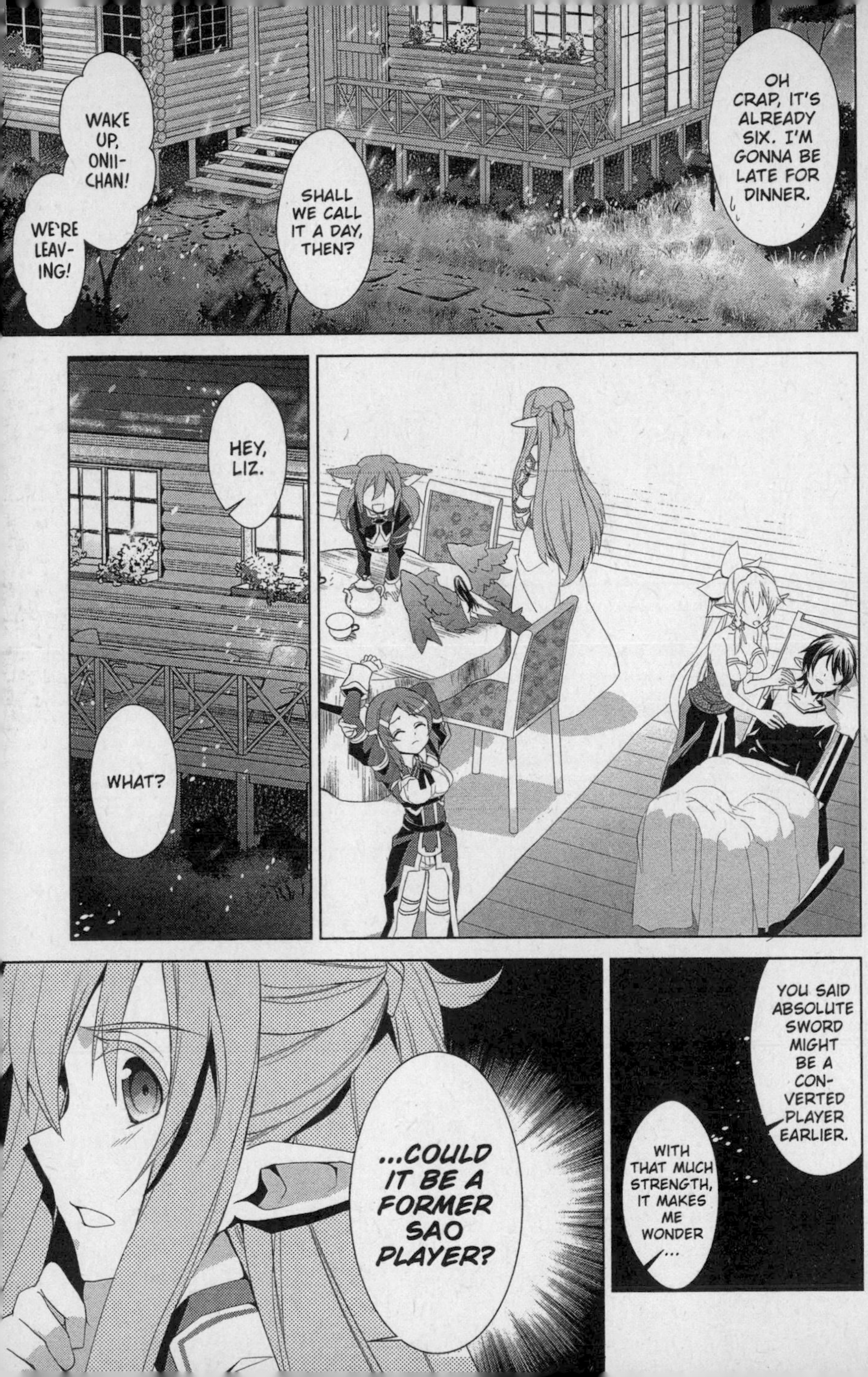
OH CRAP, IT'S ALREADY SIX. I'M GONNA BE LATE FOR DINNER.
SHALL WE CALL IT A DAY, THEN?
WAKE UP, ONII-CHAN!
WE'RE LEAV-ING!
HEY, LIZ.
WHAT?
YOU SAID ABSOLUTE SWORD MIGHT BE A CON-VERTED PLAYER EARLIER.
WITH THAT MUCH STRENGTH, IT MAKES ME WONDER...
...COULD IT BE A FORMER SAO PLAYER?

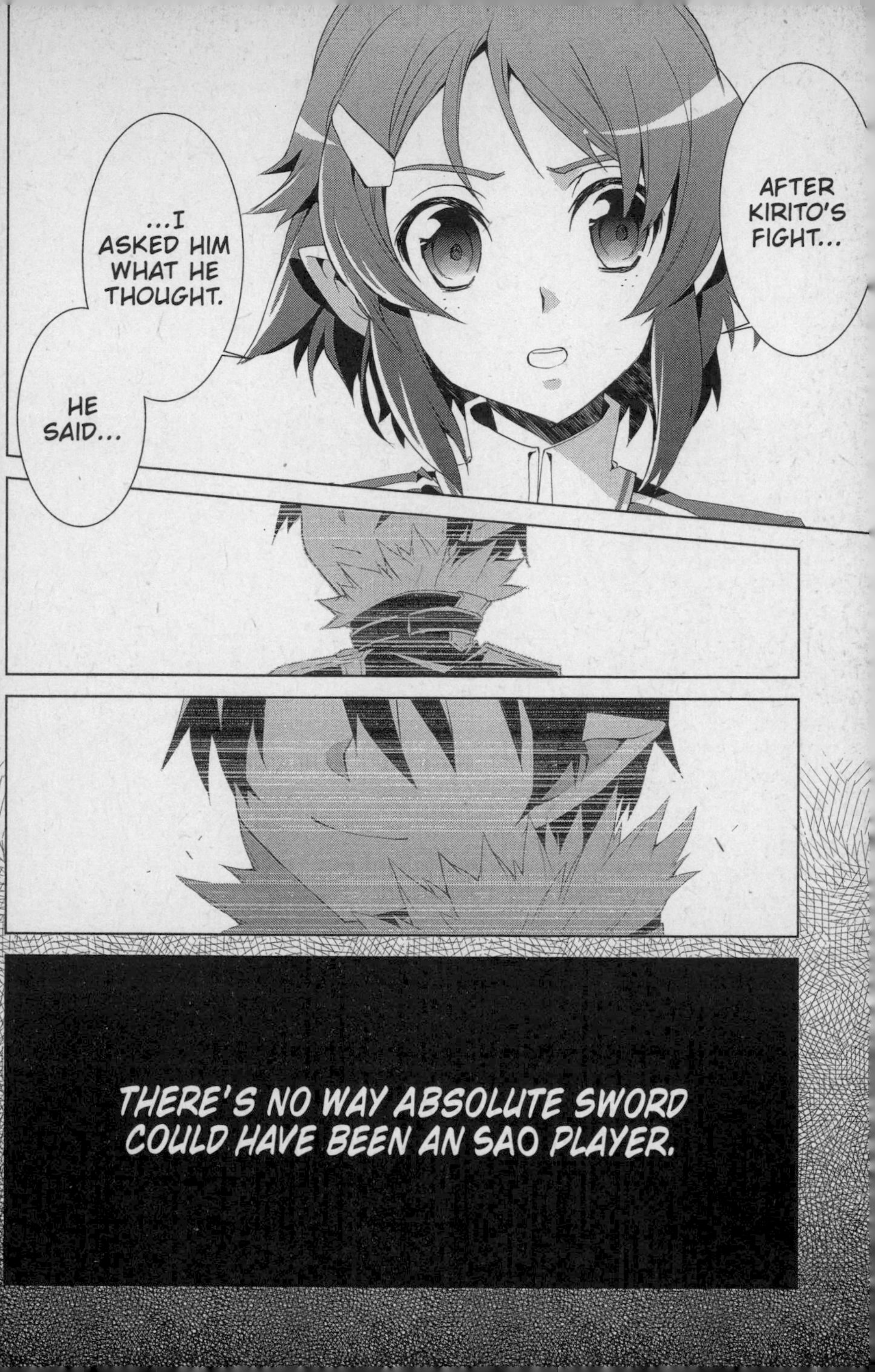
AFTER KIRITO'S FIGHT...
...I ASKED HIM WHAT HE THOUGHT.
HE SAID...
THERE'S NO WAY ABSOLUTE SWORD COULD HAVE BEEN AN SAO PLAYER.

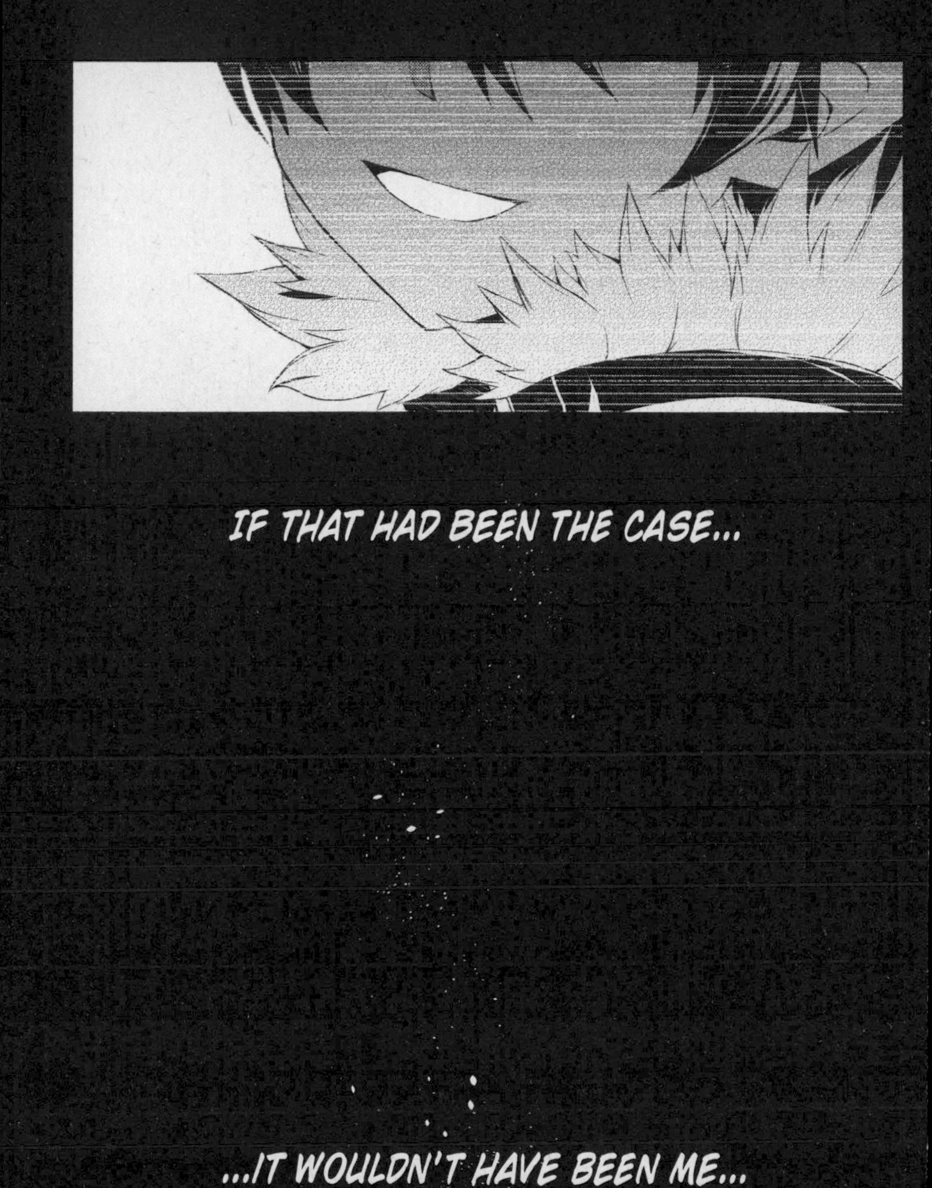
IF THAT HAD BEEN THE CASE...
...IT WOULDN'T HAVE BEEN ME...

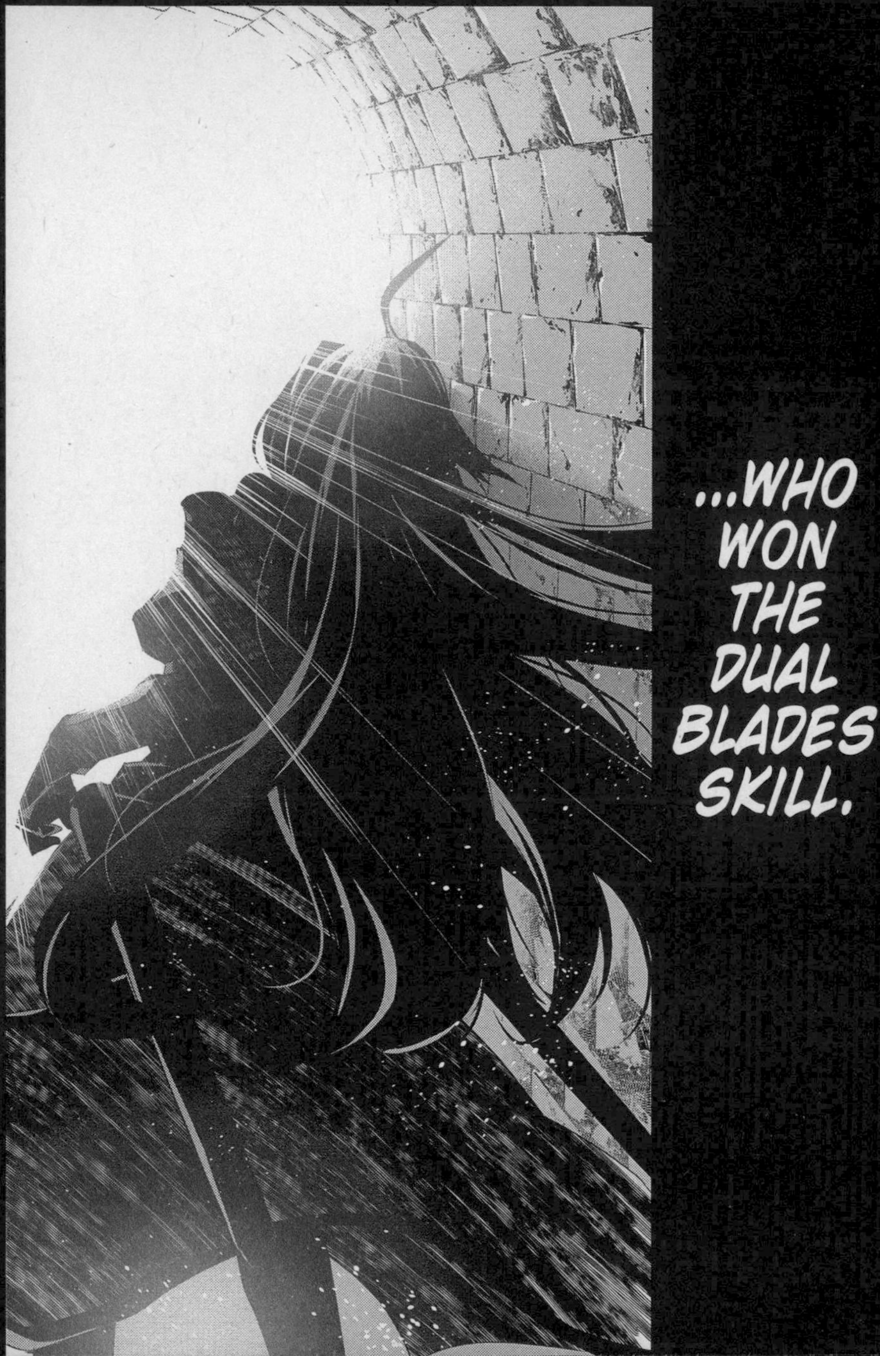
...WHO WON THE DUAL BLADES SKILL.

SWORD ART ONLINE
mother's ROSARY

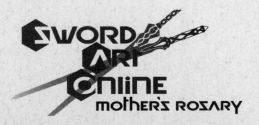

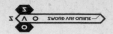

SWORD ART ONLINE mother's ROSARY 01
BACKGROUND GUIDE

NEW AINCRAD

THE OLD CASTLE OF STEEL THAT WAS THE SETTING OF SAO, BROUGHT INTO ALO BY ITS NEW ADMINISTRATORS, "YMIR." AS CAN BE SEEN FROM THE EXISTENCE OF THE LOG CABIN, THE TOWNS, TERRAIN, AND DUNGEONS ARE NEARLY ALL IDENTICAL TO BEFORE. THE BIGGEST DIFFERENCE IS ENEMY STRENGTH. GIVEN THE EXISTENCE OF MULTIPURPOSE MAGIC SPELLS FOR ATTACKING, DEFENSE, AND SUPPORT IN ALO, THE ORIGINAL SPECIFICATIONS OF SAO WOULD NO LONGER BE VERY CHALLENGING. THE BOSSES IN PARTICULAR UNDERWENT DRAMATIC BOOSTS IN DIFFICULTY, AND IT'S QUITE COMMON FOR EVEN VETERAN PARTIES TO GET WIPED OUT AGAINST THEM.

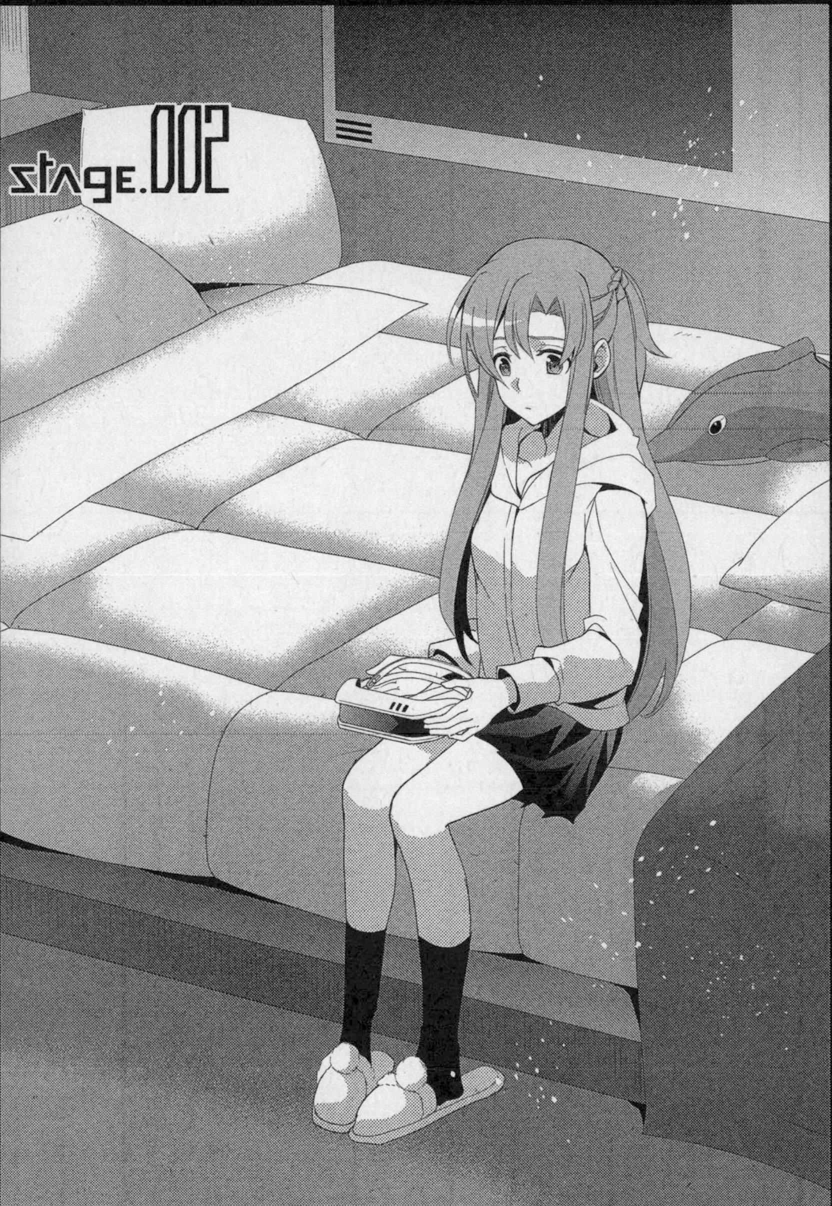
stage.002

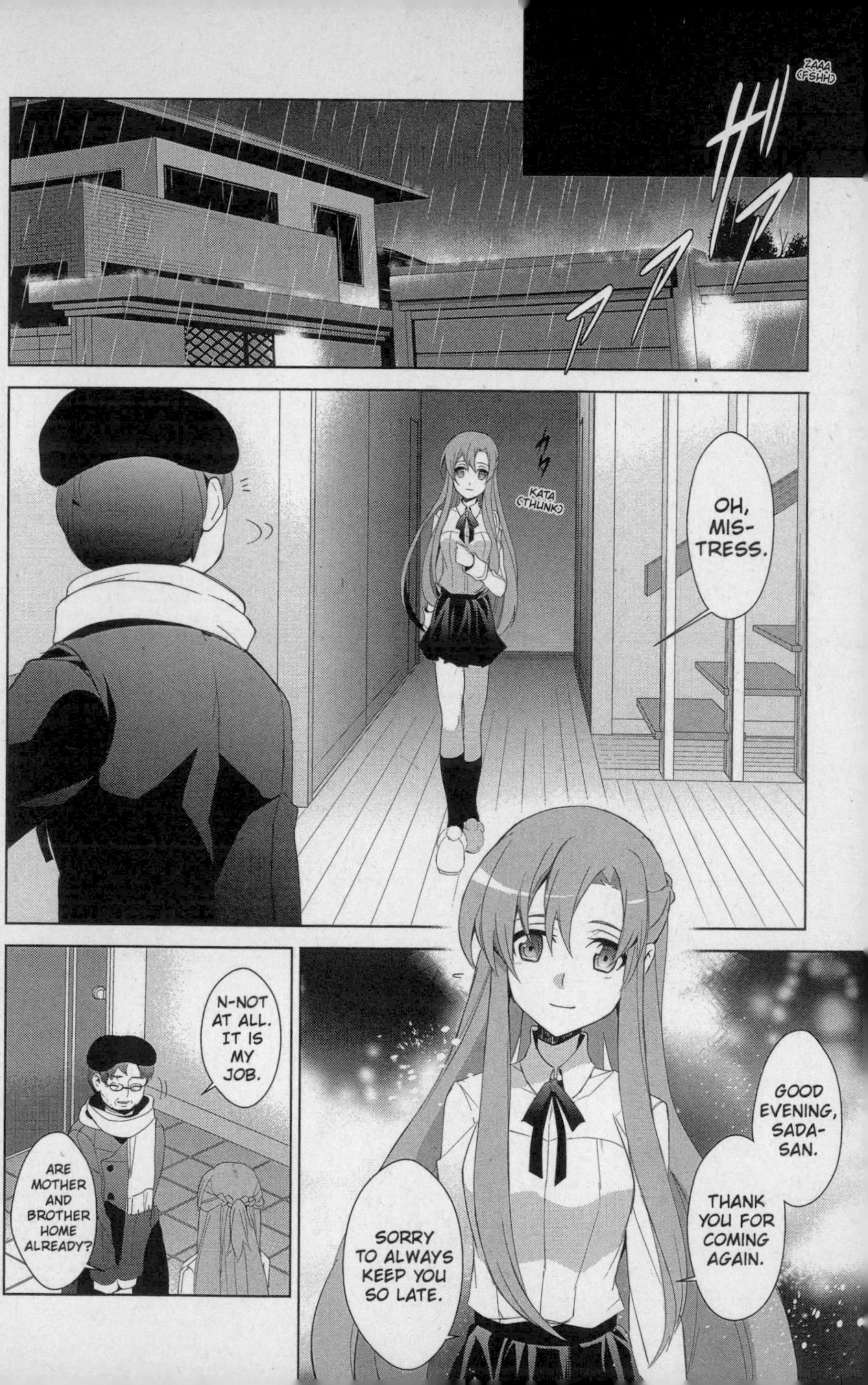
ZAAA (FSHH)
KATA (THUNK)
OH, MIS-TRESS.
GOOD EVENING, SADA-SAN.
THANK YOU FOR COMING AGAIN.
SORRY TO ALWAYS KEEP YOU SO LATE.
N-NOT AT ALL. IT IS MY JOB.
ARE MOTHER AND BROTHER HOME ALREADY?

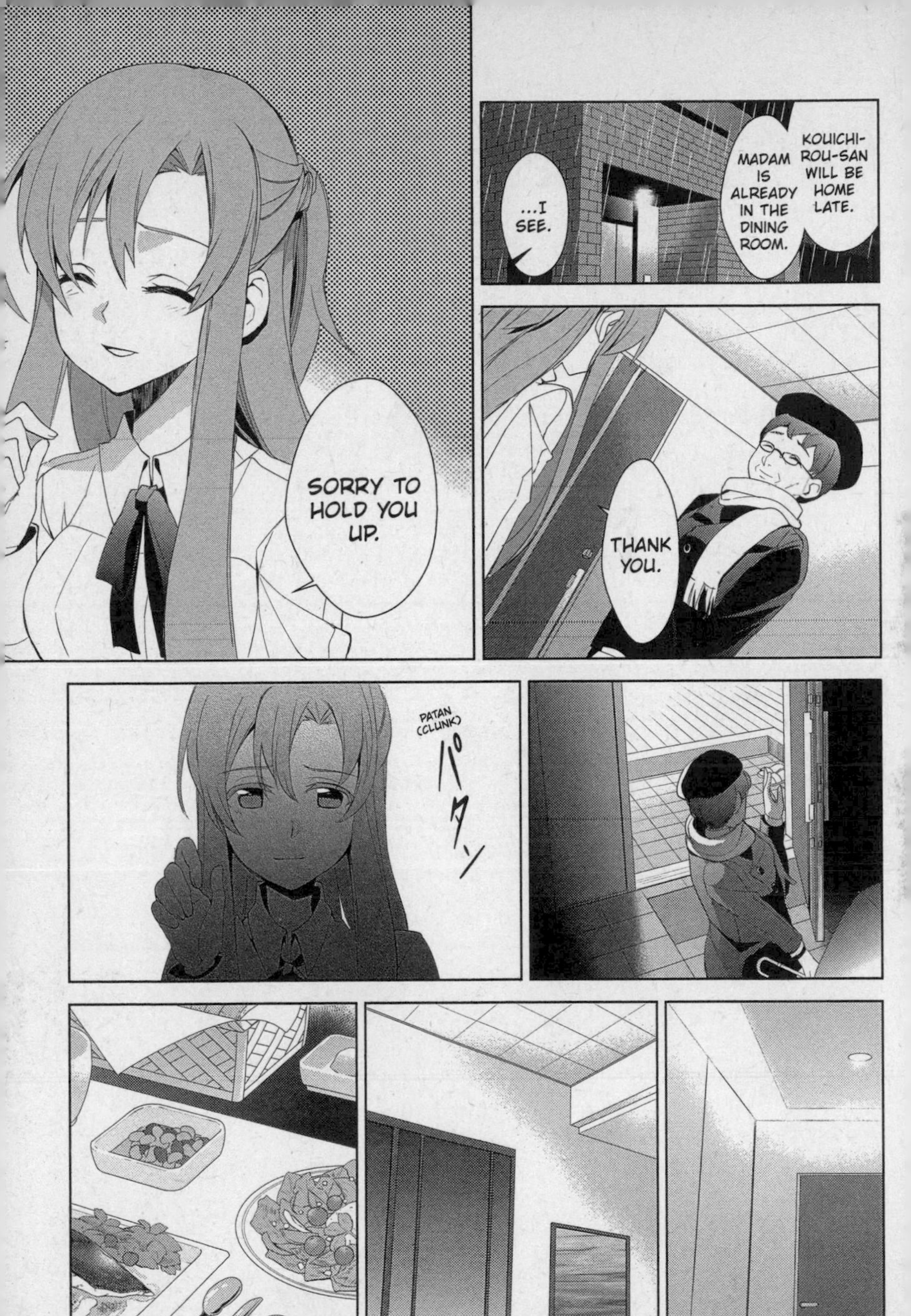
KOUICHI-ROU-SAN WILL BE HOME LATE.
MADAM IS ALREADY IN THE DINING ROOM.
...I SEE.
THANK YOU.
SORRY TO HOLD YOU UP.
PATAN (CLUNK)
パタン

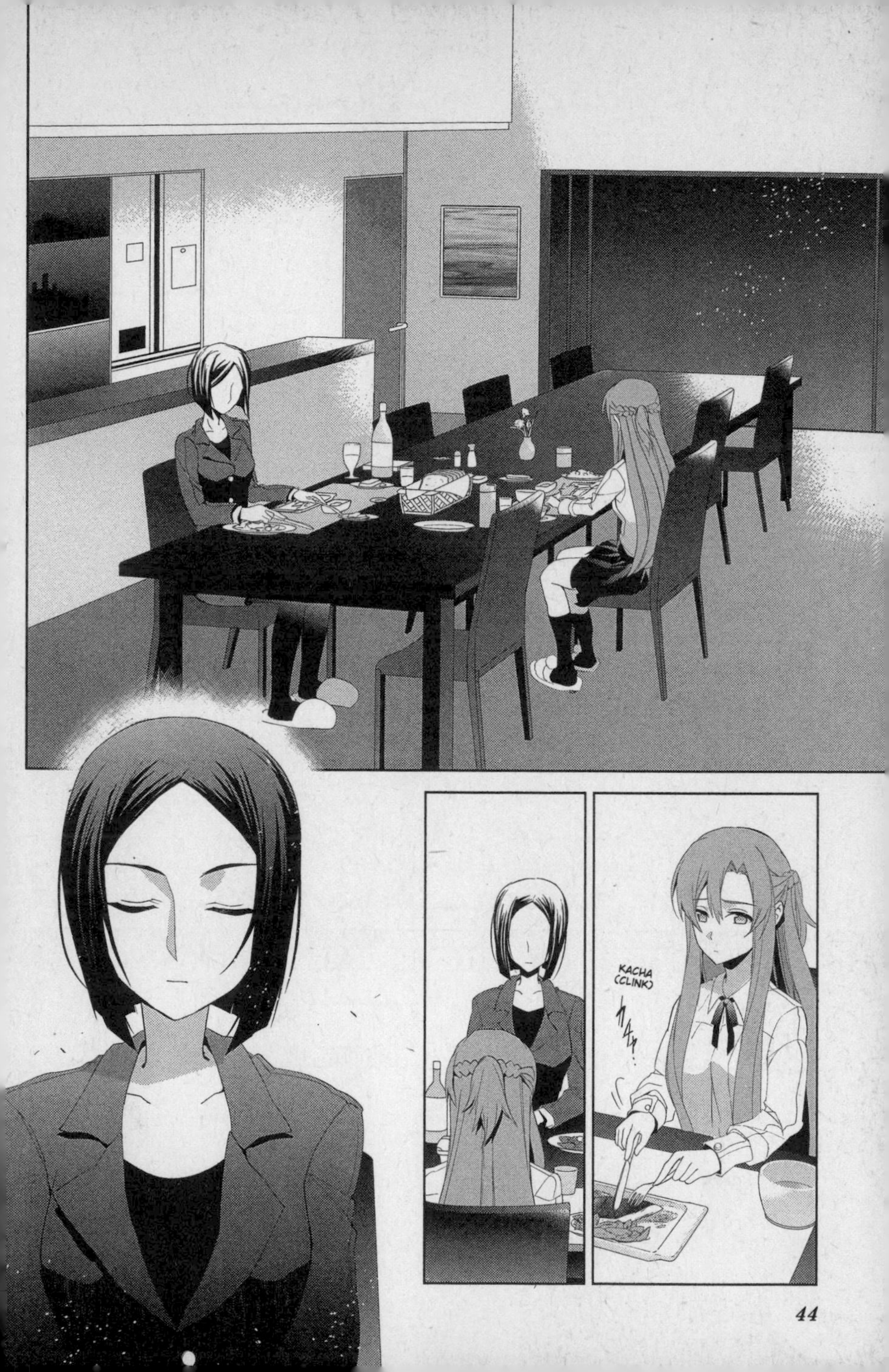
KACHA
(CLINK)

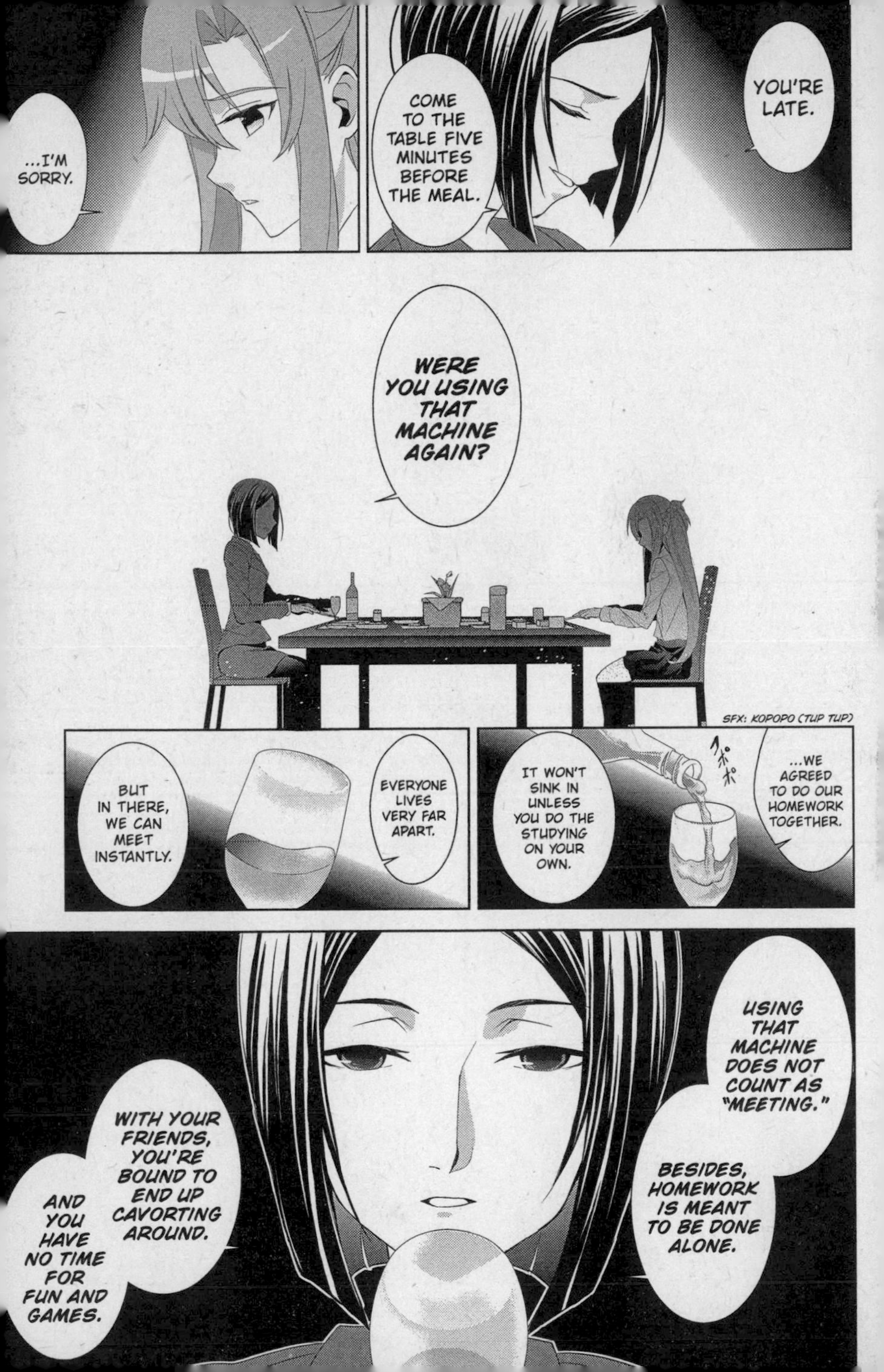
YOU'RE LATE.
COME TO THE TABLE FIVE MINUTES BEFORE THE MEAL.
...I'M SORRY.
WERE YOU USING THAT MACHINE AGAIN?
SFX: KOPOPO (TUP TUP)
...WE AGREED TO DO OUR HOMEWORK TOGETHER.
コポポ
IT WON'T SINK IN UNLESS YOU DO THE STUDYING ON YOUR OWN.
EVERYONE LIVES VERY FAR APART.
BUT IN THERE, WE CAN MEET INSTANTLY.
USING THAT MACHINE DOES NOT COUNT AS "MEETING."
BESIDES, HOMEWORK IS MEANT TO BE DONE ALONE.
WITH YOUR FRIENDS, YOU'RE BOUND TO END UP CAVORTING AROUND.
AND YOU HAVE NO TIME FOR FUN AND GAMES.

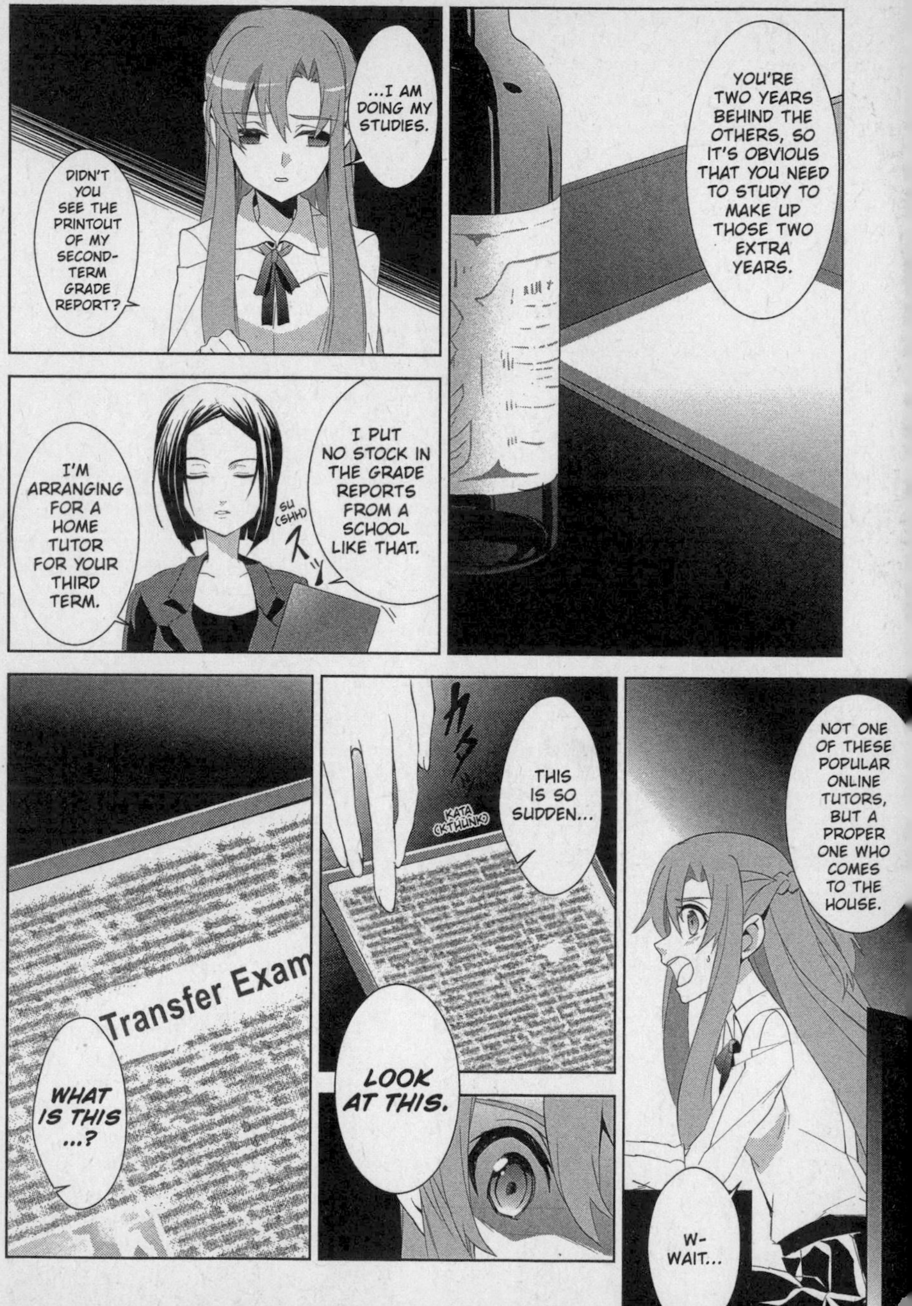
YOU'RE TWO YEARS BEHIND THE OTHERS, SO IT'S OBVIOUS THAT YOU NEED TO STUDY TO MAKE UP THOSE TWO EXTRA YEARS.
...I AM DOING MY STUDIES.
DIDN'T YOU SEE THE PRINTOUT OF MY SECOND-TERM GRADE REPORT?
I PUT NO STOCK IN THE GRADE REPORTS FROM A SCHOOL LIKE THAT.
SU (SHH)
I'M ARRANGING FOR A HOME TUTOR FOR YOUR THIRD TERM.
NOT ONE OF THESE POPULAR ONLINE TUTORS, BUT A PROPER ONE WHO COMES TO THE HOUSE.
W-WAIT...
THIS IS SO SUDDEN...
KATA (KTHUNK)
LOOK AT THIS.
Transfer Exam
WHAT IS THIS ...?

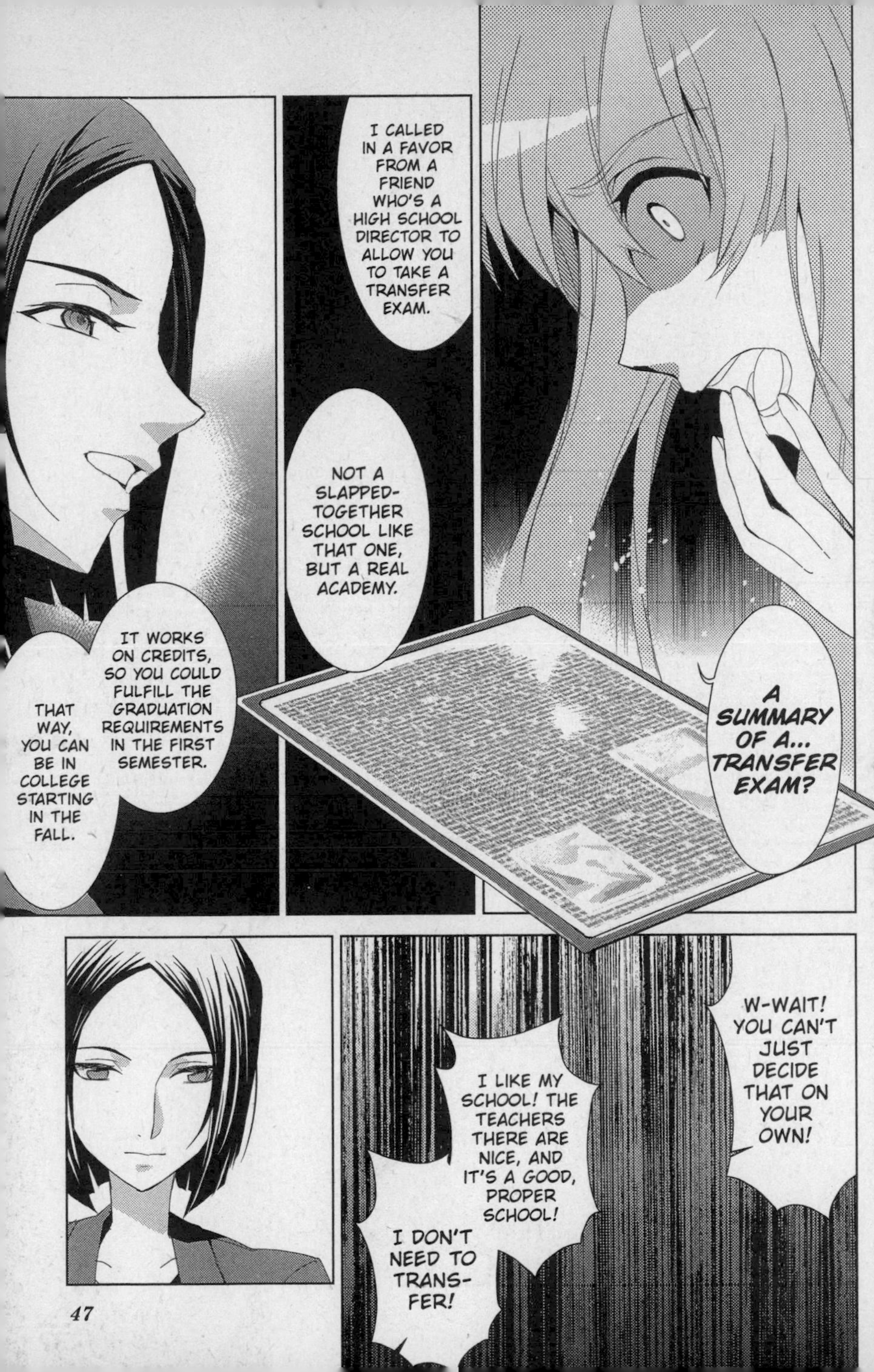
A SUMMARY OF A... TRANSFER EXAM?
I CALLED IN A FAVOR FROM A FRIEND WHO'S A HIGH SCHOOL DIRECTOR TO ALLOW YOU TO TAKE A TRANSFER EXAM.
NOT A SLAPPED-TOGETHER SCHOOL LIKE THAT ONE, BUT A REAL ACADEMY.
IT WORKS ON CREDITS, SO YOU COULD FULFILL THE GRADUATION REQUIREMENTS IN THE FIRST SEMESTER.
THAT WAY, YOU CAN BE IN COLLEGE STARTING IN THE FALL.
W-WAIT! YOU CAN'T JUST DECIDE THAT ON YOUR OWN!
I LIKE MY SCHOOL! THE TEACHERS THERE ARE NICE, AND IT'S A GOOD, PROPER SCHOOL!
I DON'T NEED TO TRANS-FER!

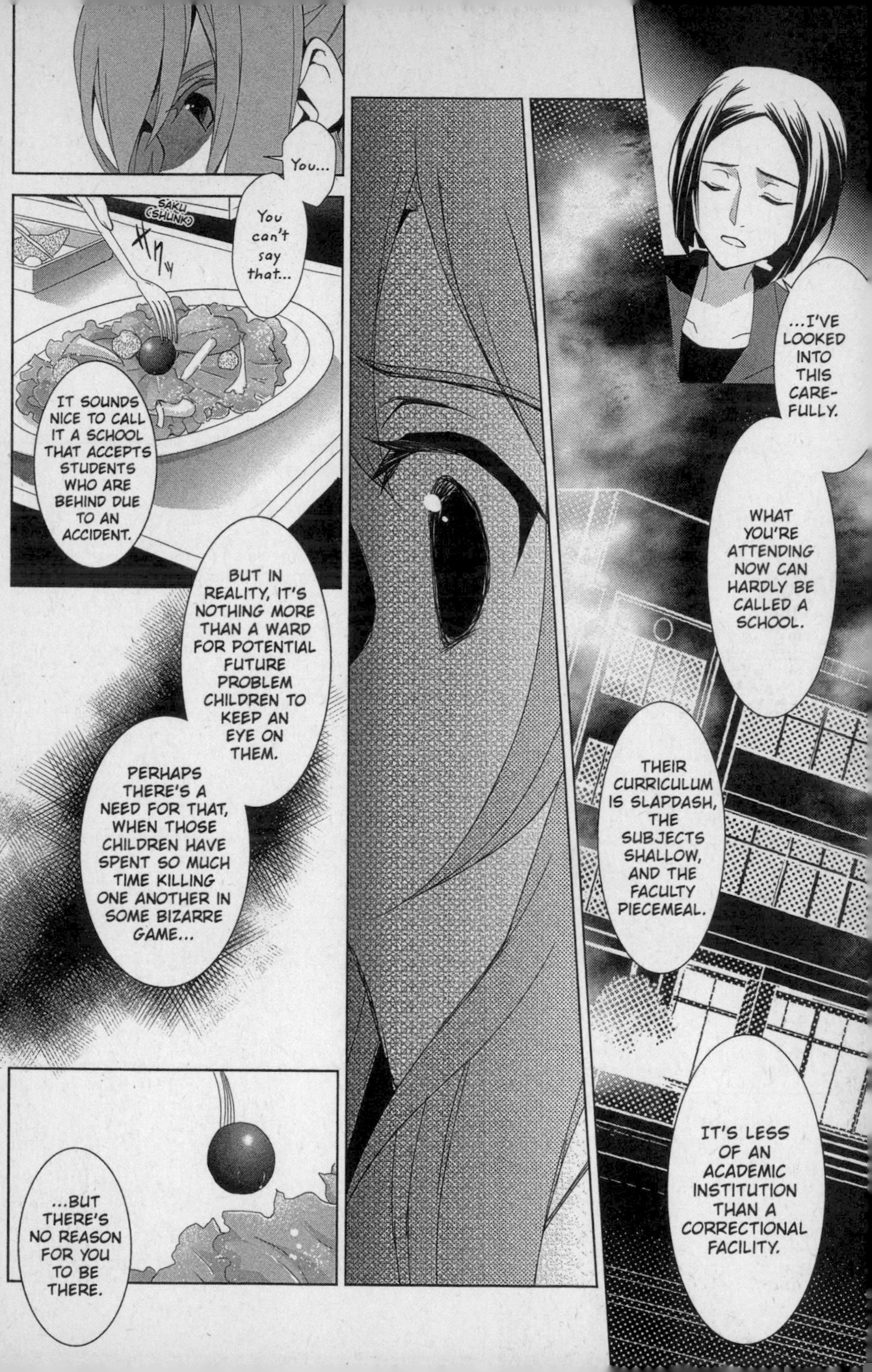
...I'VE LOOKED INTO THIS CARE-FULLY.
WHAT YOU'RE ATTENDING NOW CAN HARDLY BE CALLED A SCHOOL.
THEIR CURRICULUM IS SLAPDASH, THE SUBJECTS SHALLOW, AND THE FACULTY PIECEMEAL.
IT'S LESS OF AN ACADEMIC INSTITUTION THAN A CORRECTIONAL FACILITY.
You...
You can't say that...
SAKU (SHUNK)
IT SOUNDS NICE TO CALL IT A SCHOOL THAT ACCEPTS STUDENTS WHO ARE BEHIND DUE TO AN ACCIDENT.
BUT IN REALITY, IT'S NOTHING MORE THAN A WARD FOR POTENTIAL FUTURE PROBLEM CHILDREN TO KEEP AN EYE ON THEM.
PERHAPS THERE'S A NEED FOR THAT, WHEN THOSE CHILDREN HAVE SPENT SO MUCH TIME KILLING ONE ANOTHER IN SOME BIZARRE GAME...
...BUT THERE'S NO REASON FOR YOU TO BE THERE.

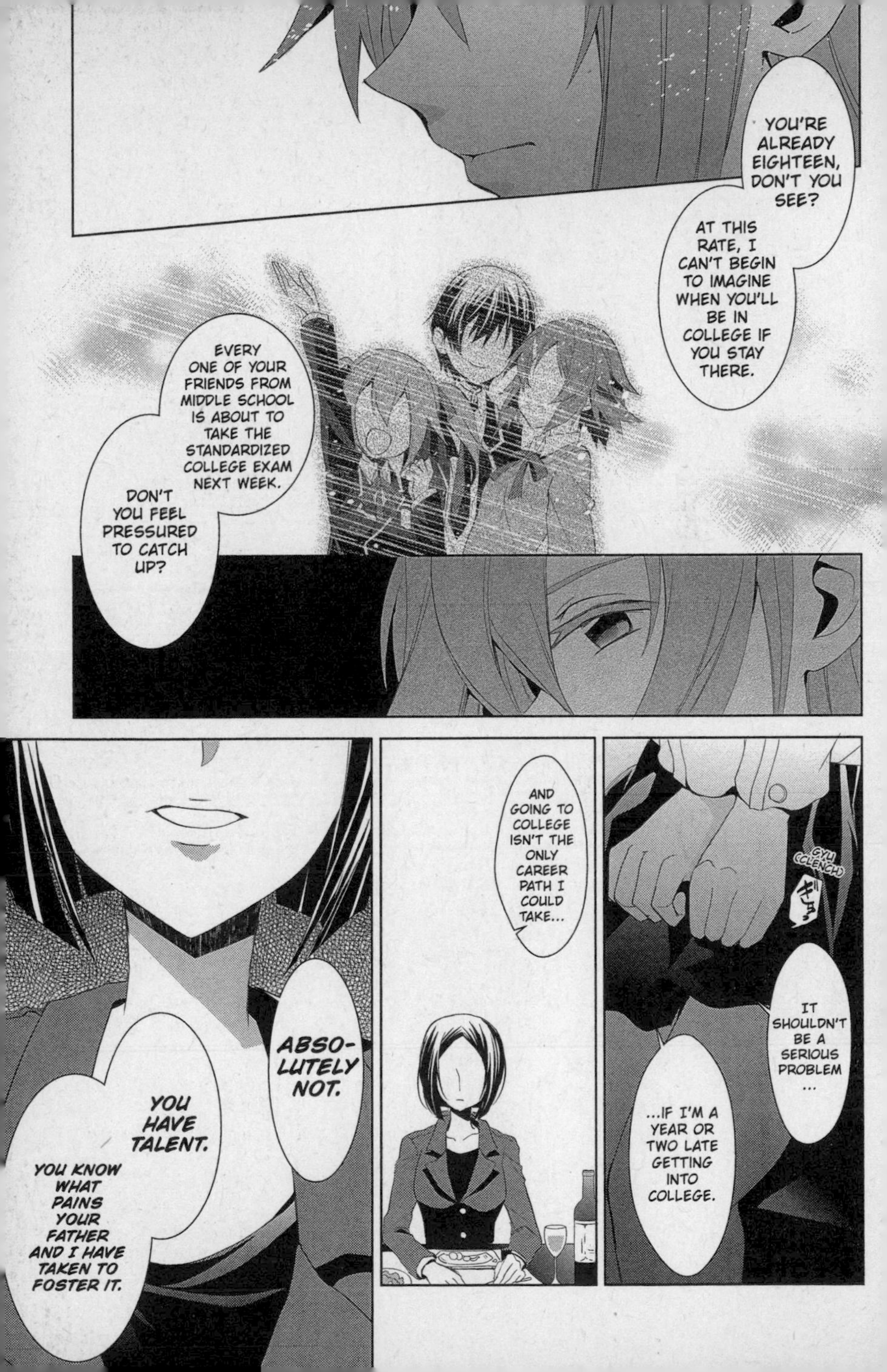
YOU'RE ALREADY EIGHTEEN, DON'T YOU SEE?
AT THIS RATE, I CAN'T BEGIN TO IMAGINE WHEN YOU'LL BE IN COLLEGE IF YOU STAY THERE.
EVERY ONE OF YOUR FRIENDS FROM MIDDLE SCHOOL IS ABOUT TO TAKE THE STANDARDIZED COLLEGE EXAM NEXT WEEK.
DON'T YOU FEEL PRESSURED TO CATCH UP?
GYU (CLENCH)
IT SHOULDN'T BE A SERIOUS PROBLEM...
...IF I'M A YEAR OR TWO LATE GETTING INTO COLLEGE.
AND GOING TO COLLEGE ISN'T THE ONLY CAREER PATH I COULD TAKE...
ABSO-LUTELY NOT.
YOU HAVE TALENT.
YOU KNOW WHAT PAINS YOUR FATHER AND I HAVE TAKEN TO FOSTER IT.

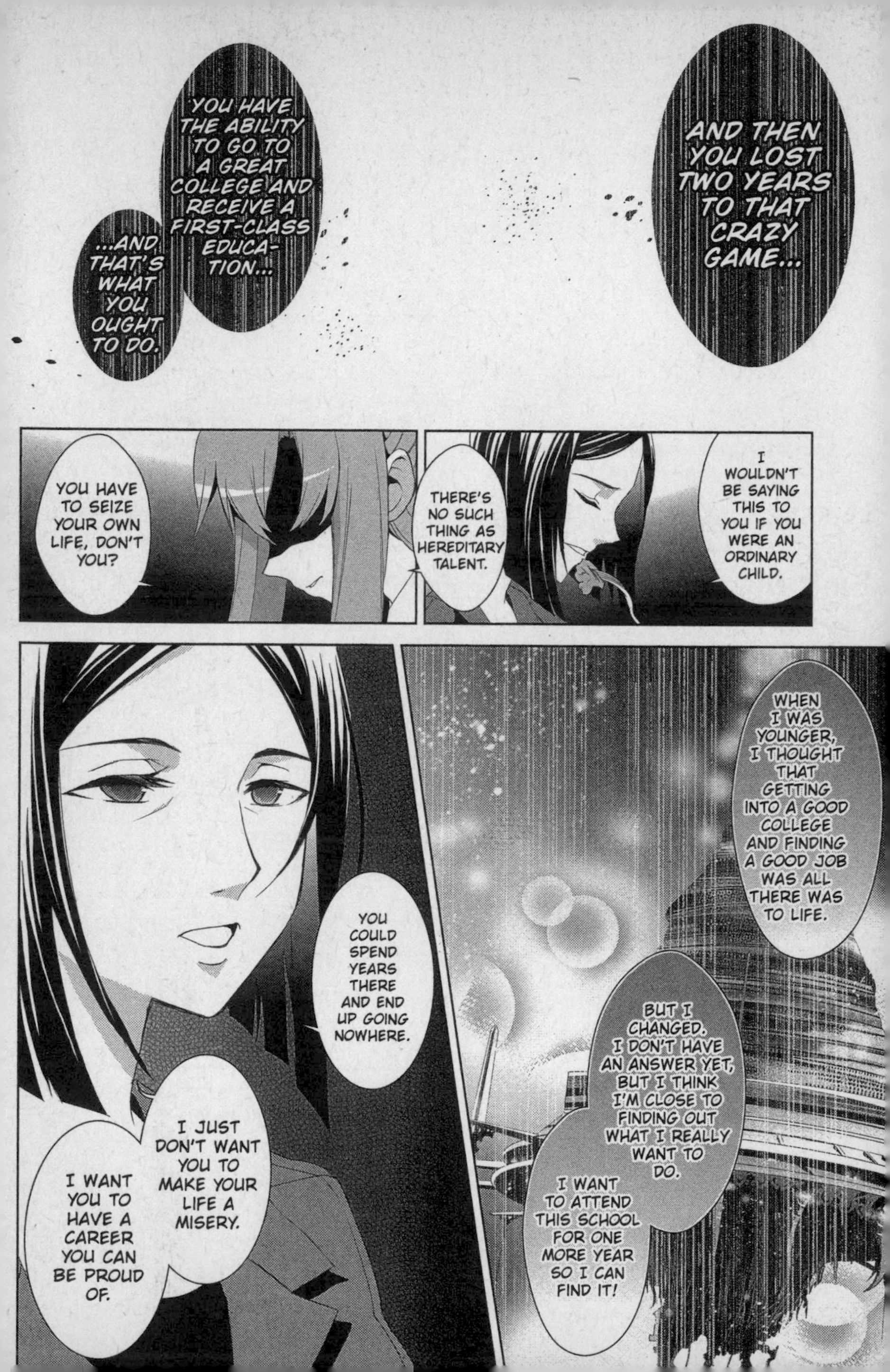
AND THEN YOU LOST TWO YEARS TO THAT CRAZY GAME...
YOU HAVE THE ABILITY TO GO TO A GREAT COLLEGE AND RECEIVE A FIRST-CLASS EDUCA-TION...
...AND THAT'S WHAT YOU OUGHT TO DO.
I WOULDN'T BE SAYING THIS TO YOU IF YOU WERE AN ORDINARY CHILD.
THERE'S NO SUCH THING AS HEREDITARY TALENT.
YOU HAVE TO SEIZE YOUR OWN LIFE, DON'T YOU?
WHEN I WAS YOUNGER, I THOUGHT THAT GETTING INTO A GOOD COLLEGE AND FINDING A GOOD JOB WAS ALL THERE WAS TO LIFE.
BUT I CHANGED. I DON'T HAVE AN ANSWER YET, BUT I THINK I'M CLOSE TO FINDING OUT WHAT I REALLY WANT TO DO.
I WANT TO ATTEND THIS SCHOOL FOR ONE MORE YEAR SO I CAN FIND IT!
YOU COULD SPEND YEARS THERE AND END UP GOING NOWHERE.
I JUST DON'T WANT YOU TO MAKE YOUR LIFE A MISERY.
I WANT YOU TO HAVE A CAREER YOU CAN BE PROUD OF.

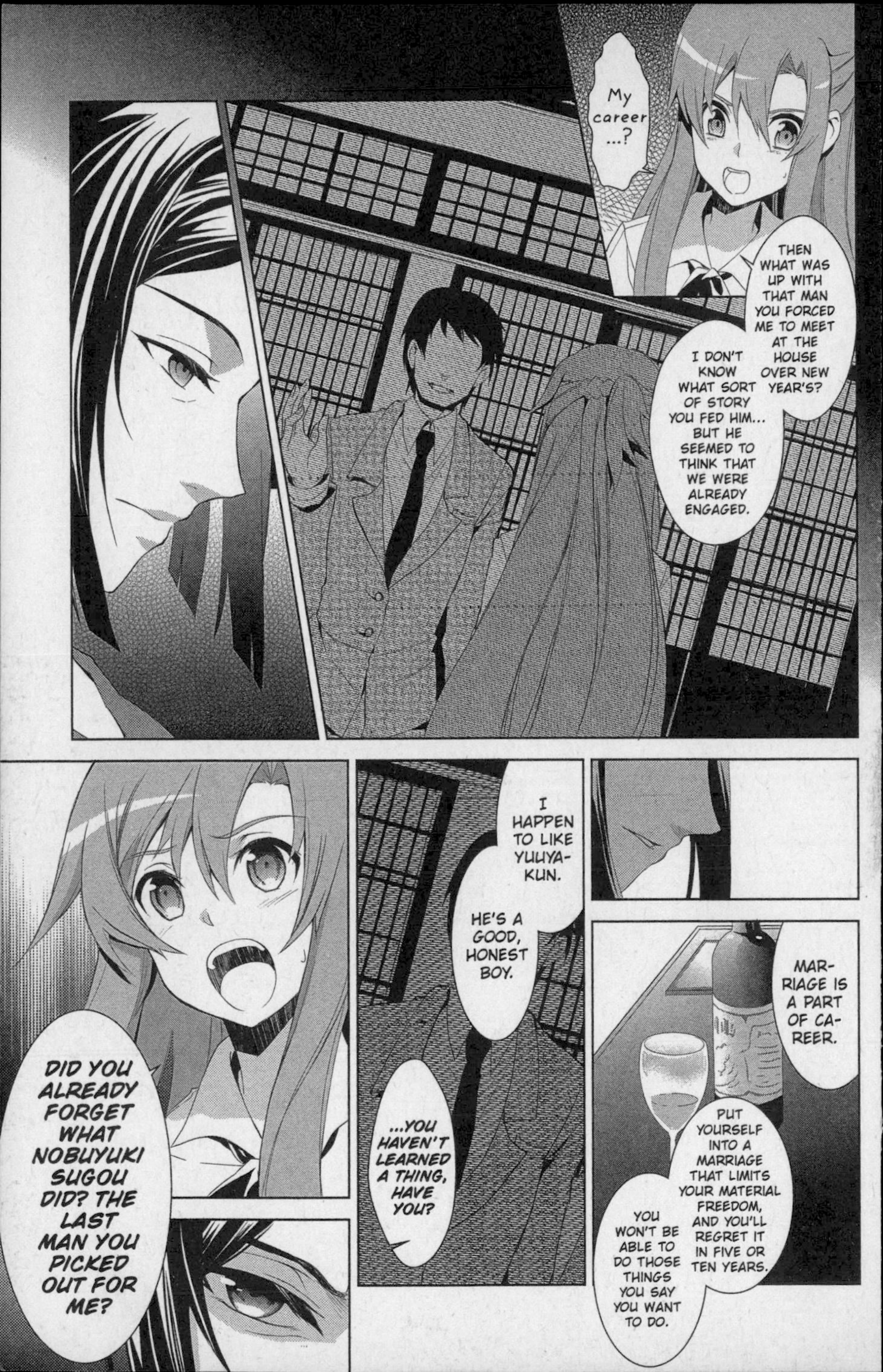
My career ...?
THEN WHAT WAS UP WITH THAT MAN YOU FORCED ME TO MEET AT THE HOUSE OVER NEW YEAR'S?
I DON'T KNOW WHAT SORT OF STORY YOU FED HIM... BUT HE SEEMED TO THINK THAT WE WERE ALREADY ENGAGED.
MAR-RIAGE IS A PART OF CA-REER.
PUT YOURSELF INTO A MARRIAGE THAT LIMITS YOUR MATERIAL FREEDOM, AND YOU'LL REGRET IT IN FIVE OR TEN YEARS.
YOU WON'T BE ABLE TO DO THOSE THINGS YOU SAY YOU WANT TO DO.
I HAPPEN TO LIKE YUUYA-KUN.
HE'S A GOOD, HONEST BOY.
...YOU HAVEN'T LEARNED A THING, HAVE YOU?
DID YOU ALREADY FORGET WHAT NOBUYUKI SUGOU DID? THE LAST MAN YOU PICKED OUT FOR ME?

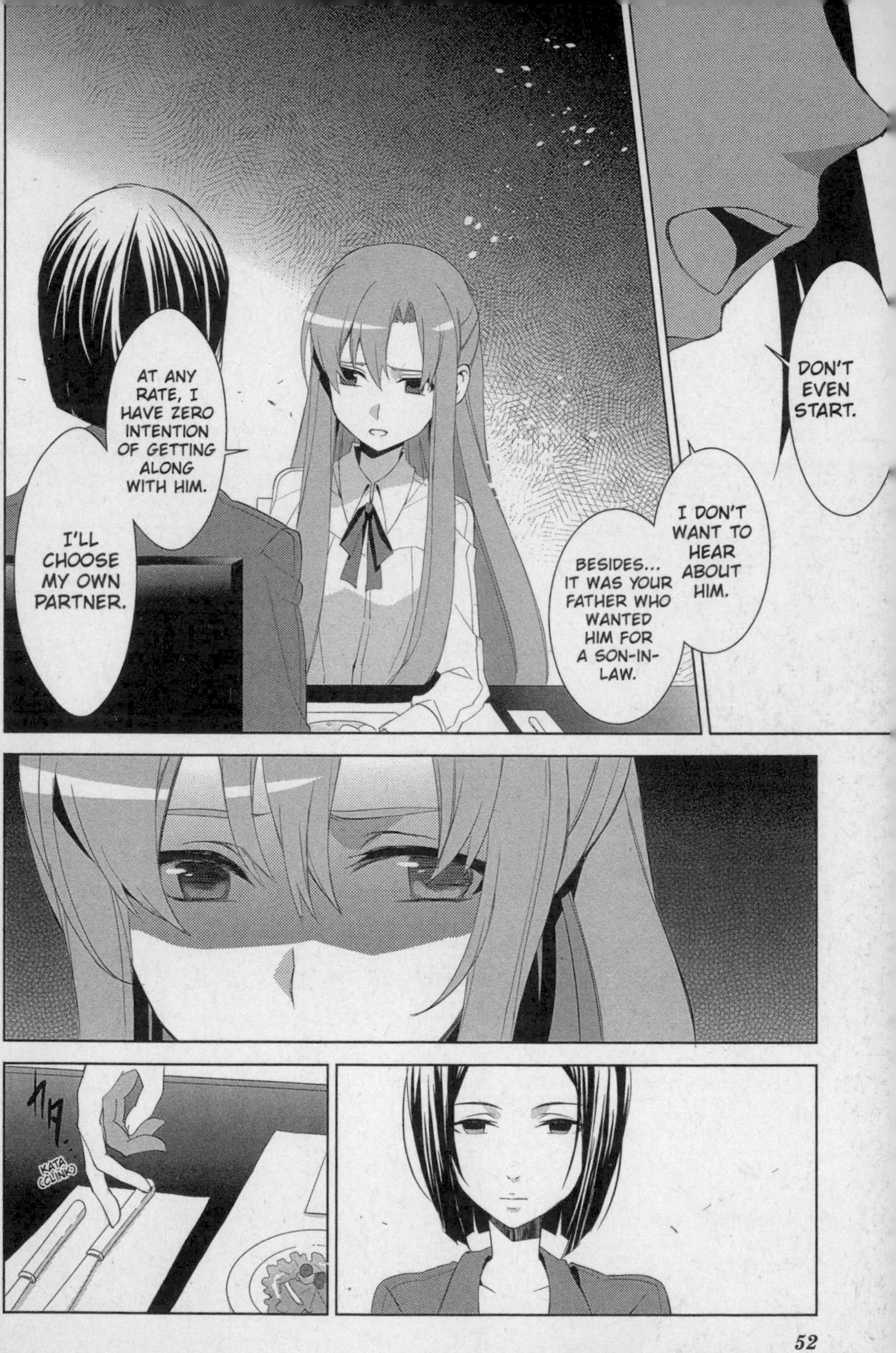
DON'T EVEN START.
I DON'T WANT TO HEAR ABOUT HIM.
BESIDES... IT WAS YOUR FATHER WHO WANTED HIM FOR A SON-IN-LAW.
AT ANY RATE, I HAVE ZERO INTENTION OF GETTING ALONG WITH HIM.
I'LL CHOOSE MY OWN PARTNER.
KATA (CLINK)

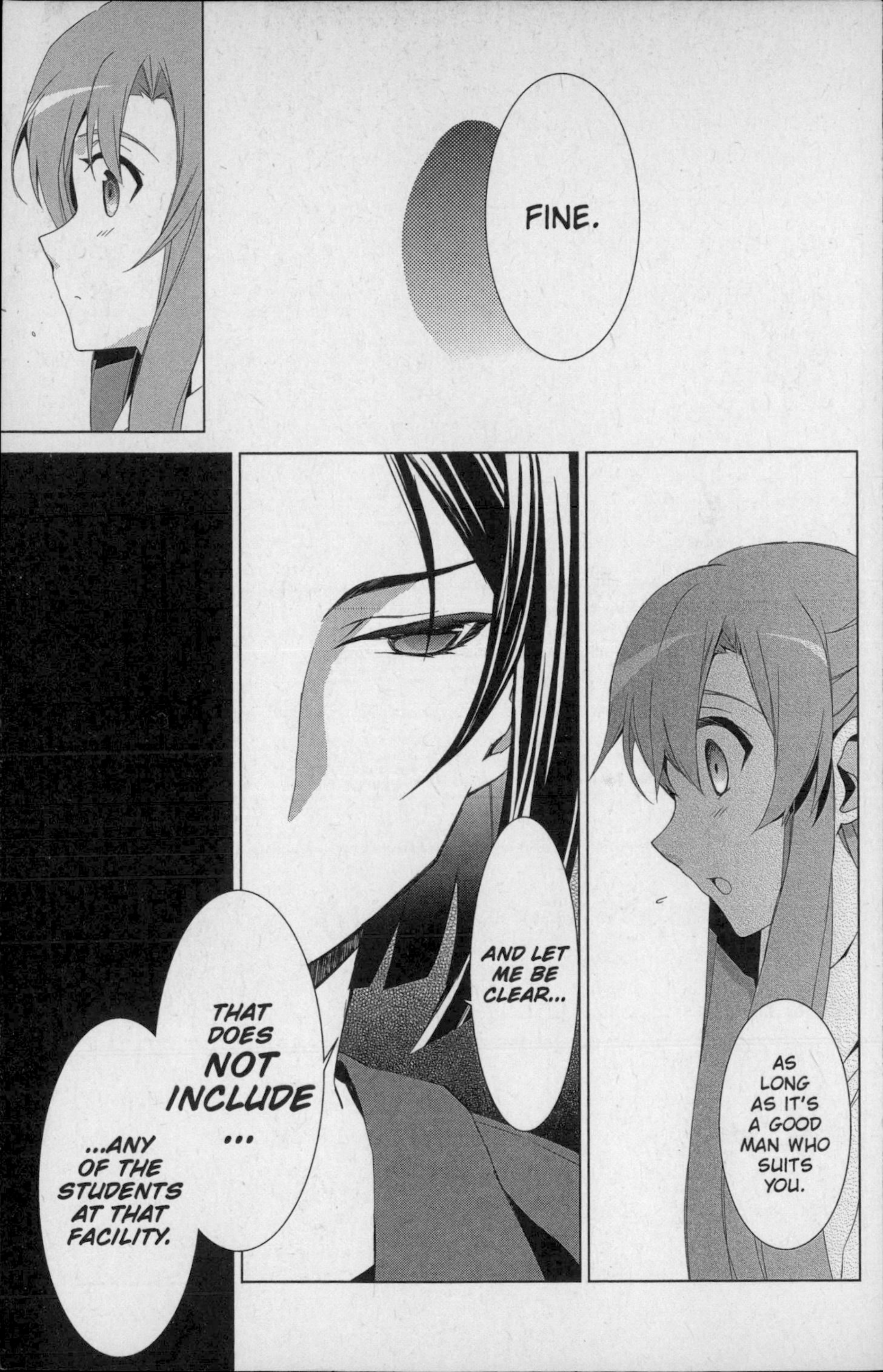
FINE.
AS LONG AS IT'S A GOOD MAN WHO SUITS YOU.
AND LET ME BE CLEAR...
THAT DOES NOT INCLUDE ...
...ANY OF THE STUDENTS AT THAT FACILITY.

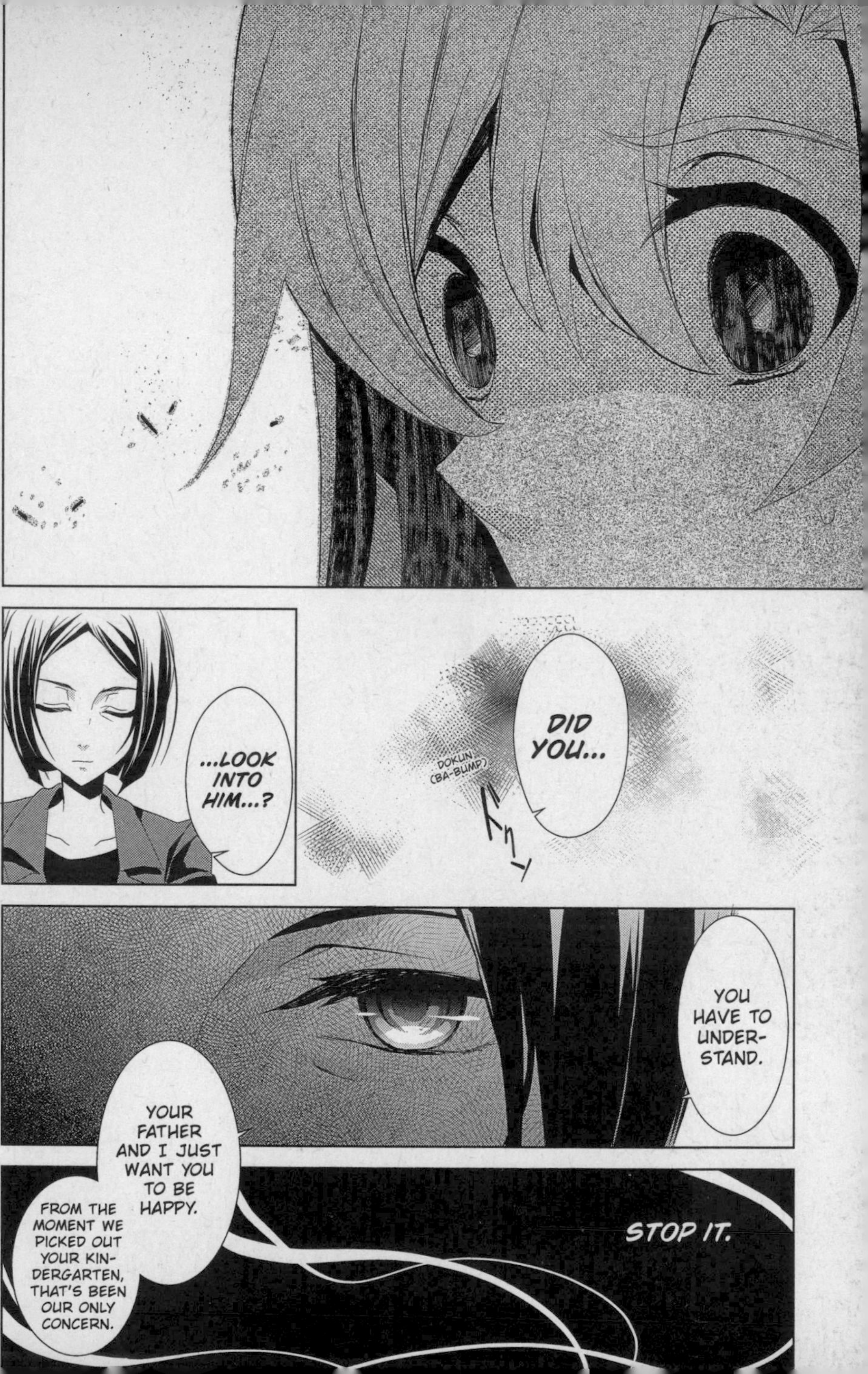
DID YOU...
DOKUN (BA-BUMP)
...LOOK INTO HIM...?
YOU HAVE TO UNDER-STAND.
YOUR FATHER AND I JUST WANT YOU TO BE HAPPY.
STOP IT.
FROM THE MOMENT WE PICKED OUT YOUR KIN-DERGARTEN, THAT'S BEEN OUR ONLY CONCERN.

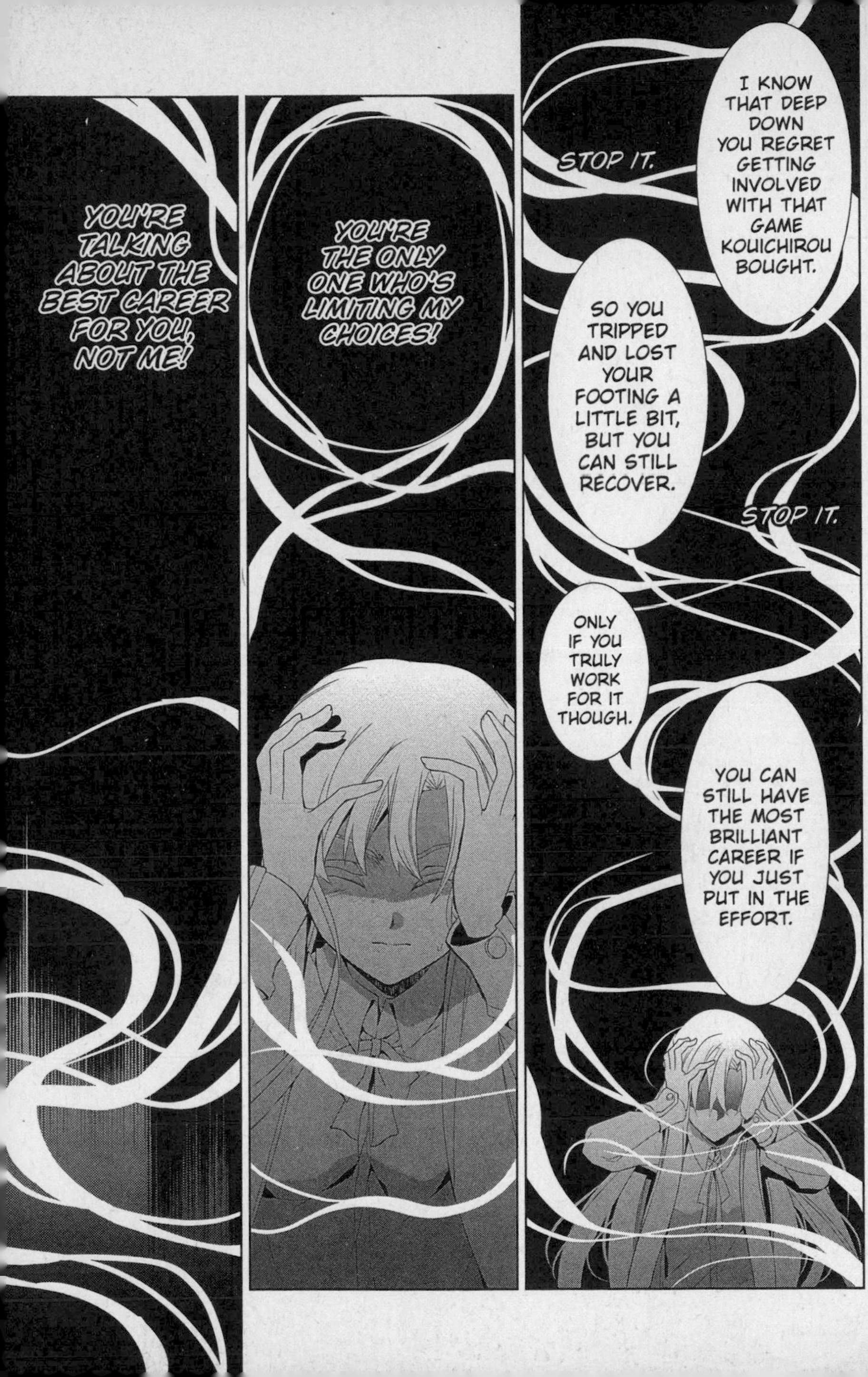

I KNOW THAT DEEP DOWN YOU REGRET GETTING INVOLVED WITH THAT GAME KOUICHIROU BOUGHT.
STOP IT.
SO YOU TRIPPED AND LOST YOUR FOOTING A LITTLE BIT, BUT YOU CAN STILL RECOVER.
STOP IT.
ONLY IF YOU TRULY WORK FOR IT THOUGH.
YOU CAN STILL HAVE THE MOST BRILLIANT CAREER IF YOU JUST PUT IN THE EFFORT.
YOU'RE THE ONLY ONE WHO'S LIMITING MY CHOICES!
YOU'RE TALKING ABOUT THE BEST CAREER FOR YOU, NOT ME!

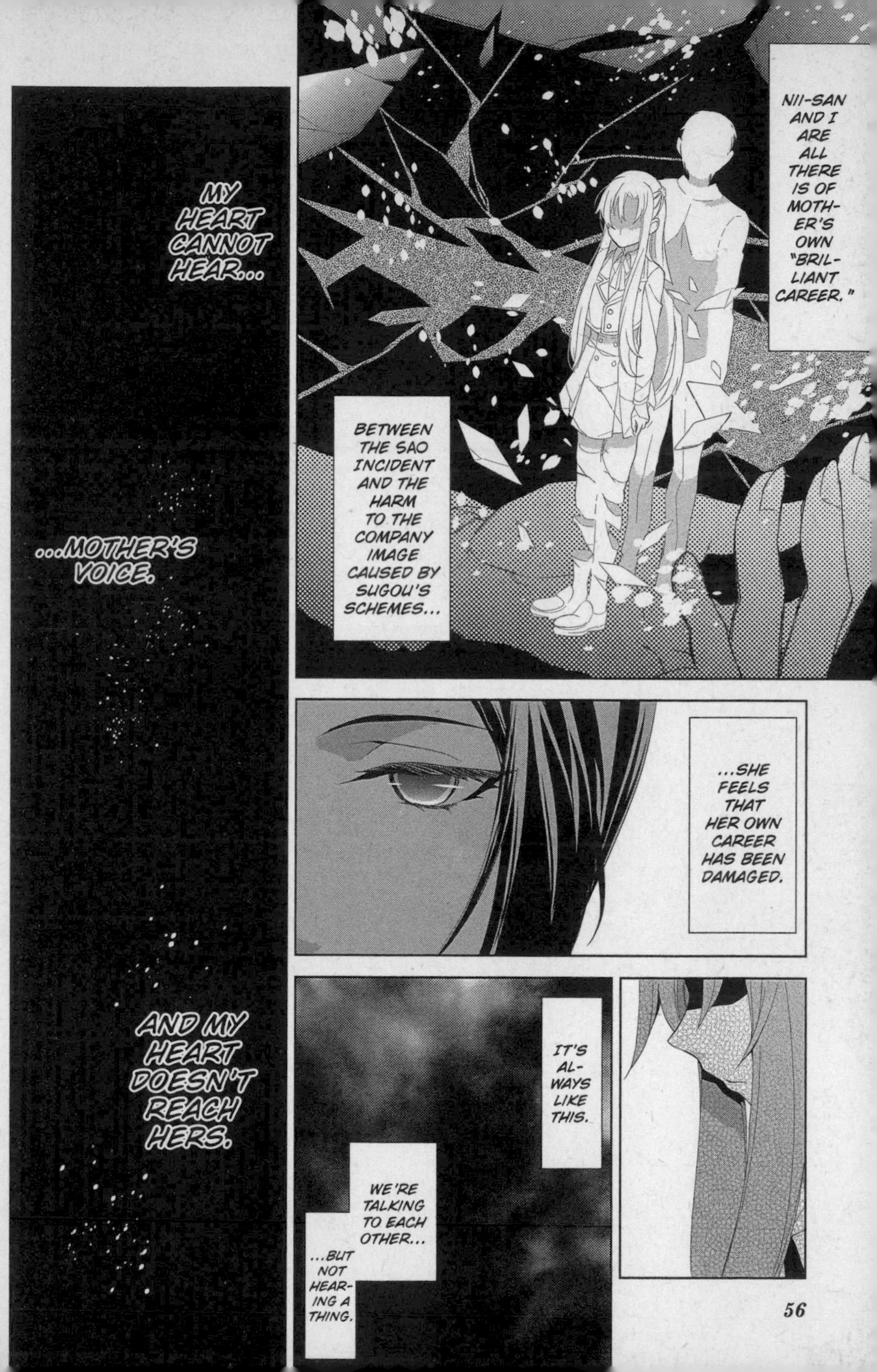
NII-SAN AND I ARE ALL THERE IS OF MOTHER'S OWN "BRILLIANT CAREER."
BETWEEN THE SAO INCIDENT AND THE HARM TO THE COMPANY IMAGE CAUSED BY SUGOU'S SCHEMES...
...SHE FEELS THAT HER OWN CAREER HAS BEEN DAMAGED.
IT'S ALWAYS LIKE THIS.
WE'RE TALKING TO EACH OTHER...
...BUT NOT HEARING A THING.
MY HEART CANNOT HEAR...
...MOTHER'S VOICE.
AND MY HEART DOESN'T REACH HERS.

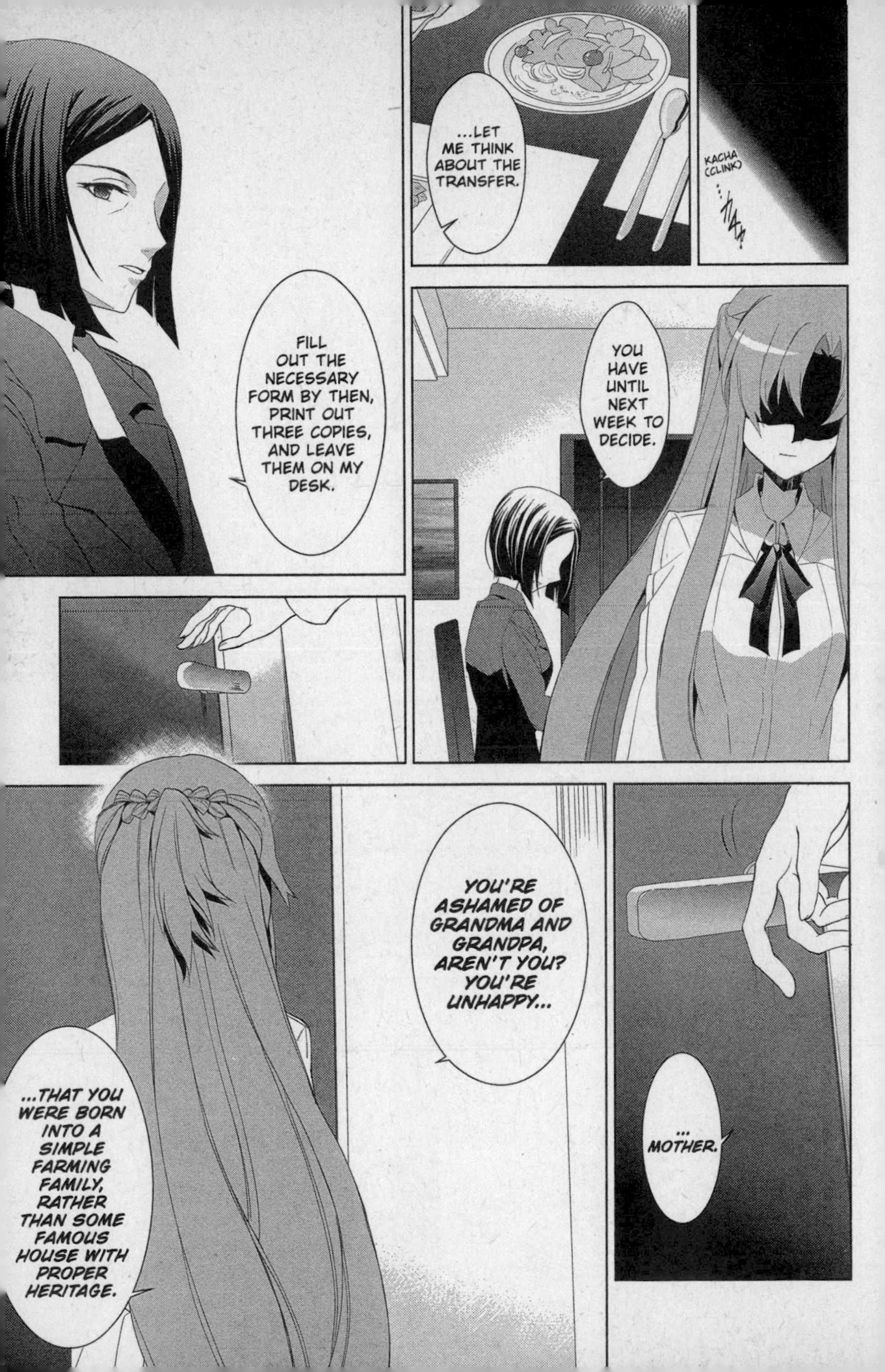
KACHA (CLINK)
...LET ME THINK ABOUT THE TRANSFER.
YOU HAVE UNTIL NEXT WEEK TO DECIDE.
FILL OUT THE NECESSARY FORM BY THEN, PRINT OUT THREE COPIES, AND LEAVE THEM ON MY DESK.
... MOTHER.
YOU'RE ASHAMED OF GRANDMA AND GRANDPA, AREN'T YOU? YOU'RE UNHAPPY...
...THAT YOU WERE BORN INTO A SIMPLE FARMING FAMILY, RATHER THAN SOME FAMOUS HOUSE WITH PROPER HERITAGE.

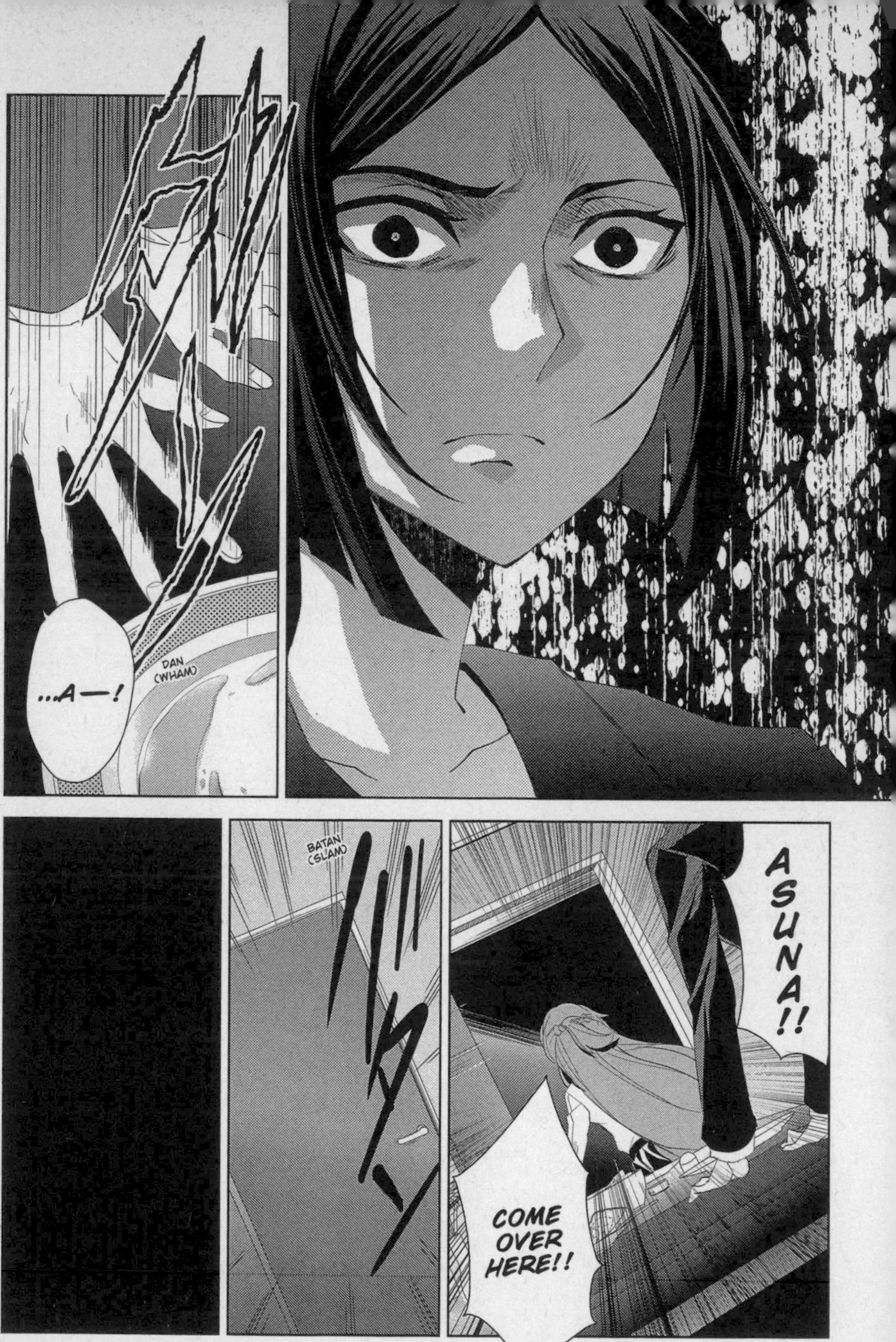
DAN
(WHAM)
...A—!
ASUNA!!
COME OVER HERE!!
BATAN
(SLAM)

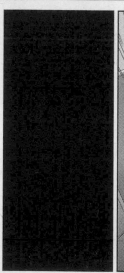

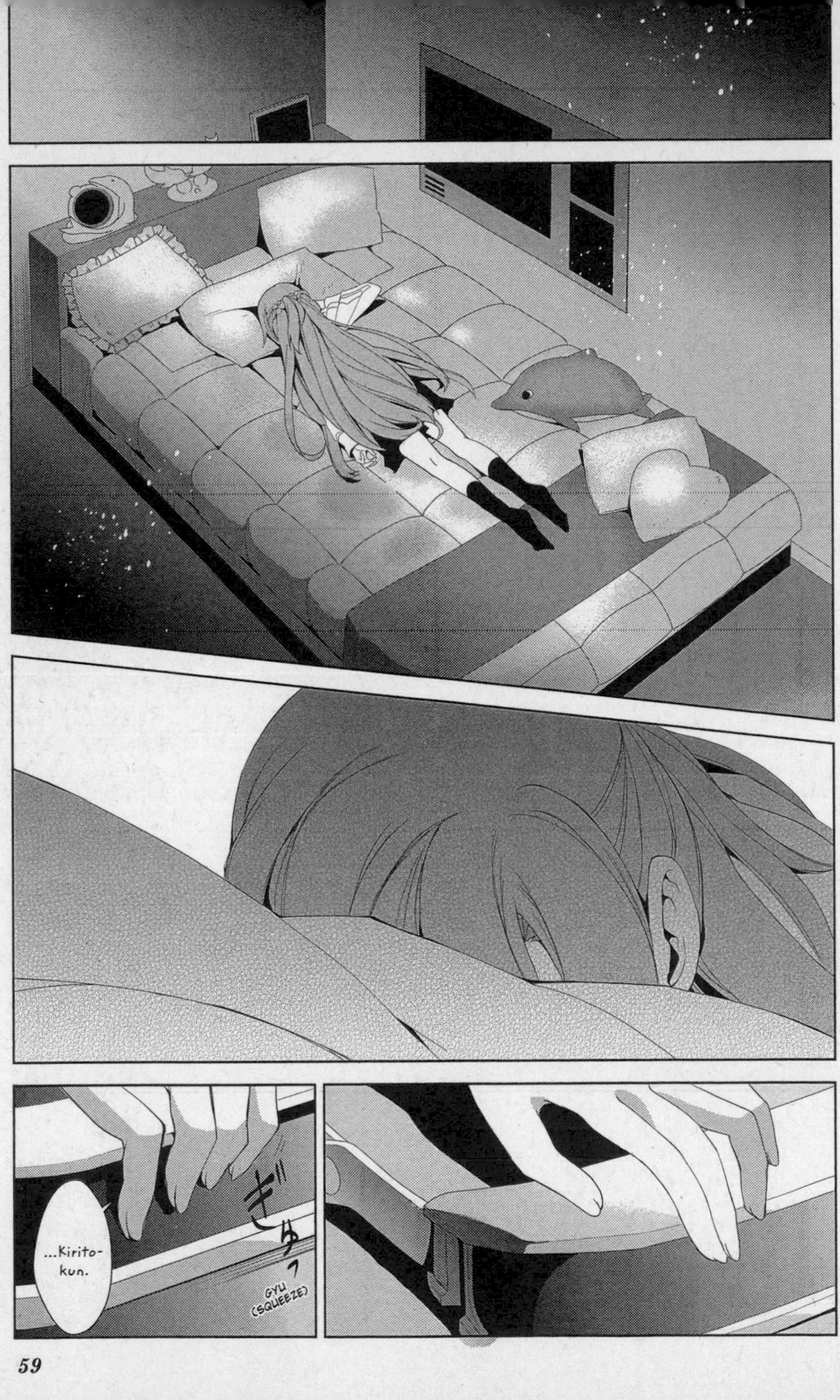
ぎゅっ
GYU (SQUEEZE)
...Kirito-kun.

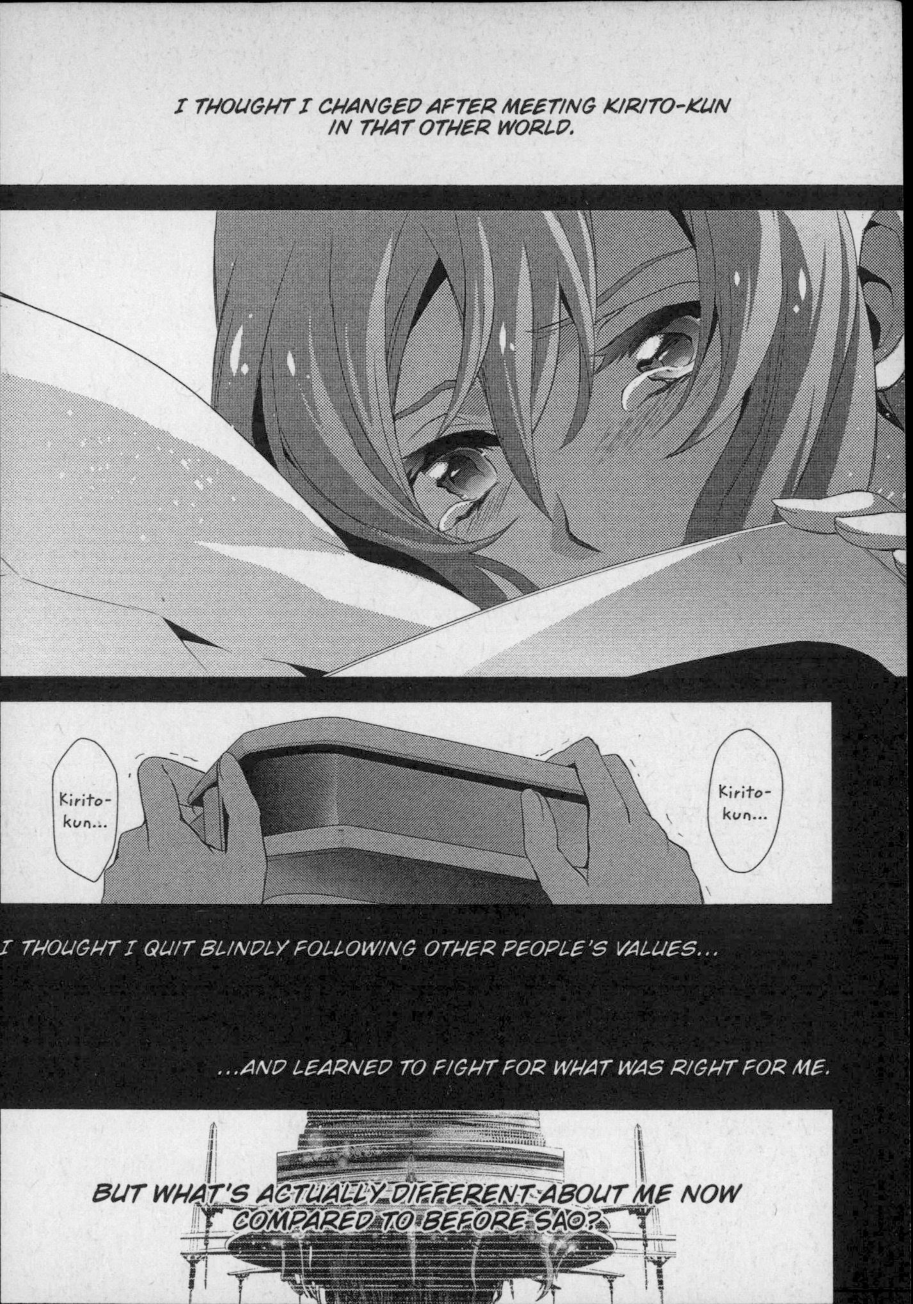
I THOUGHT I CHANGED AFTER MEETING KIRITO-KUN IN THAT OTHER WORLD.
Kirito-kun...
Kirito-kun...
I THOUGHT I QUIT BLINDLY FOLLOWING OTHER PEOPLE'S VALUES...
...AND LEARNED TO FIGHT FOR WHAT WAS RIGHT FOR ME.
BUT WHAT'S ACTUALLY DIFFERENT ABOUT ME NOW COMPARED TO BEFORE SAO?

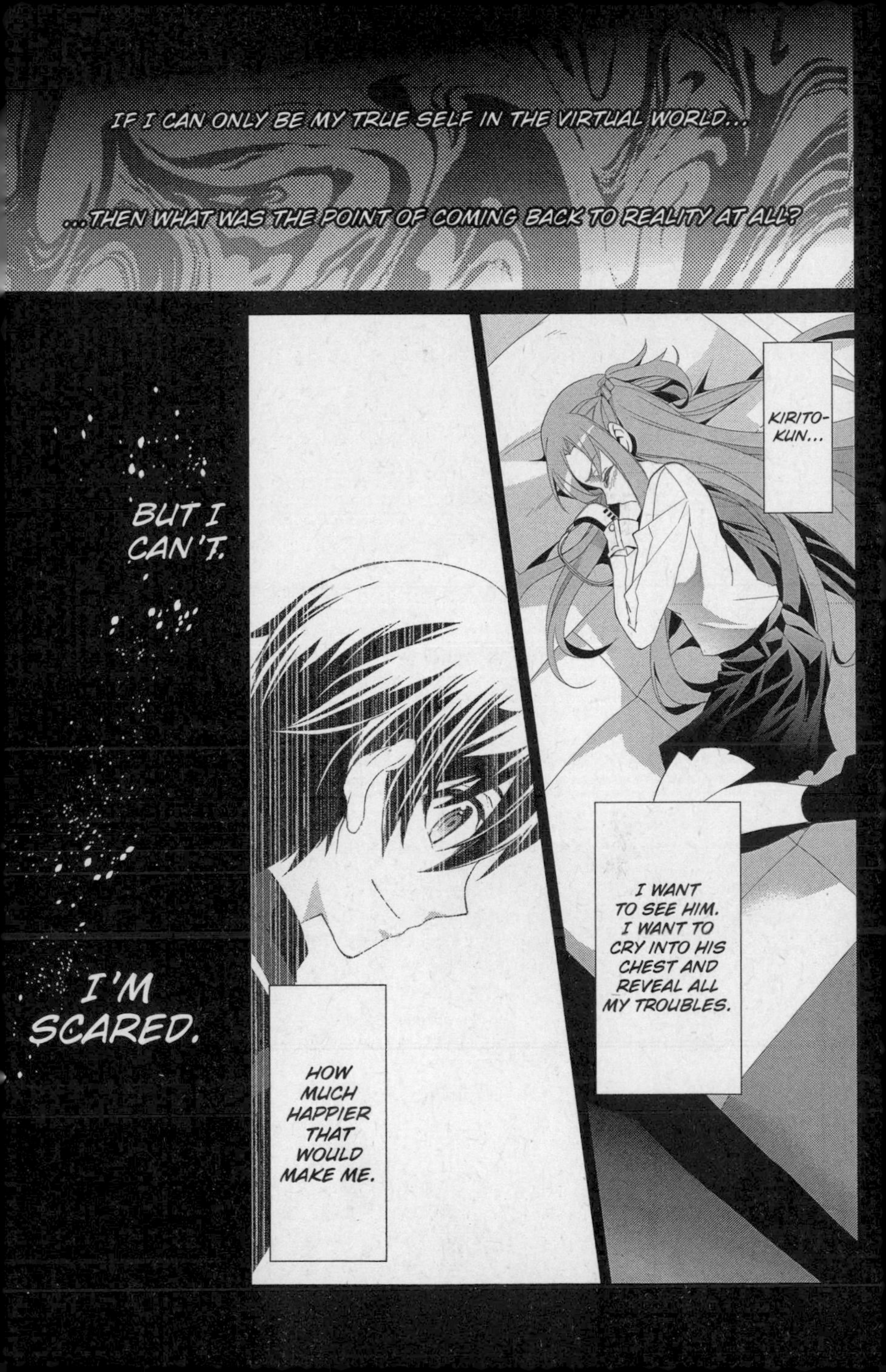
IF I CAN ONLY BE MY TRUE SELF IN THE VIRTUAL WORLD...
...THEN WHAT WAS THE POINT OF COMING BACK TO REALITY AT ALL?
KIRITO-KUN...
I WANT TO SEE HIM. I WANT TO CRY INTO HIS CHEST AND REVEAL ALL MY TROUBLES.
HOW MUCH HAPPIER THAT WOULD MAKE ME.
BUT I CAN'T.
I'M SCARED.

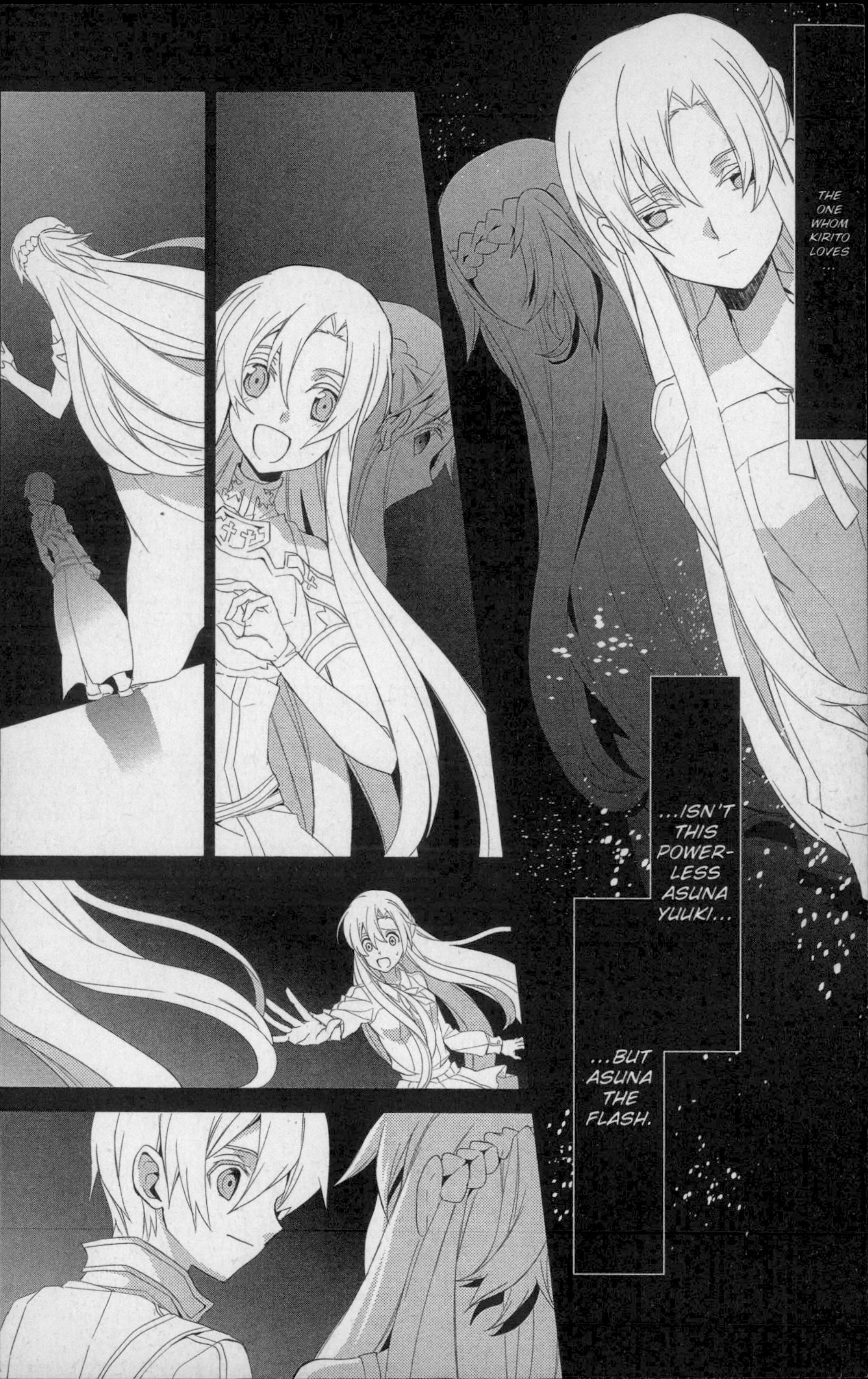
THE ONE WHOM KIRITO LOVES ...
...ISN'T THIS POWER-LESS ASUNA YUUKI...
...BUT ASUNA THE FLASH.

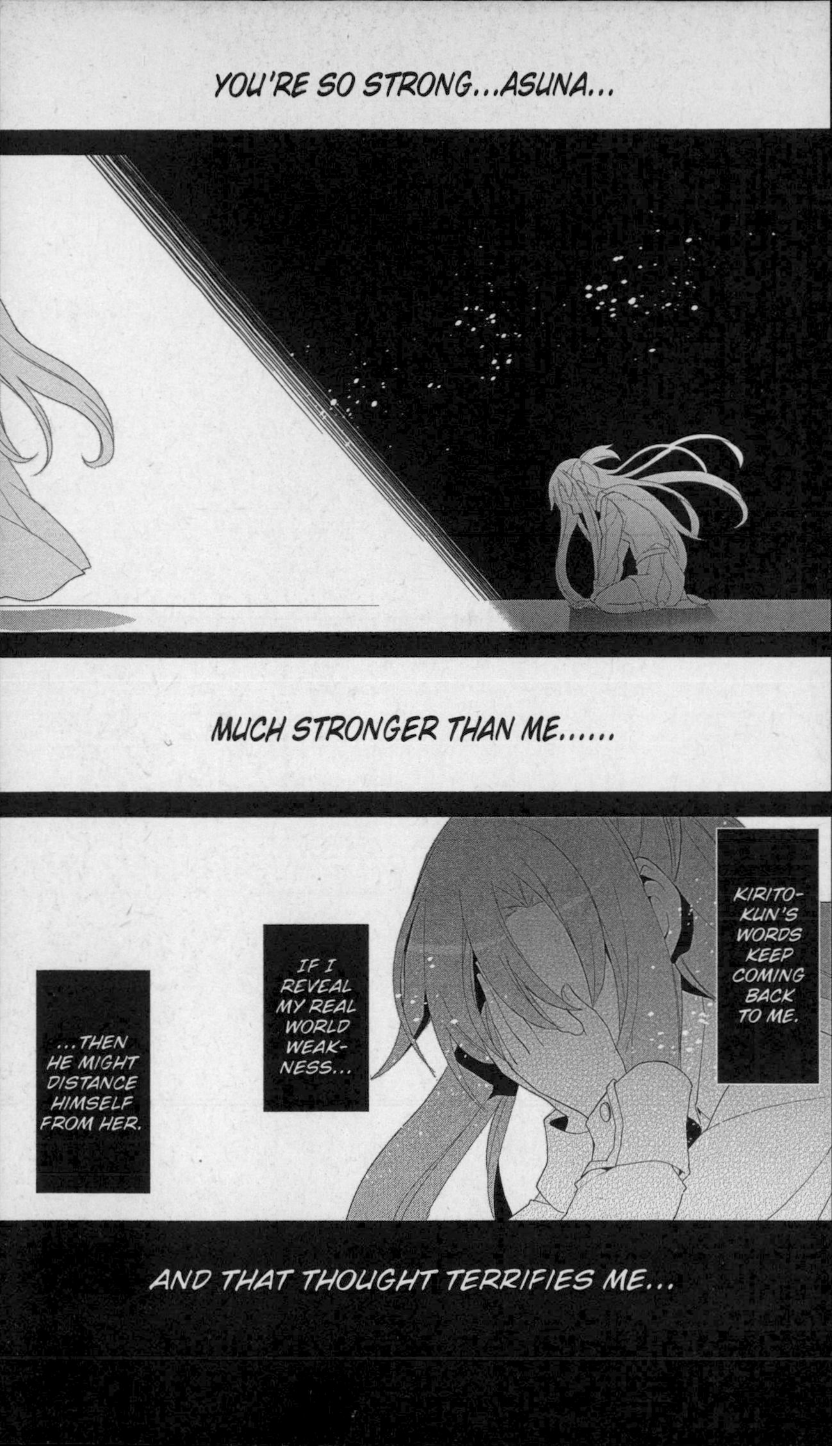
YOU'RE SO STRONG...ASUNA...
MUCH STRONGER THAN ME......
KIRITO-KUN'S WORDS KEEP COMING BACK TO ME.
IF I REVEAL MY REAL WORLD WEAKNESS...
...THEN HE MIGHT DISTANCE HIMSELF FROM HER.
AND THAT THOUGHT TERRIFIES ME...

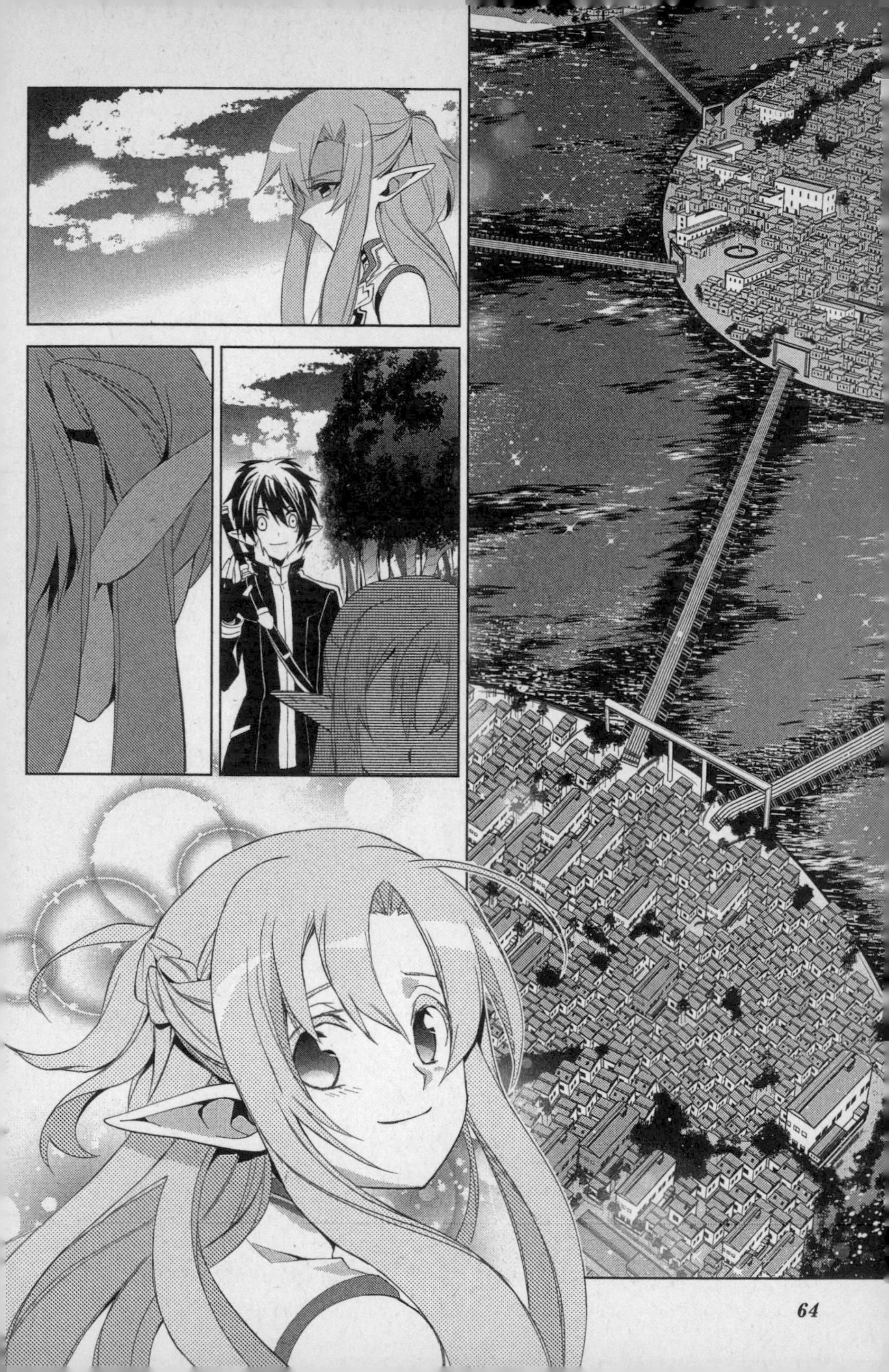

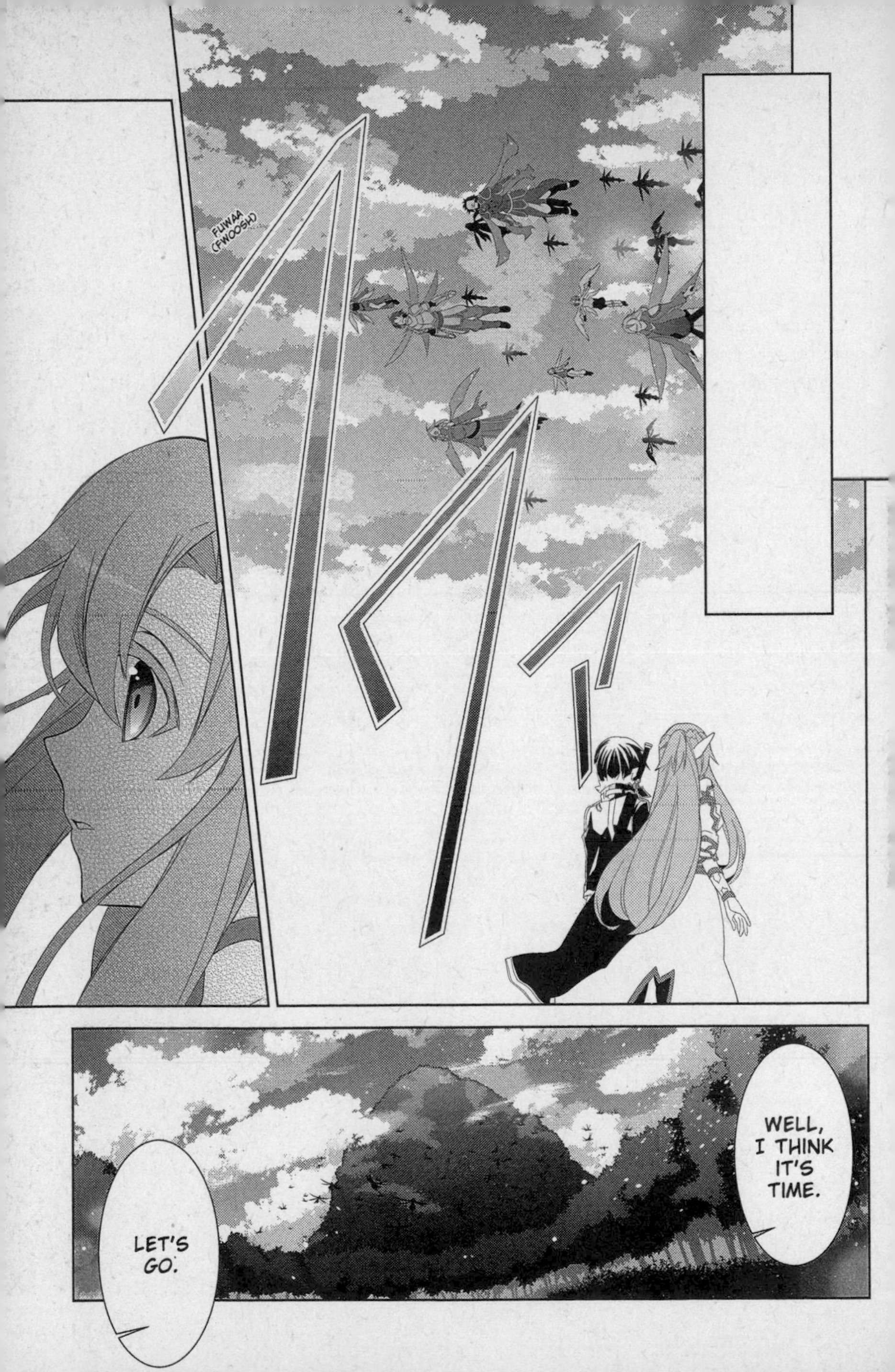
FUWAA (FWOOSH)
WELL, I THINK IT'S TIME.
LET'S GO.

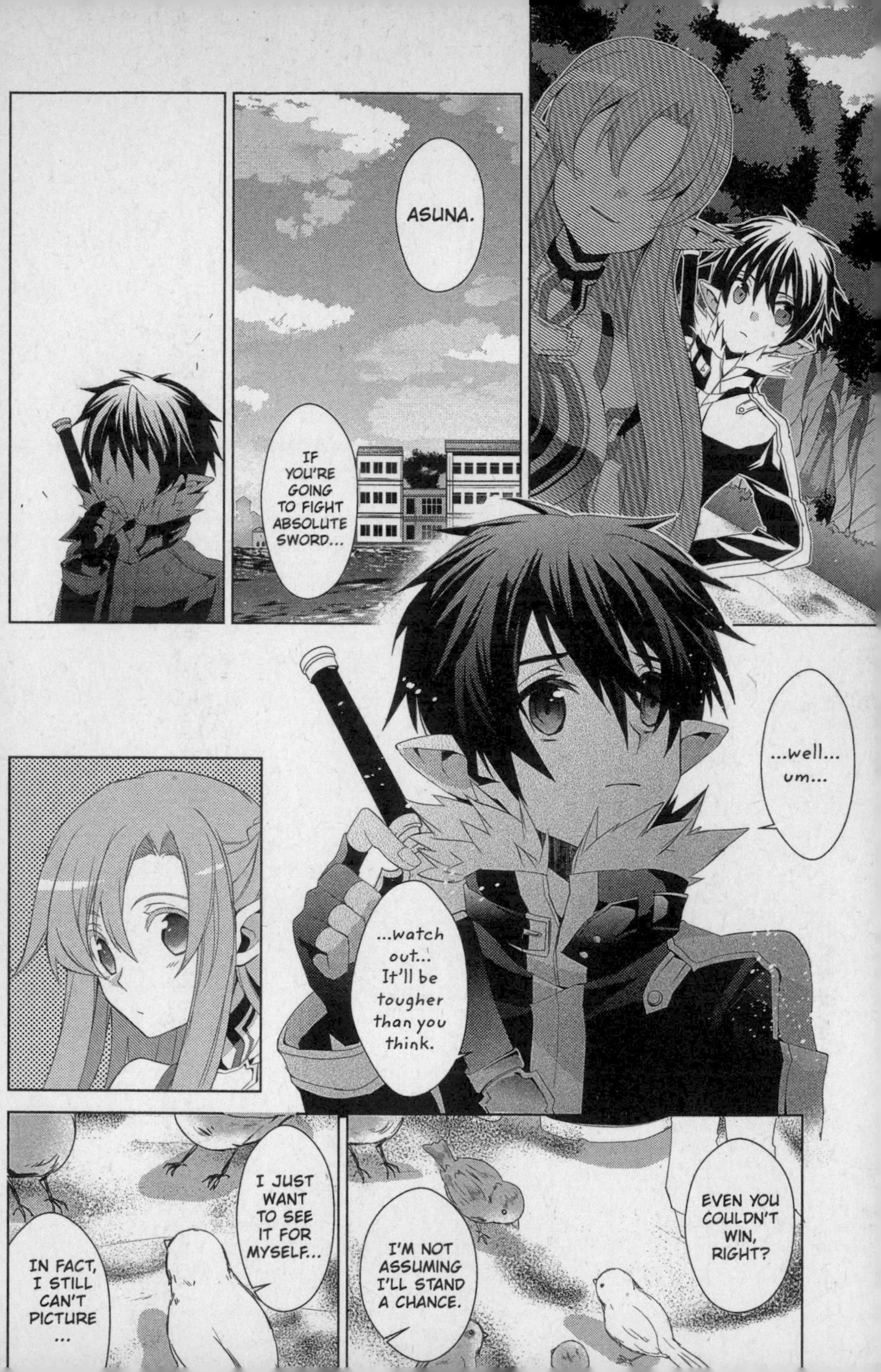
ASUNA.
IF YOU'RE GOING TO FIGHT ABSOLUTE SWORD...
...well... um...
...watch out... It'll be tougher than you think.
EVEN YOU COULDN'T WIN, RIGHT?
I'M NOT ASSUMING I'LL STAND A CHANCE.
I JUST WANT TO SEE IT FOR MYSELF...
IN FACT, I STILL CAN'T PICTURE ...

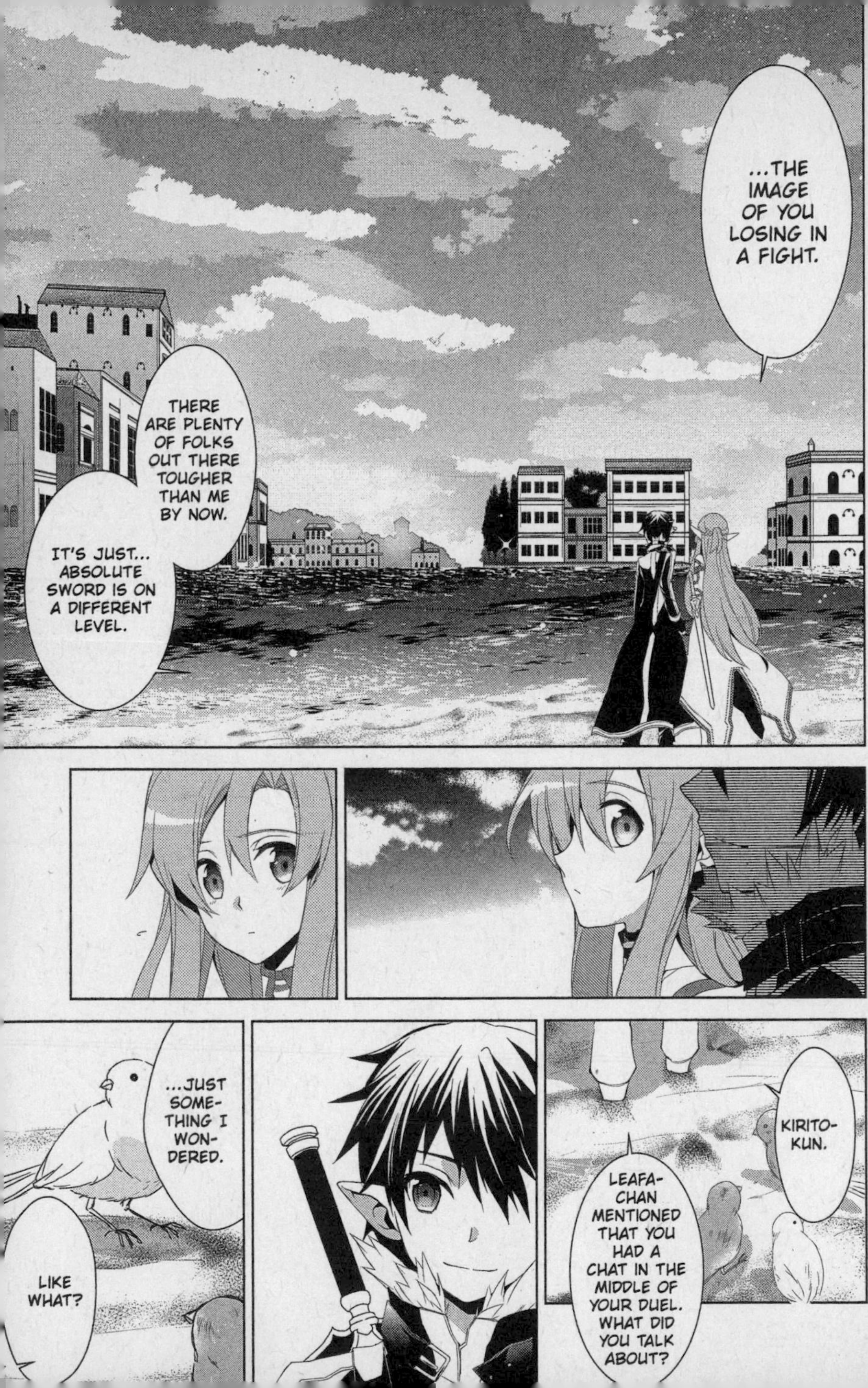
...THE IMAGE OF YOU LOSING IN A FIGHT.
THERE ARE PLENTY OF FOLKS OUT THERE TOUGHER THAN ME BY NOW.
IT'S JUST... ABSOLUTE SWORD IS ON A DIFFERENT LEVEL.
KIRITO-KUN.
LEAFA-CHAN MENTIONED THAT YOU HAD A CHAT IN THE MIDDLE OF YOUR DUEL. WHAT DID YOU TALK ABOUT?
...JUST SOME-THING I WON-DERED.
LIKE WHAT?

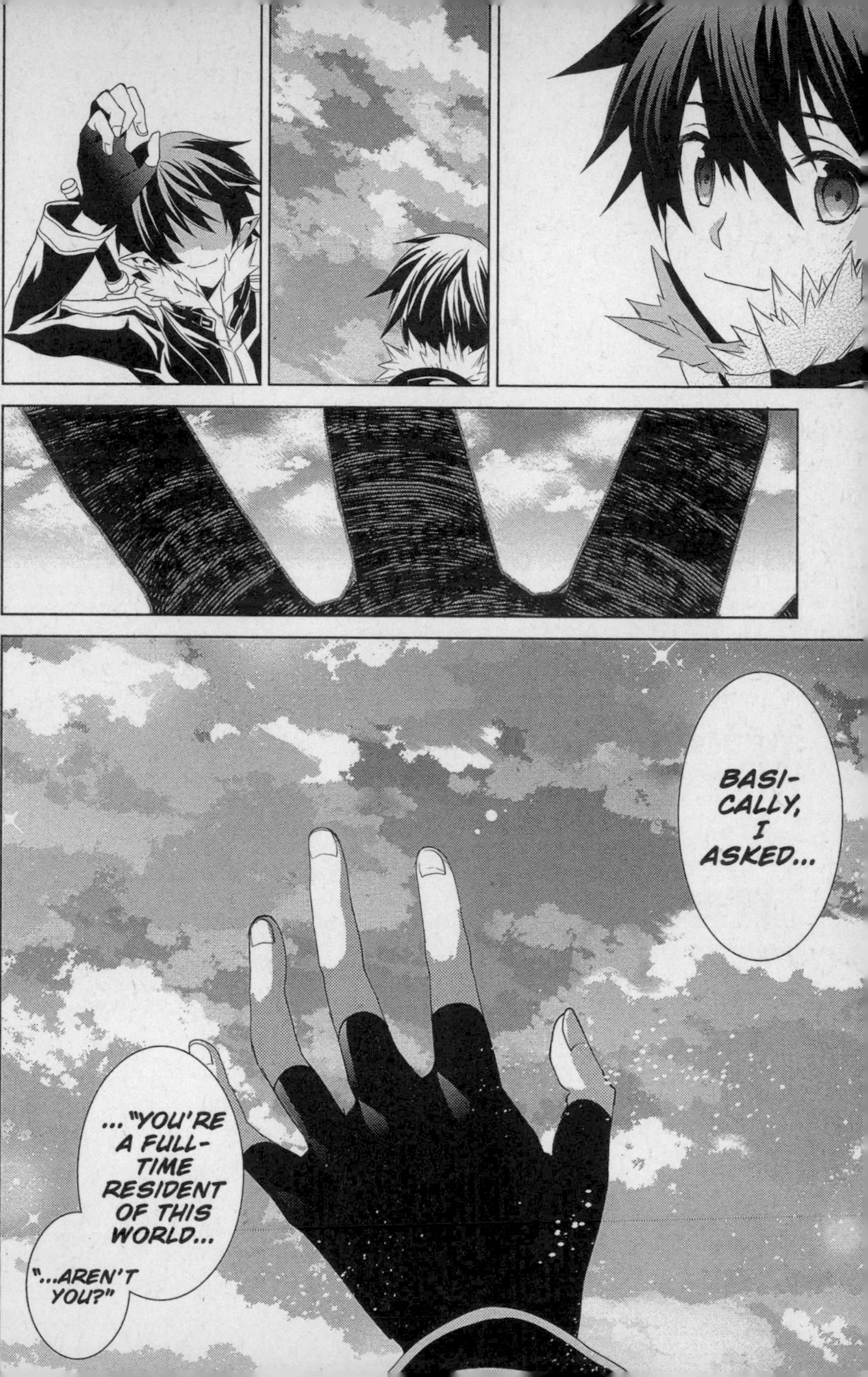
BASI-CALLY, I ASKED...
..."YOU'RE A FULL-TIME RESIDENT OF THIS WORLD...
"...AREN'T YOU?"

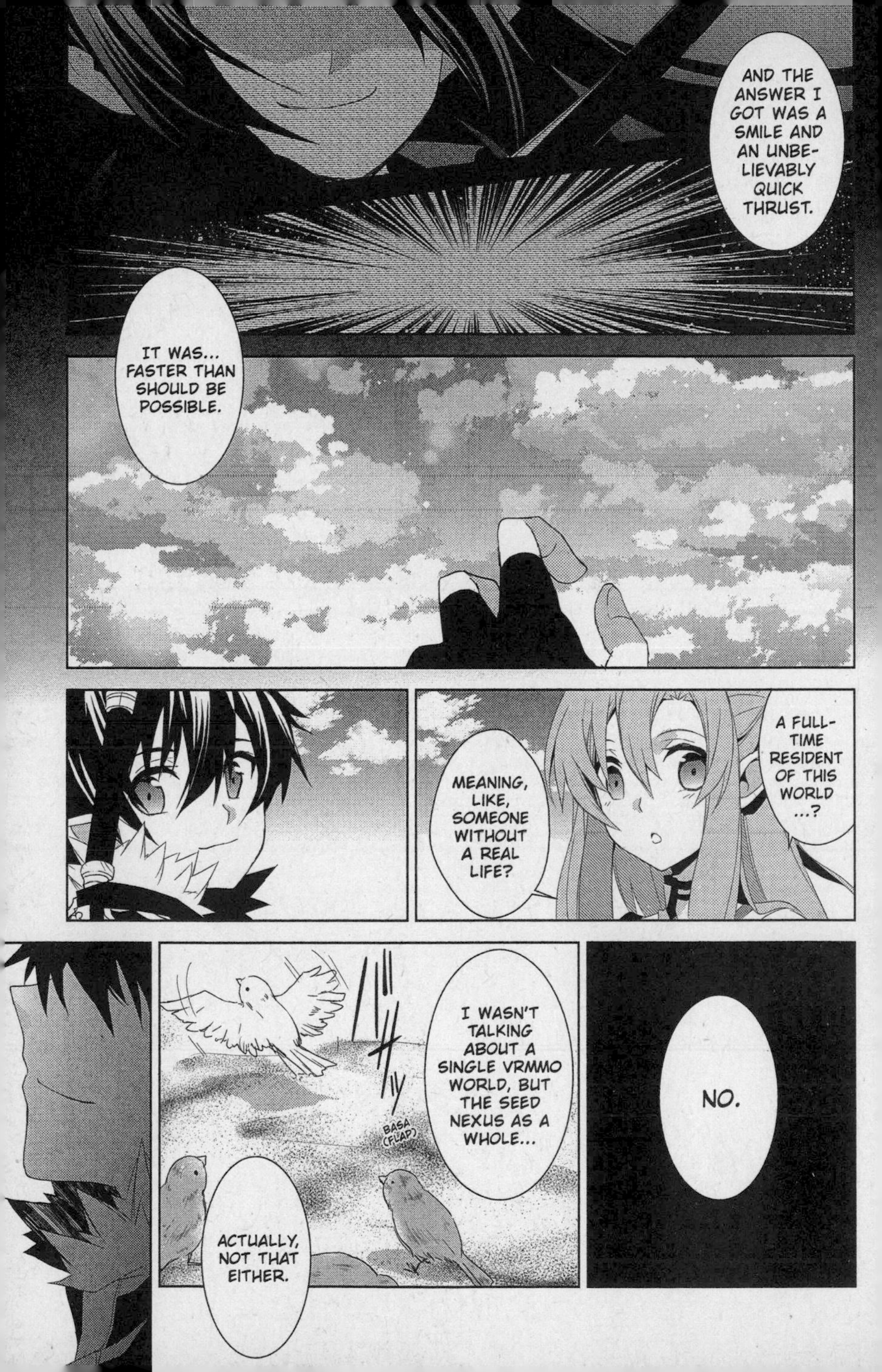
AND THE ANSWER I GOT WAS A SMILE AND AN UNBE-LIEVABLY QUICK THRUST.
IT WAS... FASTER THAN SHOULD BE POSSIBLE.
A FULL-TIME RESIDENT OF THIS WORLD ...?
MEANING, LIKE, SOMEONE WITHOUT A REAL LIFE?
NO.
I WASN'T TALKING ABOUT A SINGLE VRMMO WORLD, BUT THE SEED NEXUS AS A WHOLE...
BASA (FLAP)
ACTUALLY, NOT THAT EITHER.

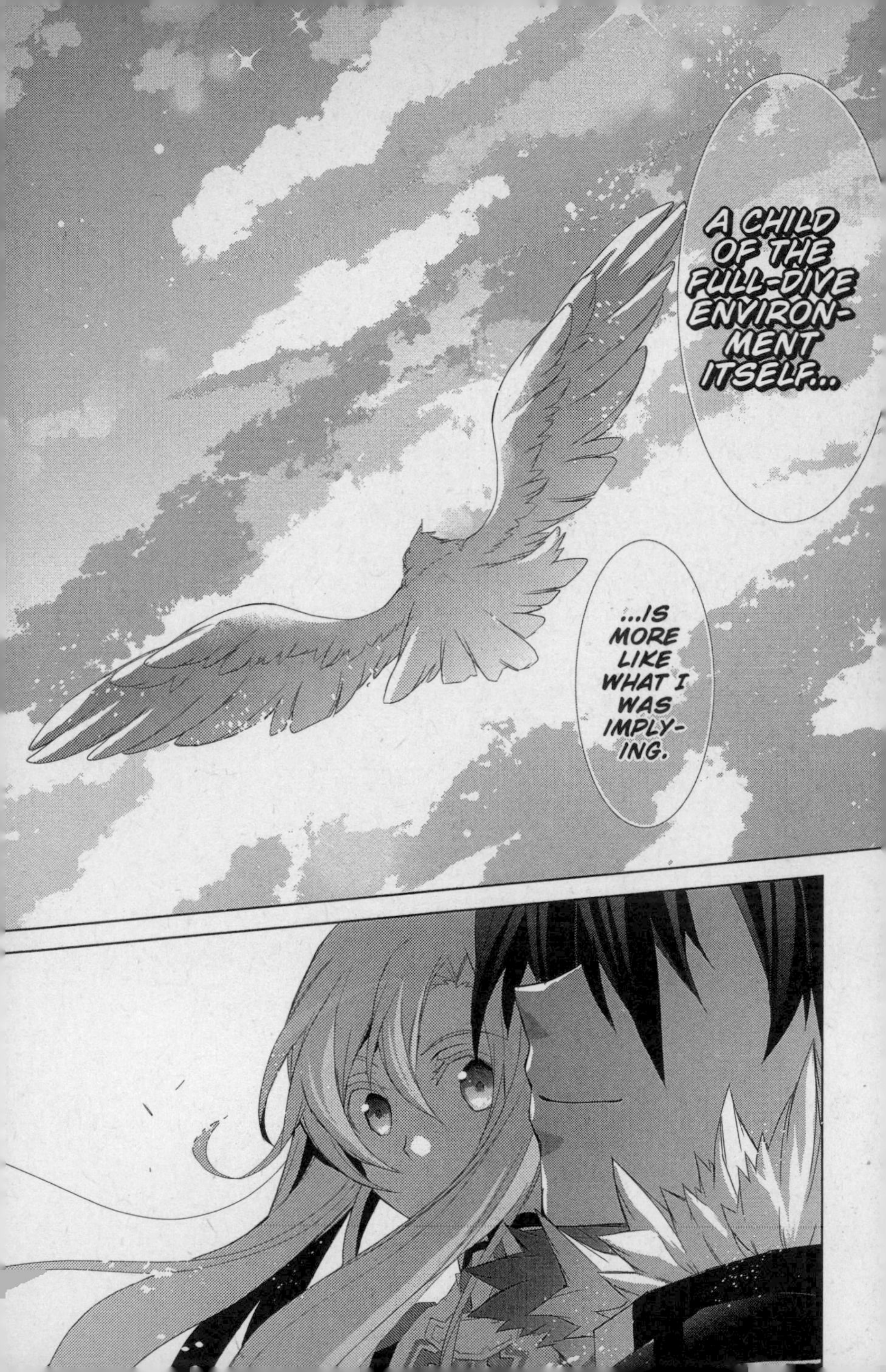
A CHILD OF THE FULL-DIVE ENVIRONMENT ITSELF...
...IS MORE LIKE WHAT I WAS IMPLYING.

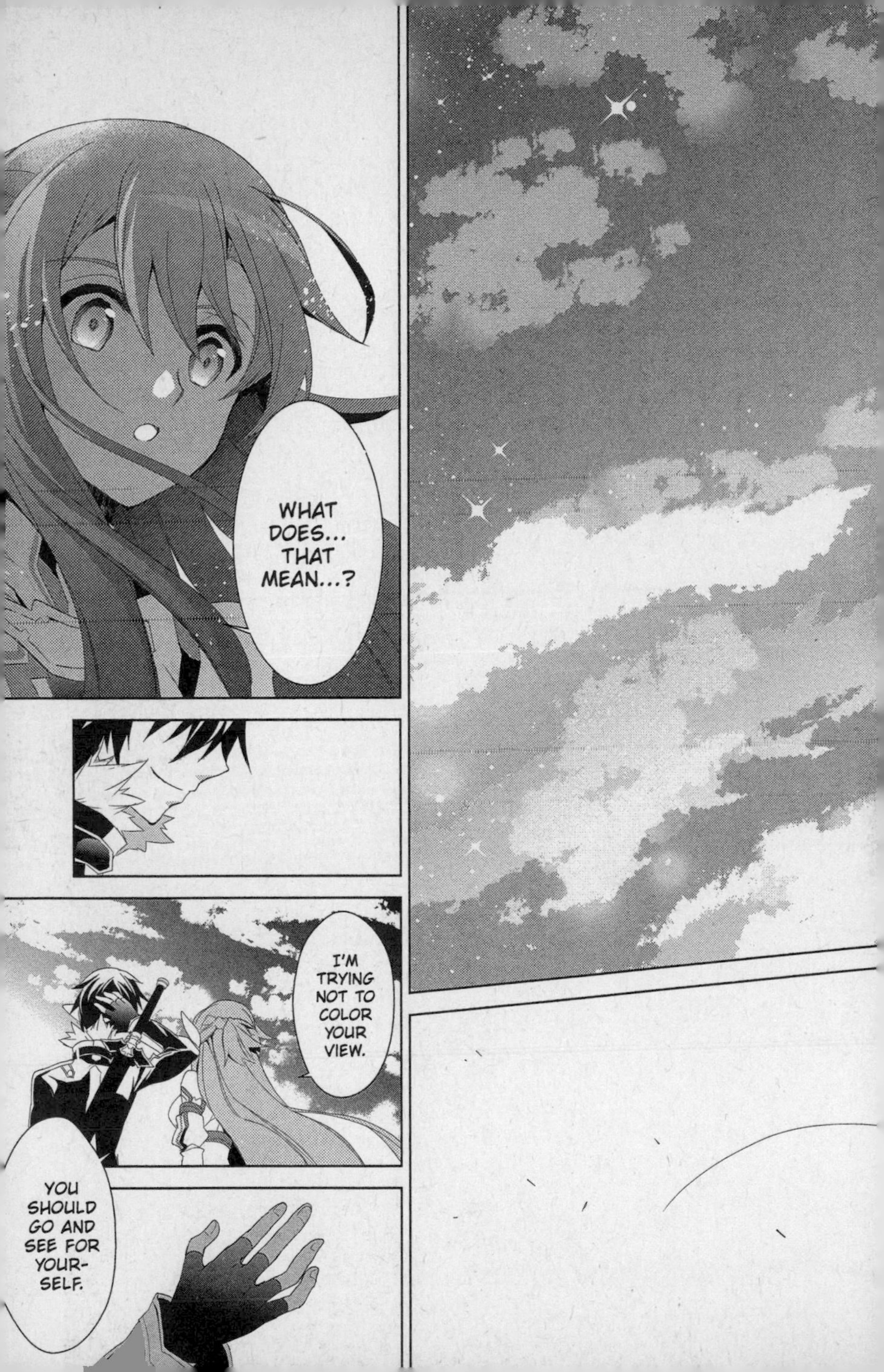
WHAT DOES… THAT MEAN…?
I'M TRYING NOT TO COLOR YOUR VIEW.
YOU SHOULD GO AND SEE FOR YOUR-SELF.

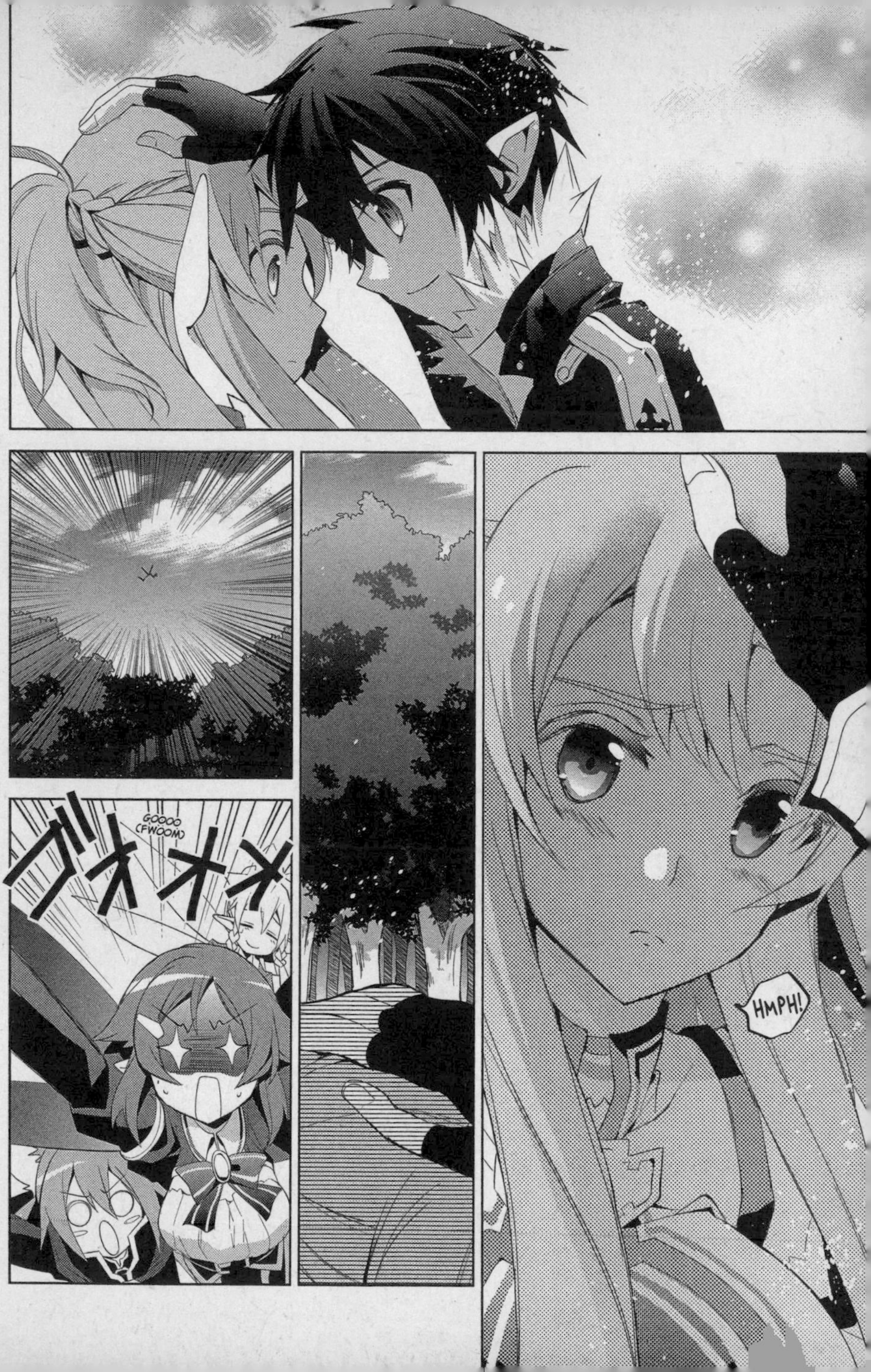
HMPH!
ゴオオオ
GOOOO
(FWOOM)

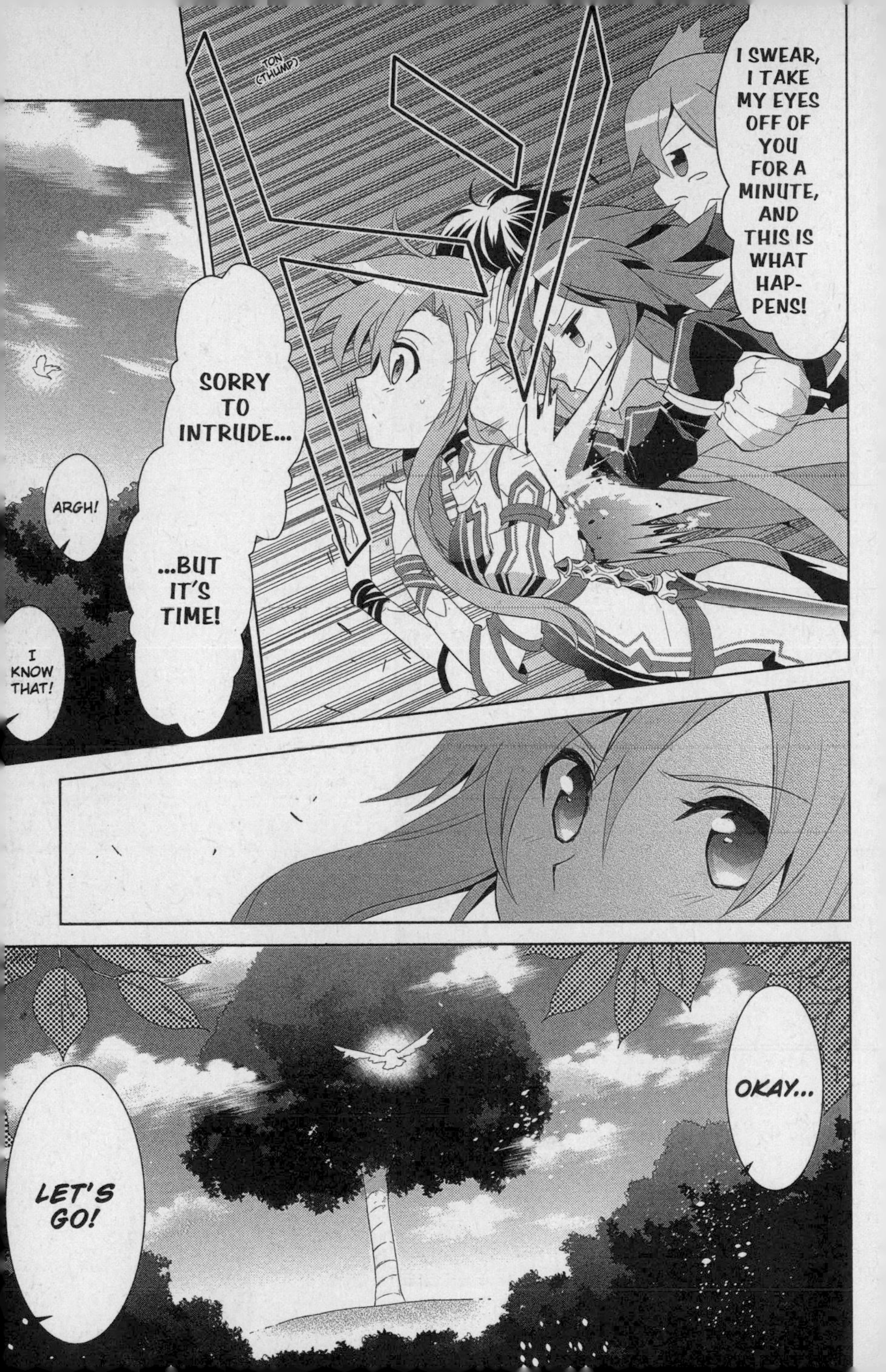
I SWEAR, I TAKE MY EYES OFF OF YOU FOR A MINUTE, AND THIS IS WHAT HAP-PENS!
TON (THUMP)
SORRY TO INTRUDE...
...BUT IT'S TIME!
ARGH!
I KNOW THAT!
OKAY...
LET'S GO!

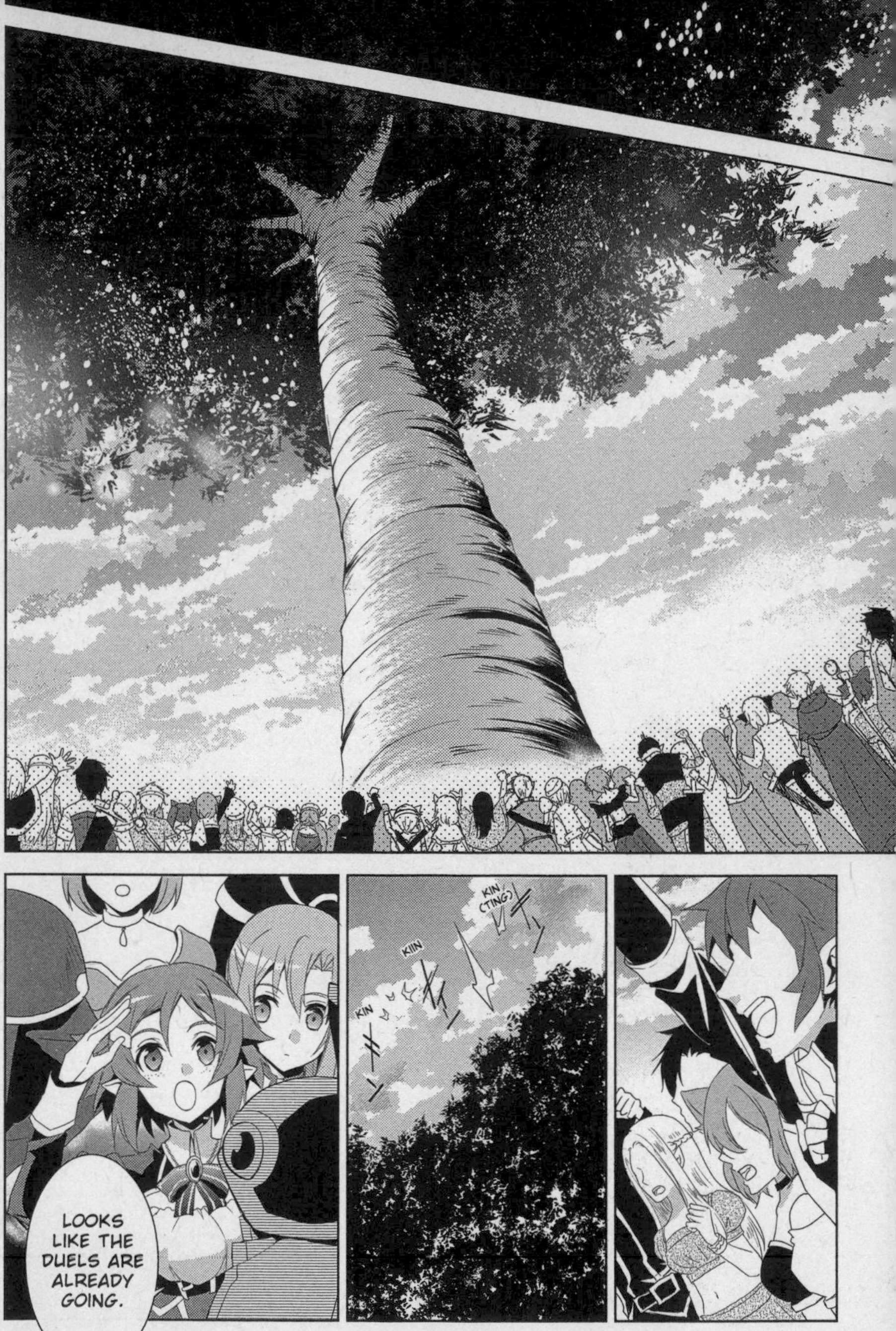
KIN (TING)
KIIN
KIN
LOOKS LIKE THE DUELS ARE ALREADY GOING.

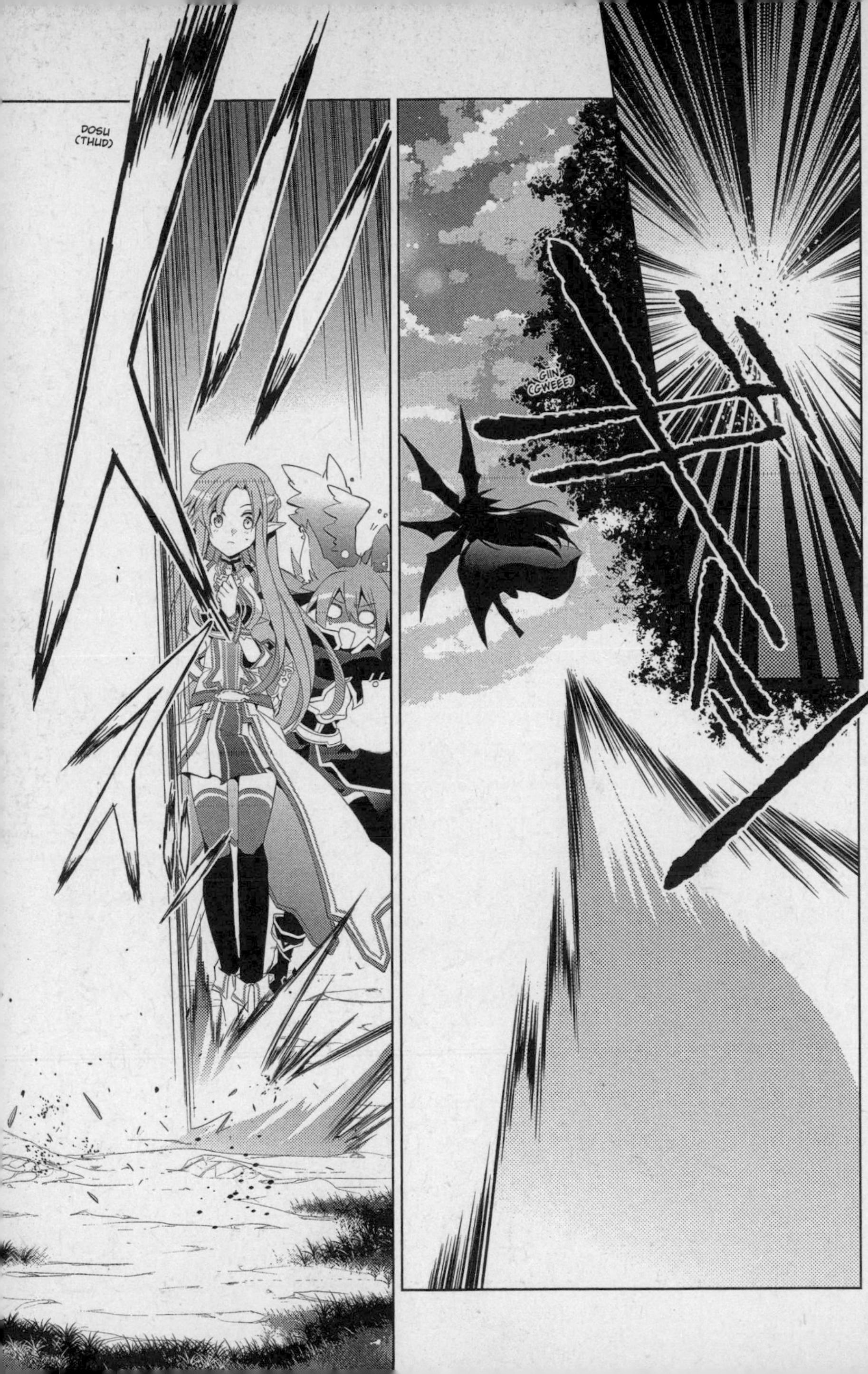
GIIN
(GWEEE)
DOSU
(THUD)

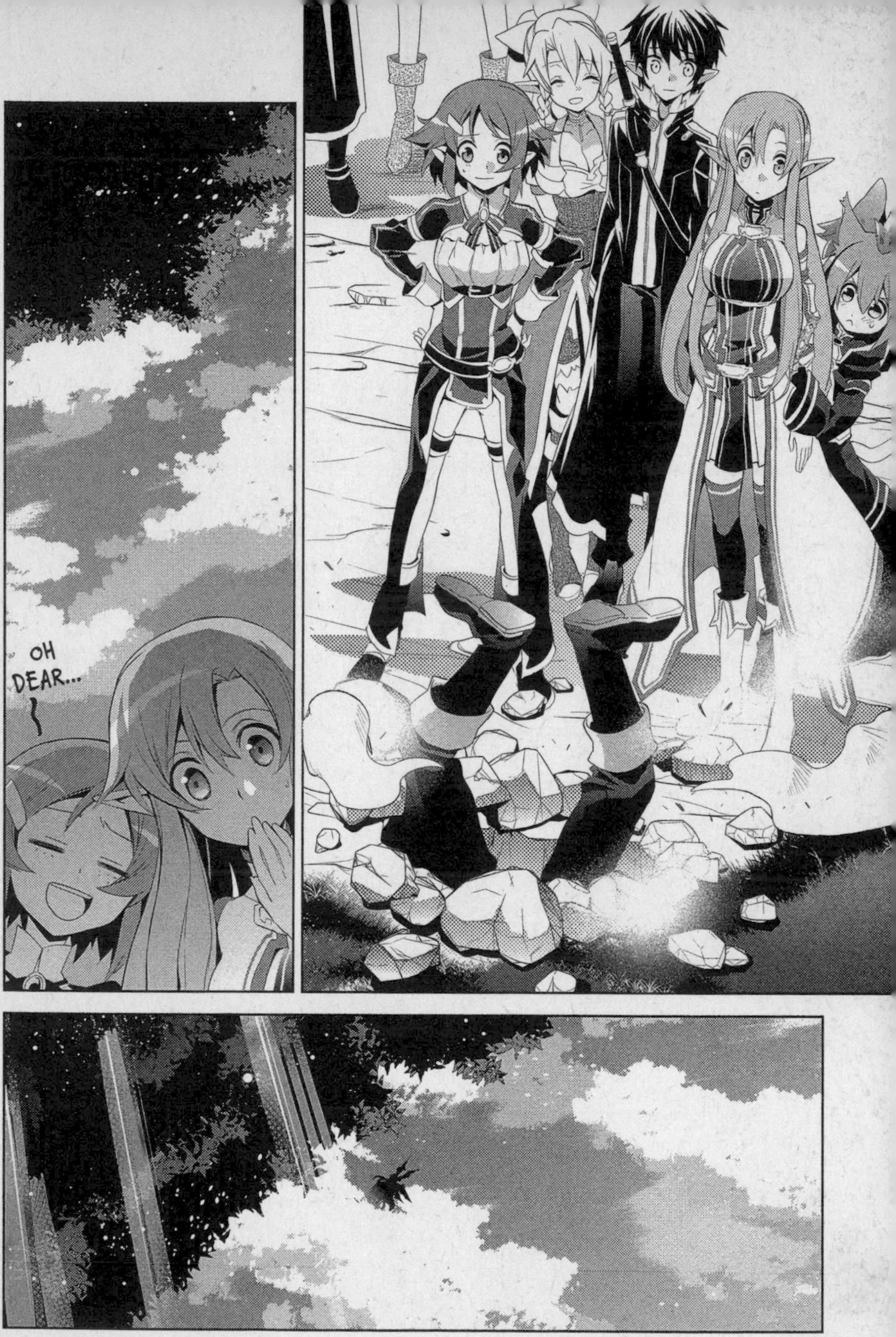
OH DEAR...

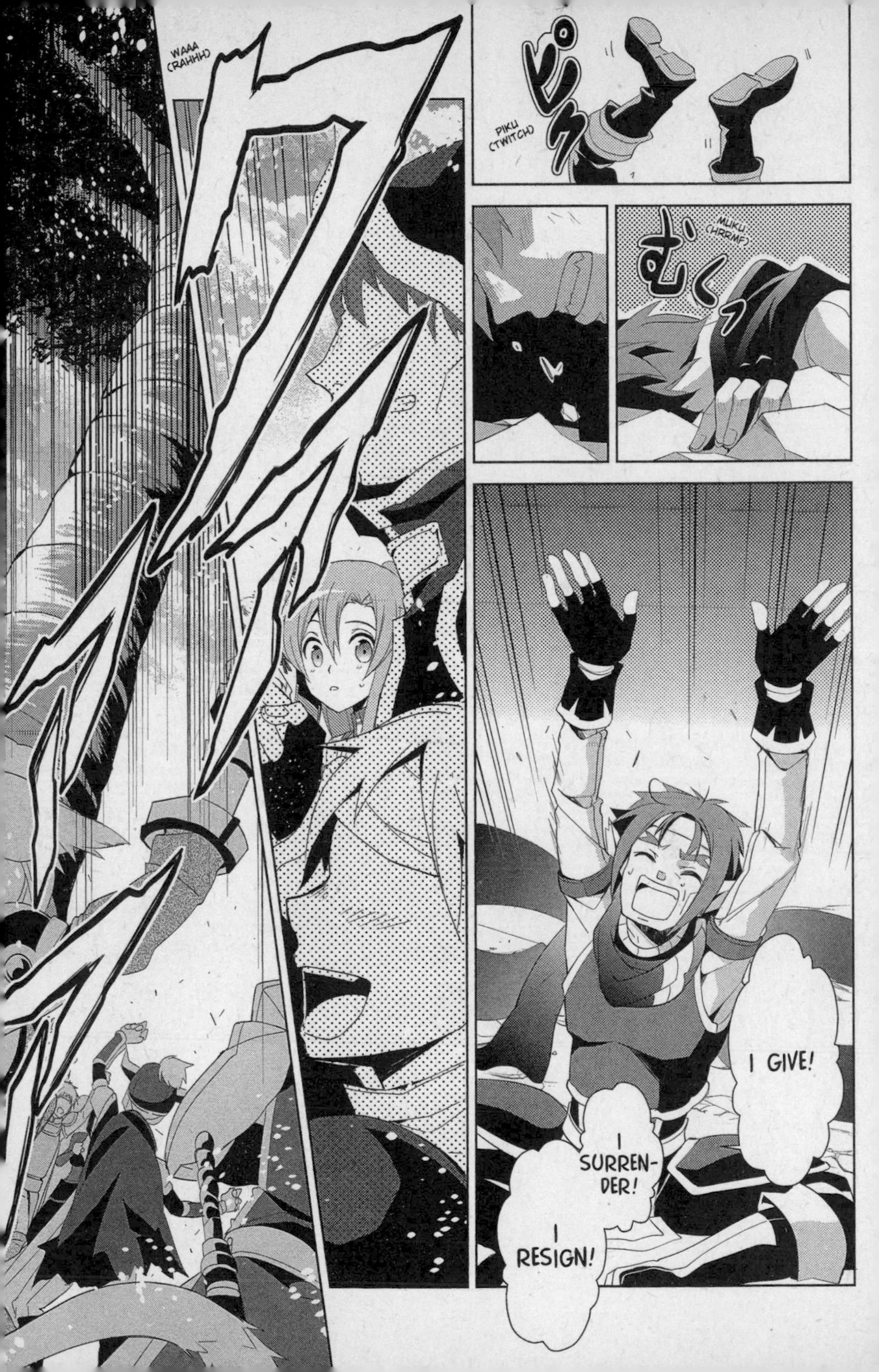
ピク
PIKU (TWITCH)
むくっ
MUKU (HRRMF)
I GIVE!
I SURREN-DER!
I RESIGN!
WAAA (RAHHH)

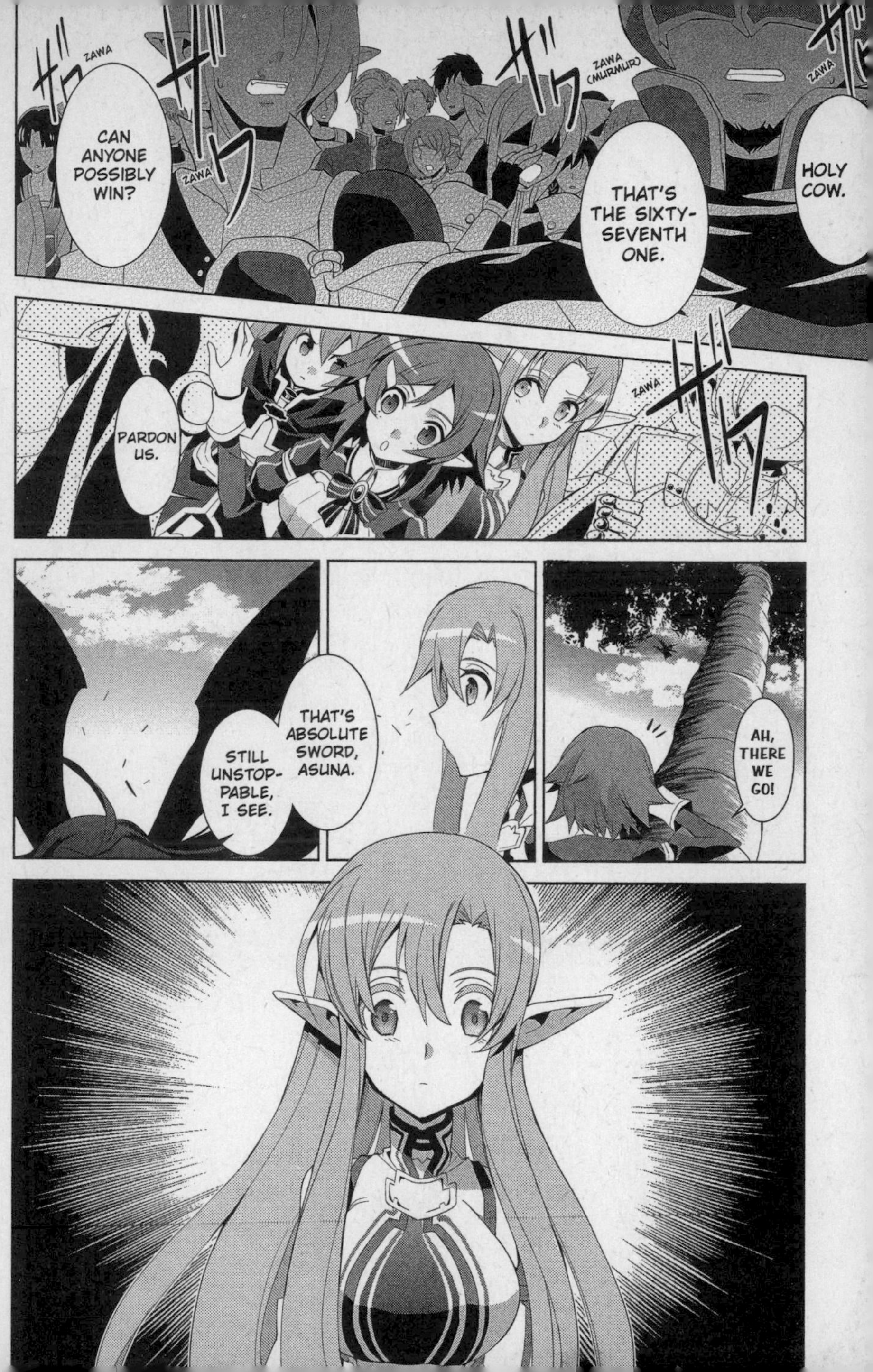
HOLY COW.
ZAWA
ZAWA (MURMUR)
THAT'S THE SIXTY-SEVENTH ONE.
ZAWA
CAN ANYONE POSSIBLY WIN?
ZAWA
ZAWA
PARDON US.
AH, THERE WE GO!
THAT'S ABSOLUTE SWORD, ASUNA.
STILL UNSTOP-PABLE, I SEE.

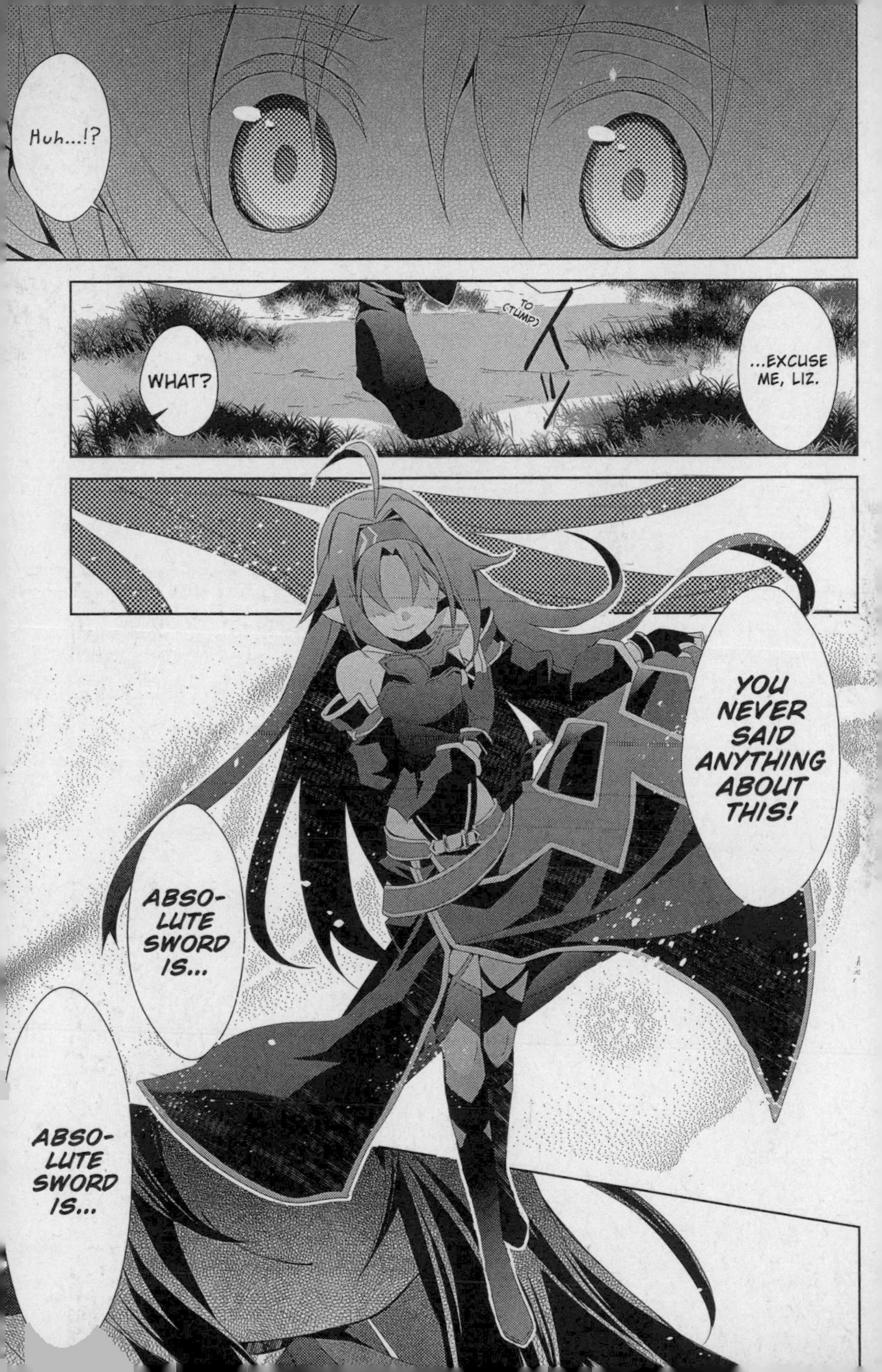
Huh...!?
...EXCUSE ME, LIZ.
TO (TUMP)
WHAT?
YOU NEVER SAID ANYTHING ABOUT THIS!
ABSO-LUTE SWORD IS...
ABSO-LUTE SWORD IS...

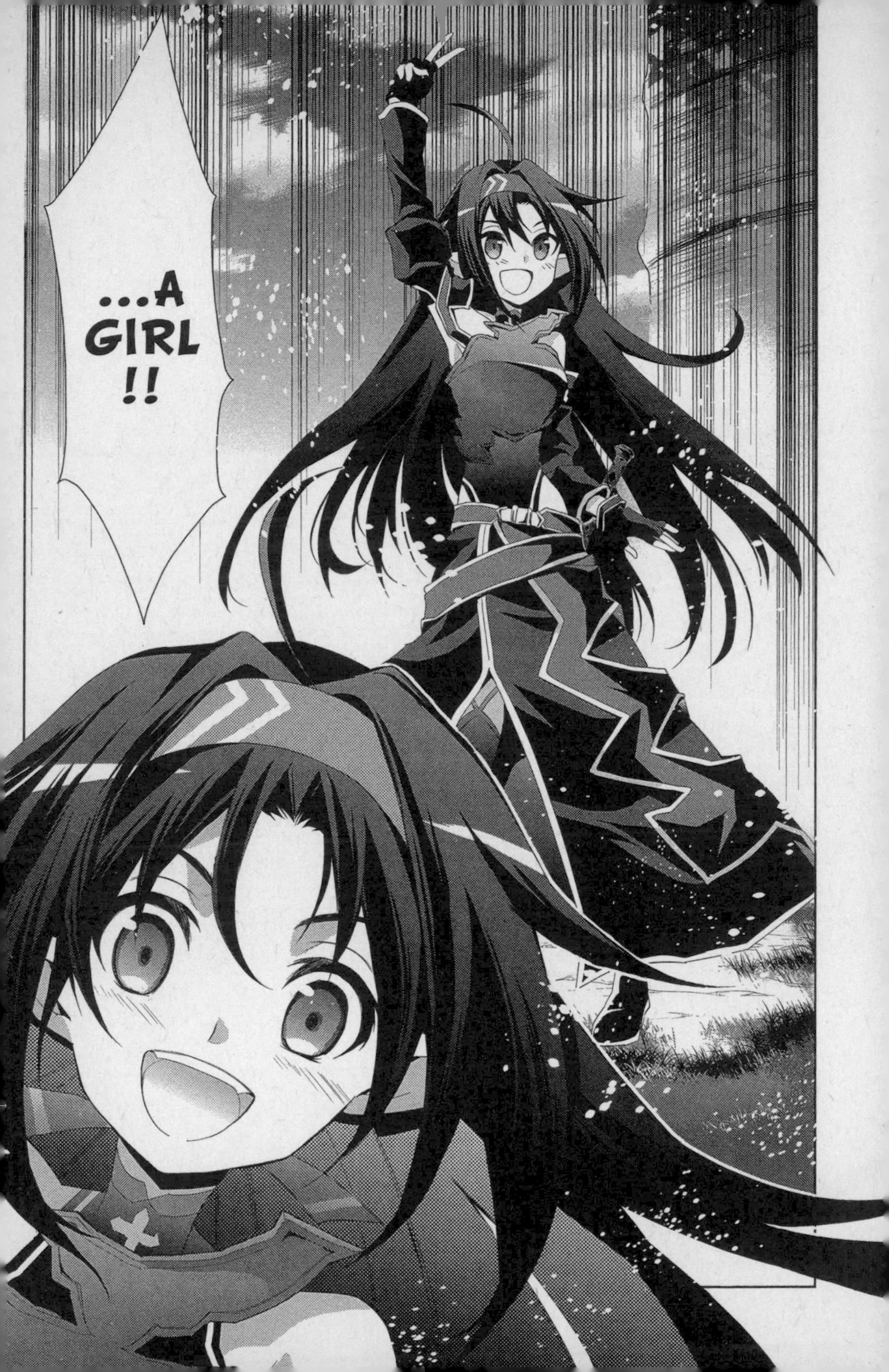
...A GIRL !!

SWORD ART ONLINE
mother's ROSARY

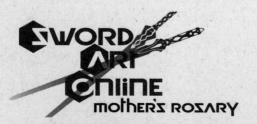

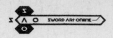

ΣWORD ARƚ ONIINE moƚheR'Σ ROΣARY
BACKGROUND GUIDE 02

THE GROUP'S AVATARS

AT THIS TIME, IT'S POSSIBLE TO USE OLD *SAO* CHARACTER DATA IN THE GAME OF *ALO*, SO ASUNA, SILICA, AND THE OTHERS ARE PLAYING AVATARS BASED ON THEIR OLD *SAO* DATA. (KIRITO WAS THE ONLY ONE TO RESET HIS SKILLS AND LEVELS, AFTER THE INCIDENT WITH SUGOU.) FURTHERMORE, THOUGH SHE DOESN'T APPEAR IN THIS ARC, SINON DECIDED TO START HER OWN *ALO* CHARACTER FROM SCRATCH, RATHER THAN CONVERT FROM *GGO*. PERHAPS SHE HAD UNFINISHED BUSINESS IN THE WORLD OF GUNS AND STEEL.

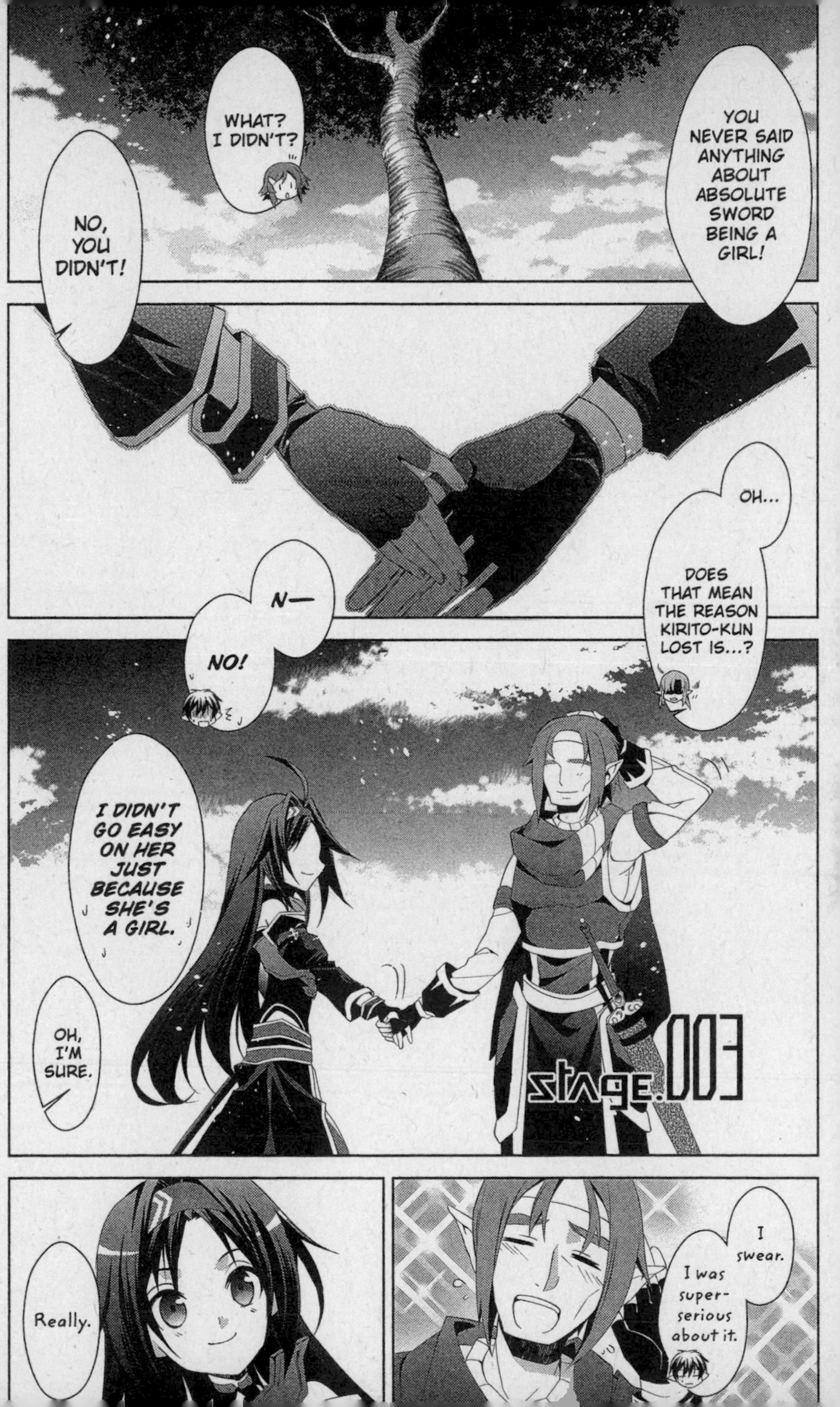
YOU NEVER SAID ANYTHING ABOUT ABSOLUTE SWORD BEING A GIRL!
WHAT? I DIDN'T?
NO, YOU DIDN'T!
OH...
DOES THAT MEAN THE REASON KIRITO-KUN LOST IS...?
N— NO!
I DIDN'T GO EASY ON HER JUST BECAUSE SHE'S A GIRL.
OH, I'M SURE.
stage.003
I swear. I was super-serious about it.
Really.

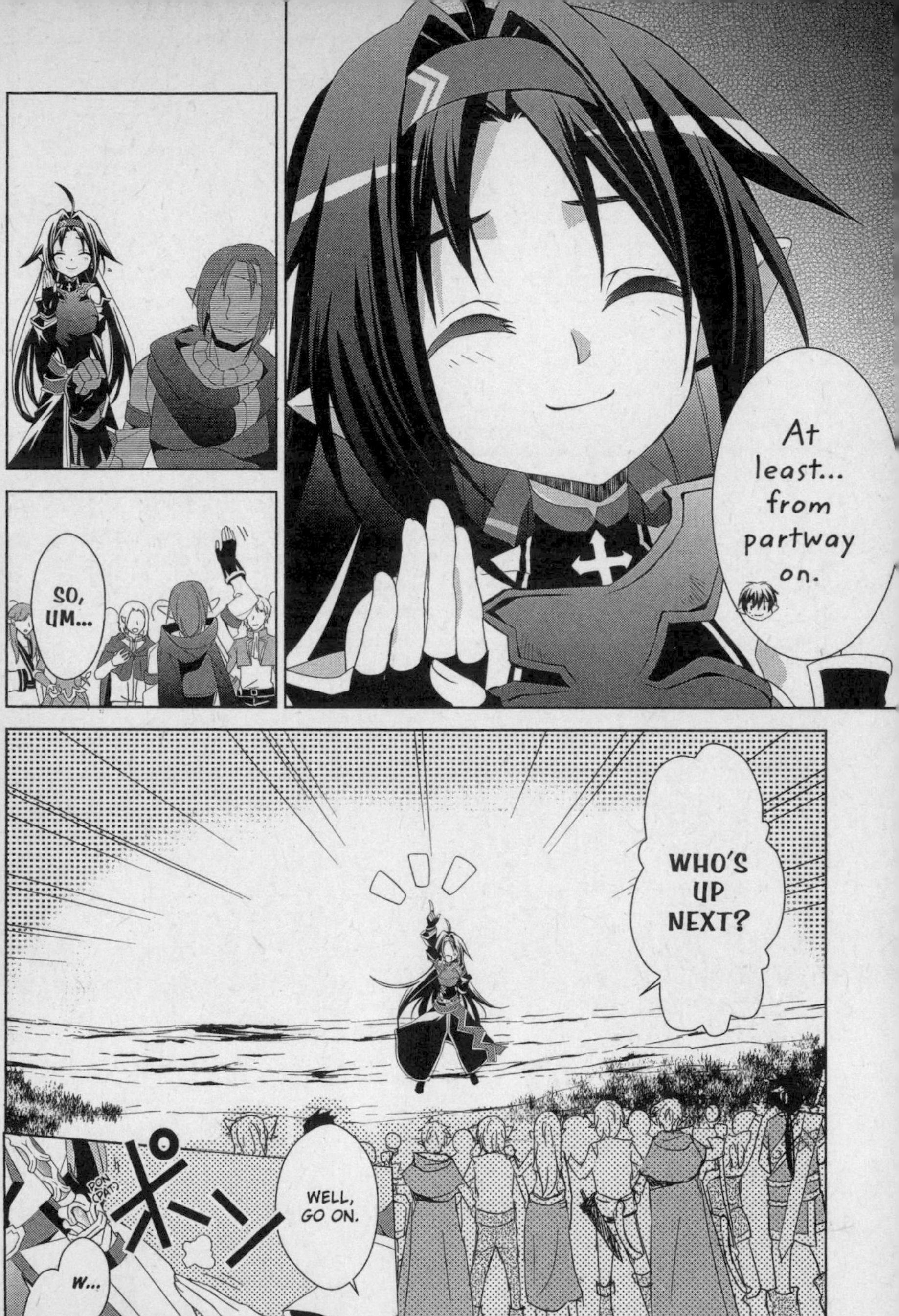
At least... from partway on.
SO, UM...
WHO'S UP NEXT?
WELL, GO ON.
ポーン
PON (PAT)
W... WAIT!

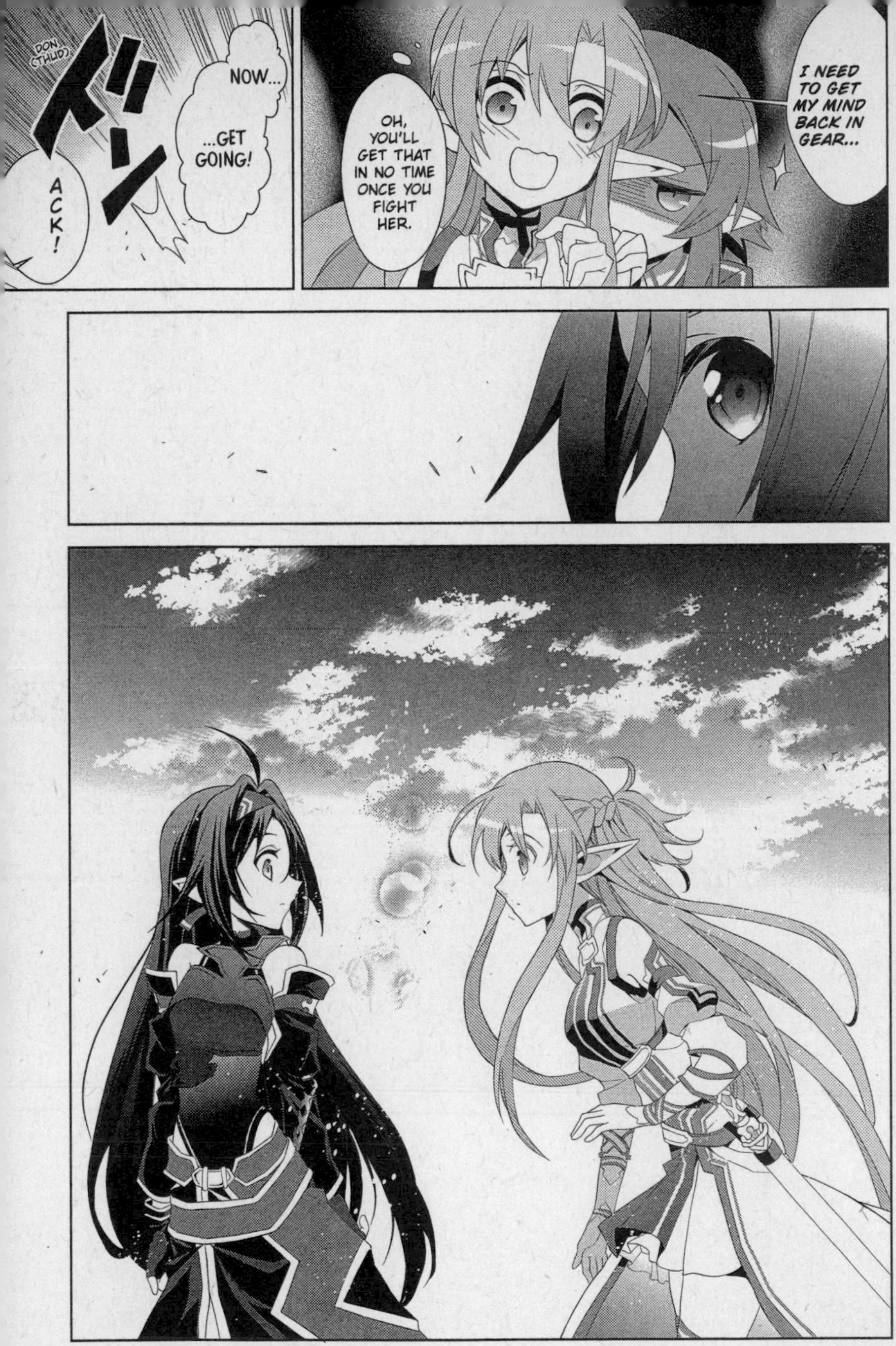
I NEED TO GET MY MIND BACK IN GEAR...
OH, YOU'LL GET THAT IN NO TIME ONCE YOU FIGHT HER.
NOW...
...GET GOING!
DON (THUD)
ACK!

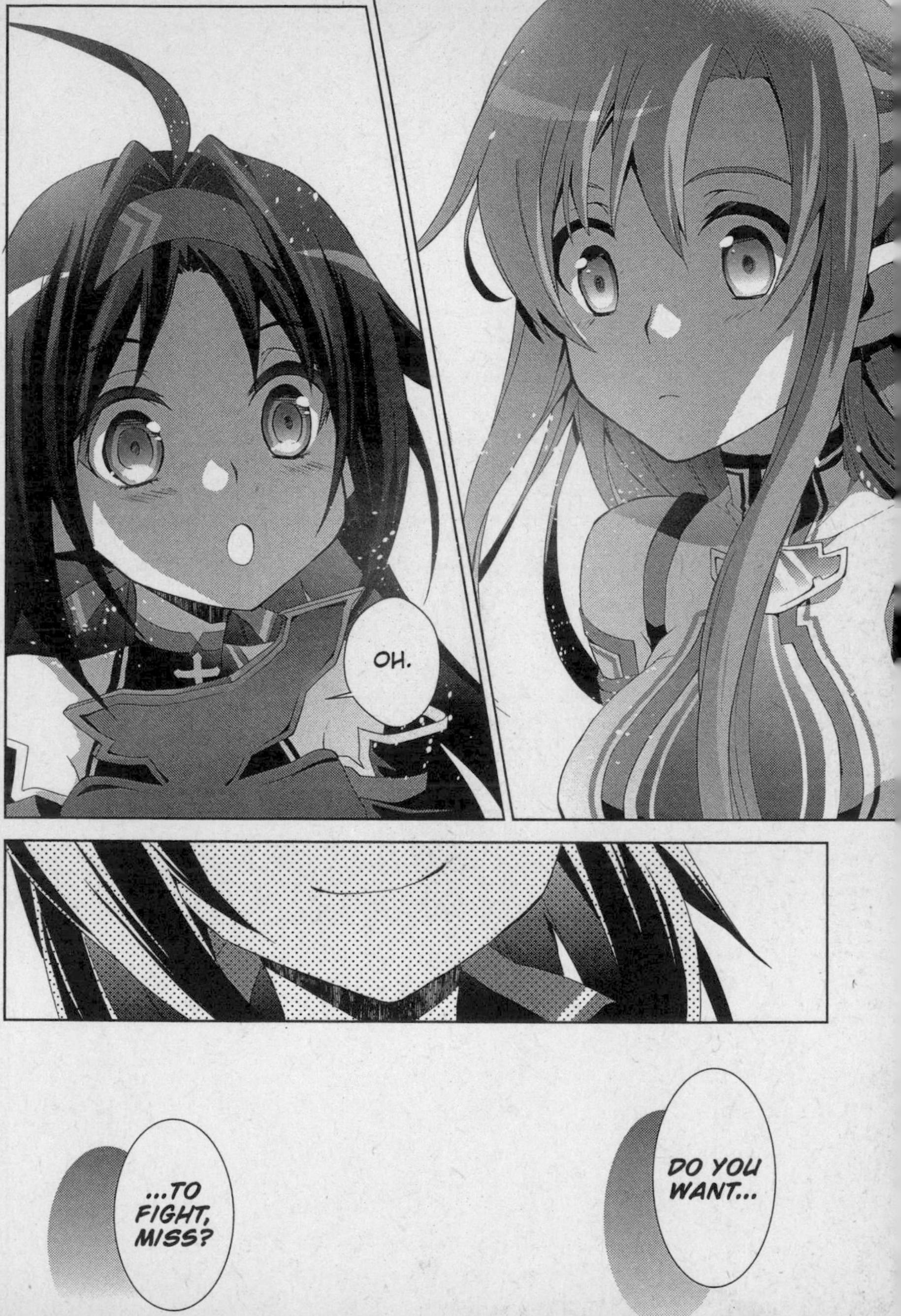
OH.
DO YOU WANT...
...TO FIGHT, MISS?

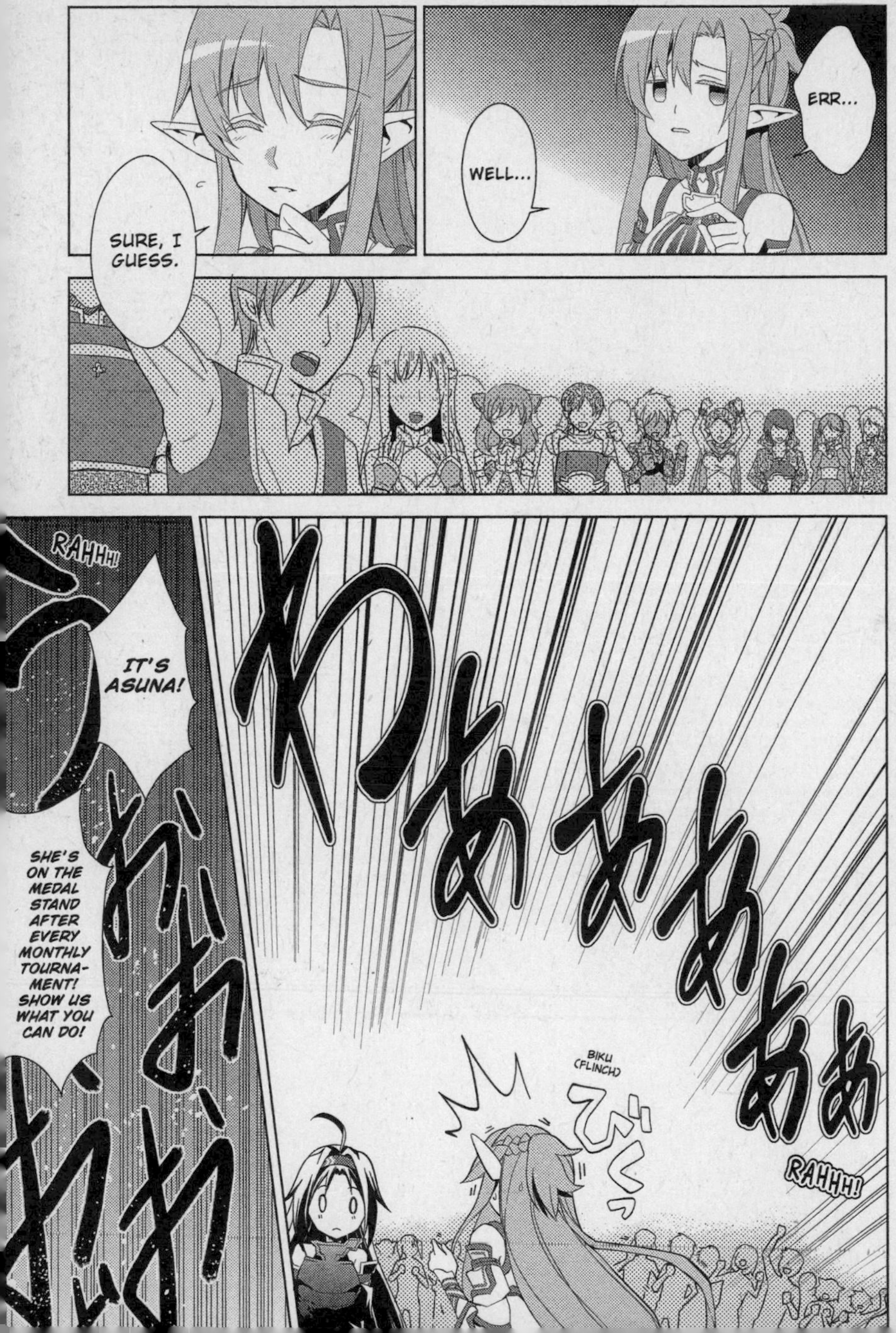
ERR...
WELL...
SURE, I GUESS.
わああああああ
BIKU (FLINCH)
びくっ
RAHHH!
RAHHH!
IT'S ASUNA!
SHE'S ON THE MEDAL STAND AFTER EVERY MONTHLY TOURNA-MENT! SHOW US WHAT YOU CAN DO!
うおおお

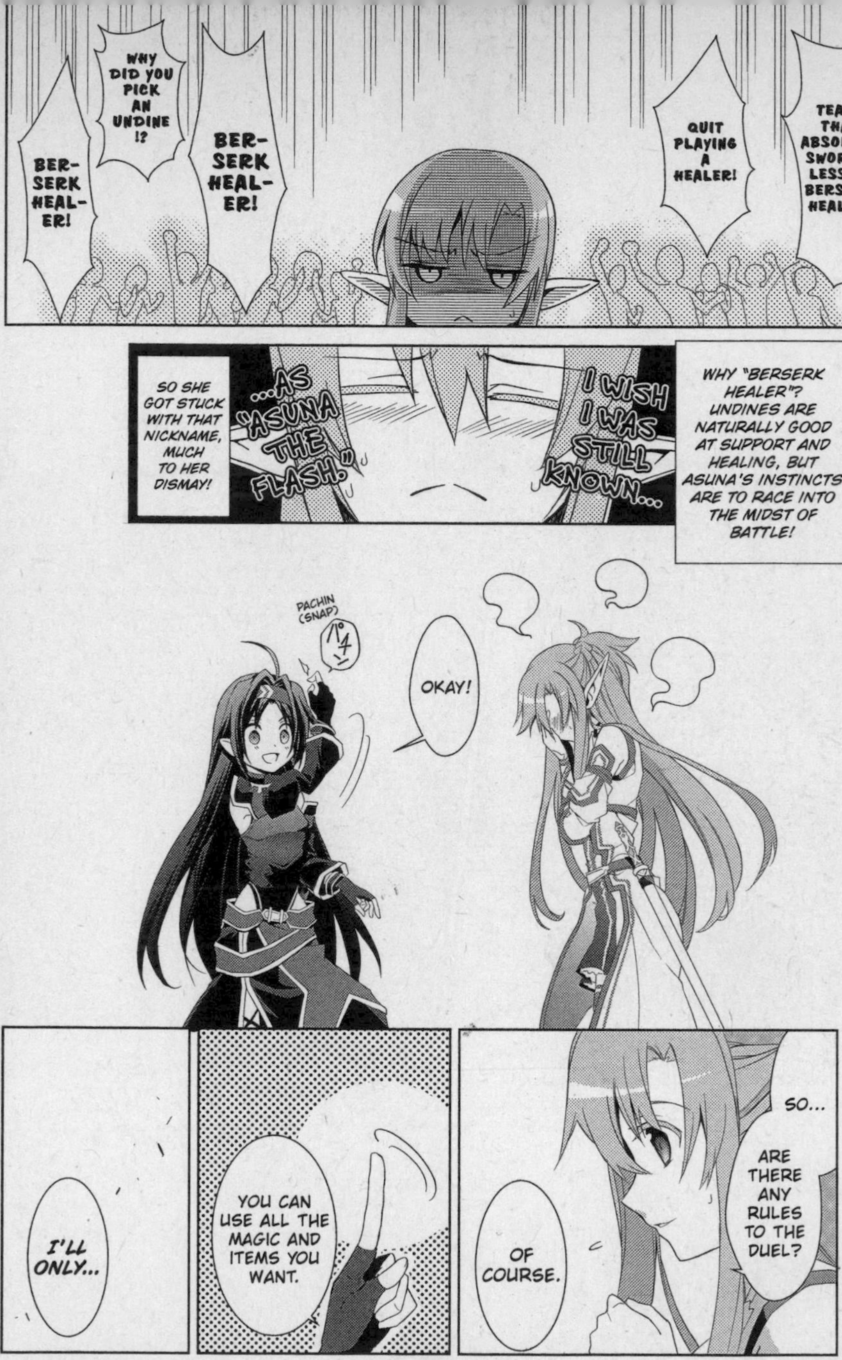
TEACH THAT ABSOLUTE SWORD A LESSON, BERSERK HEALER!
QUIT PLAYING A HEALER!
BER-SERK HEAL-ER!
WHY DID YOU PICK AN UNDINE !?
BER-SERK HEAL-ER!
WHY "BERSERK HEALER"? UNDINES ARE NATURALLY GOOD AT SUPPORT AND HEALING, BUT ASUNA'S INSTINCTS ARE TO RACE INTO THE MIDST OF BATTLE!
I WISH I WAS STILL KNOWN...
...AS "ASUNA THE FLASH."
SO SHE GOT STUCK WITH THAT NICKNAME, MUCH TO HER DISMAY!
OKAY!
PACHIN (SNAP)
SO...
ARE THERE ANY RULES TO THE DUEL?
OF COURSE.
YOU CAN USE ALL THE MAGIC AND ITEMS YOU WANT.
I'LL ONLY...

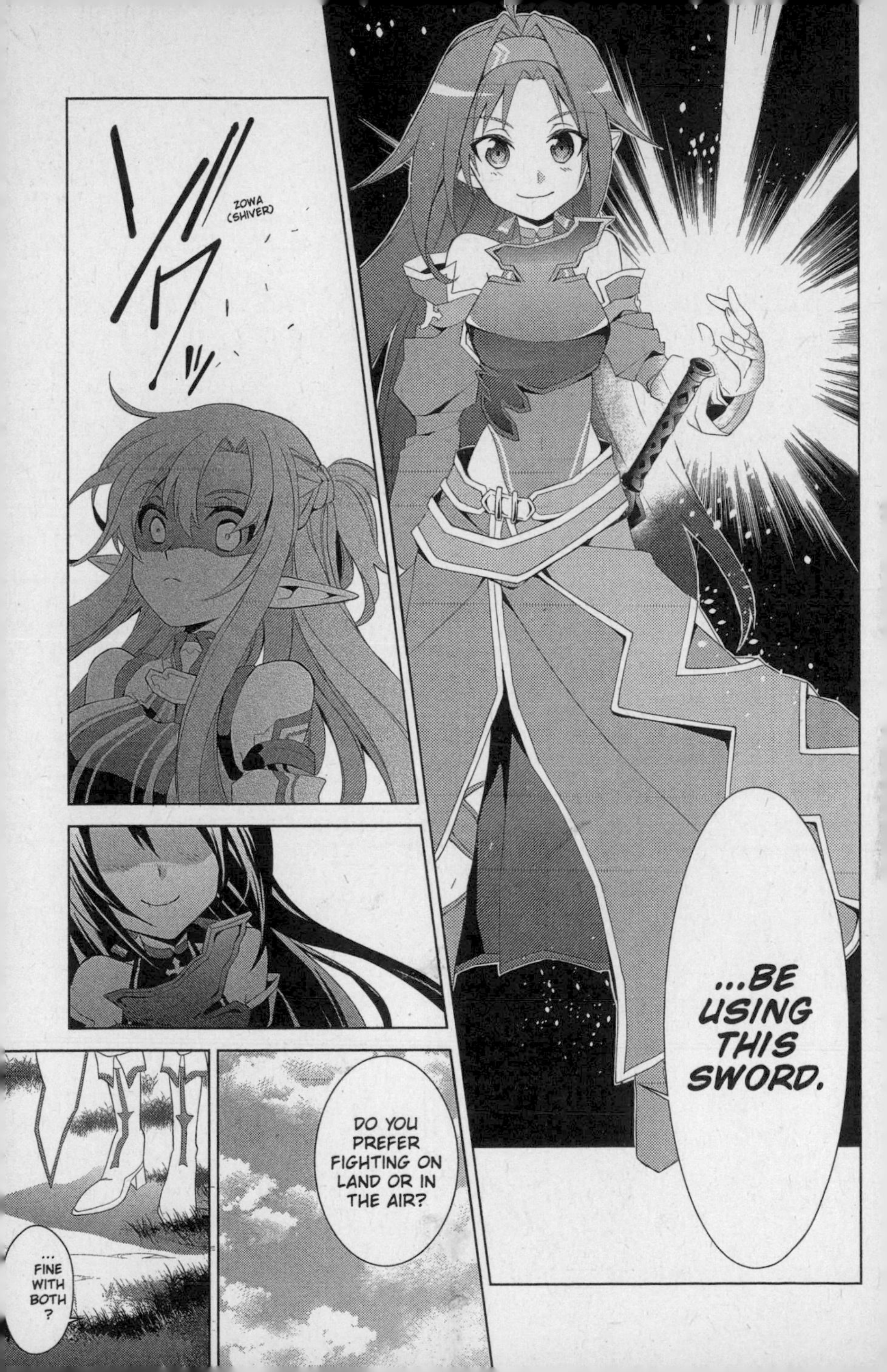
...BE USING THIS SWORD.
ZOWA (SHIVER)
DO YOU PREFER FIGHTING ON LAND OR IN THE AIR?
... FINE WITH BOTH ?

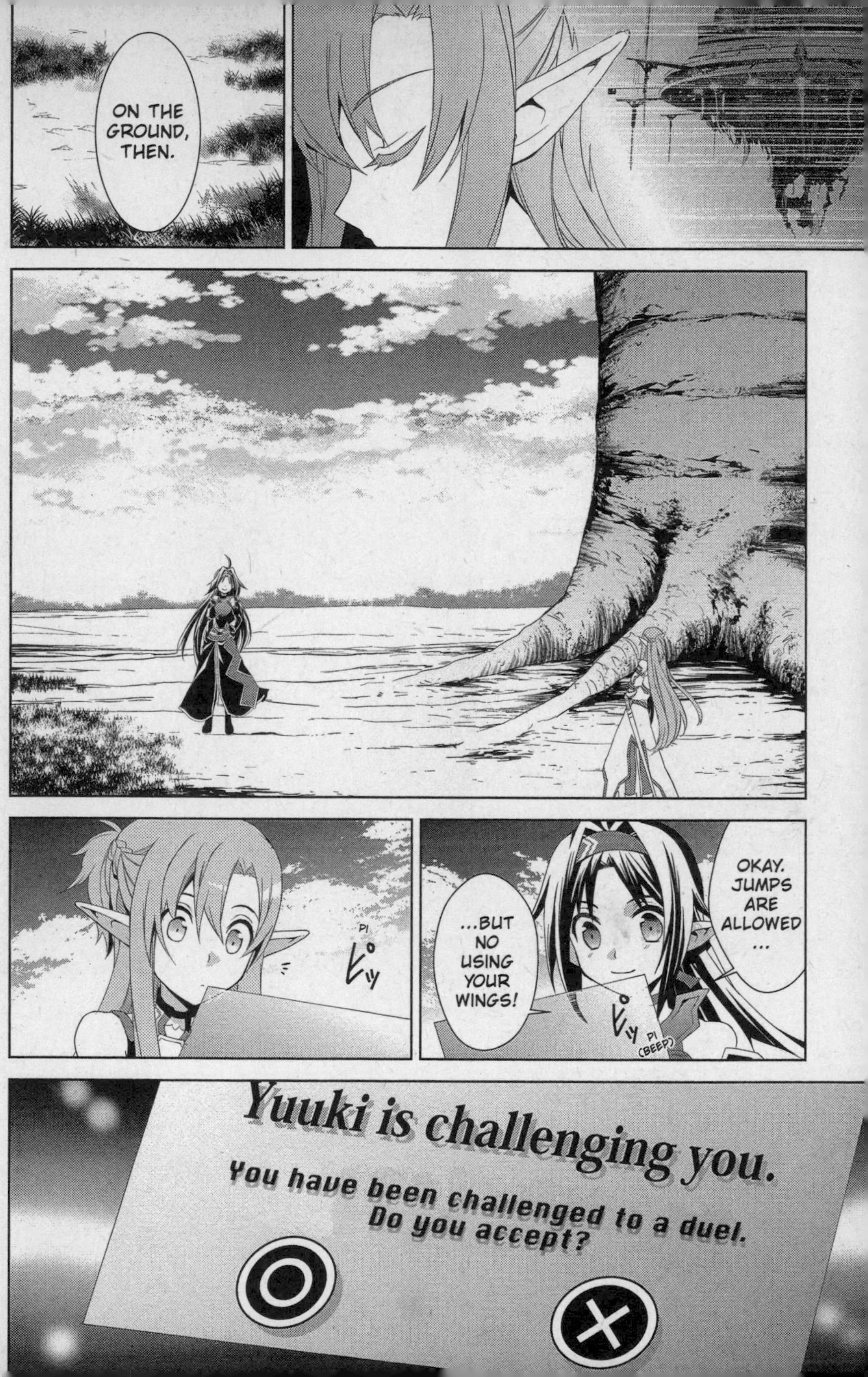
ON THE GROUND, THEN.
OKAY. JUMPS ARE ALLOWED ...
...BUT NO USING YOUR WINGS!
PI (BEEP)
PI
Yuuki is challenging you.
You have been challenged to a duel. Do you accept?

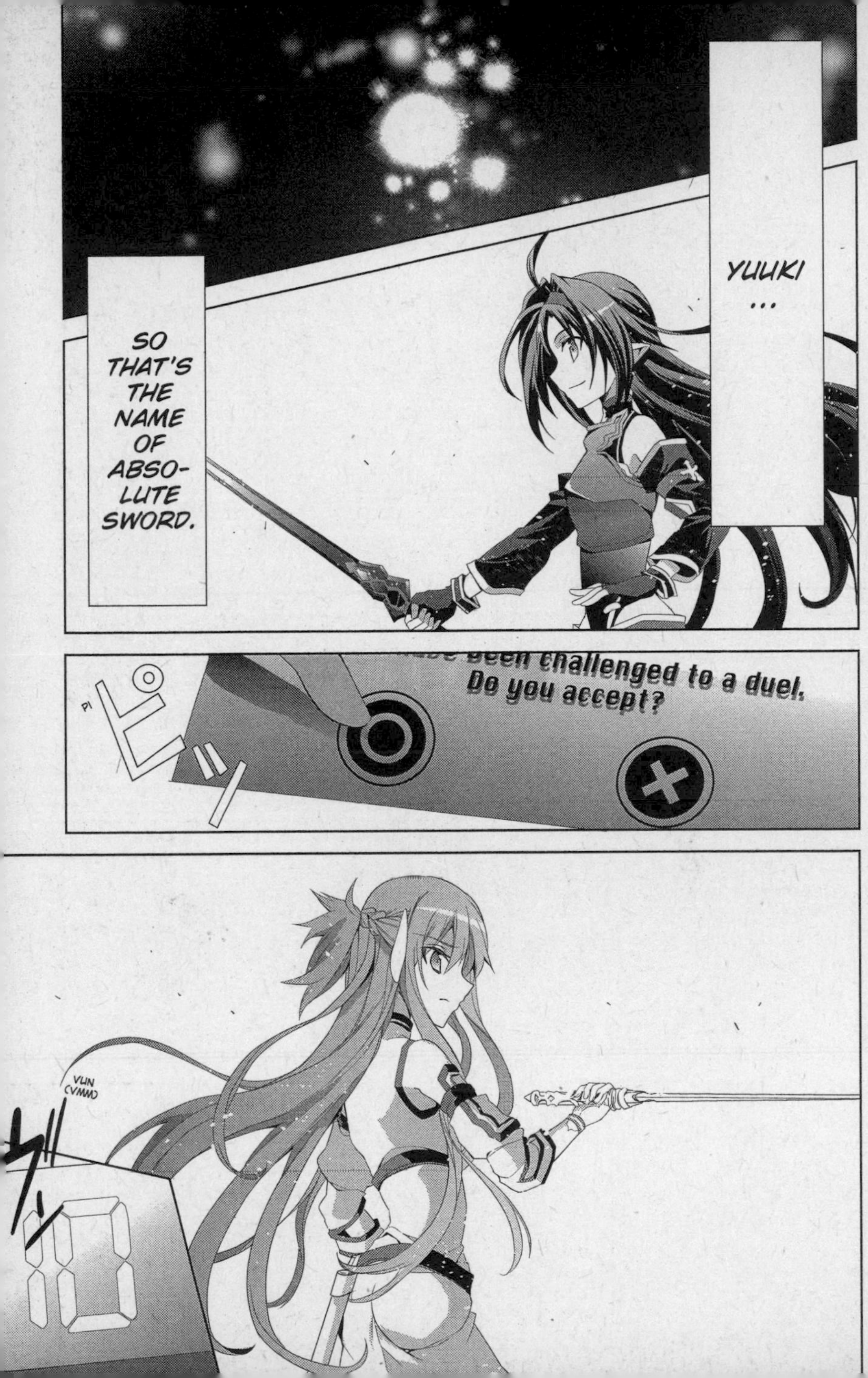
YUUKI
...
SO THAT'S THE NAME OF ABSOLUTE SWORD.
PI
been challenged to a duel.
Do you accept?
VUN
(VMM)

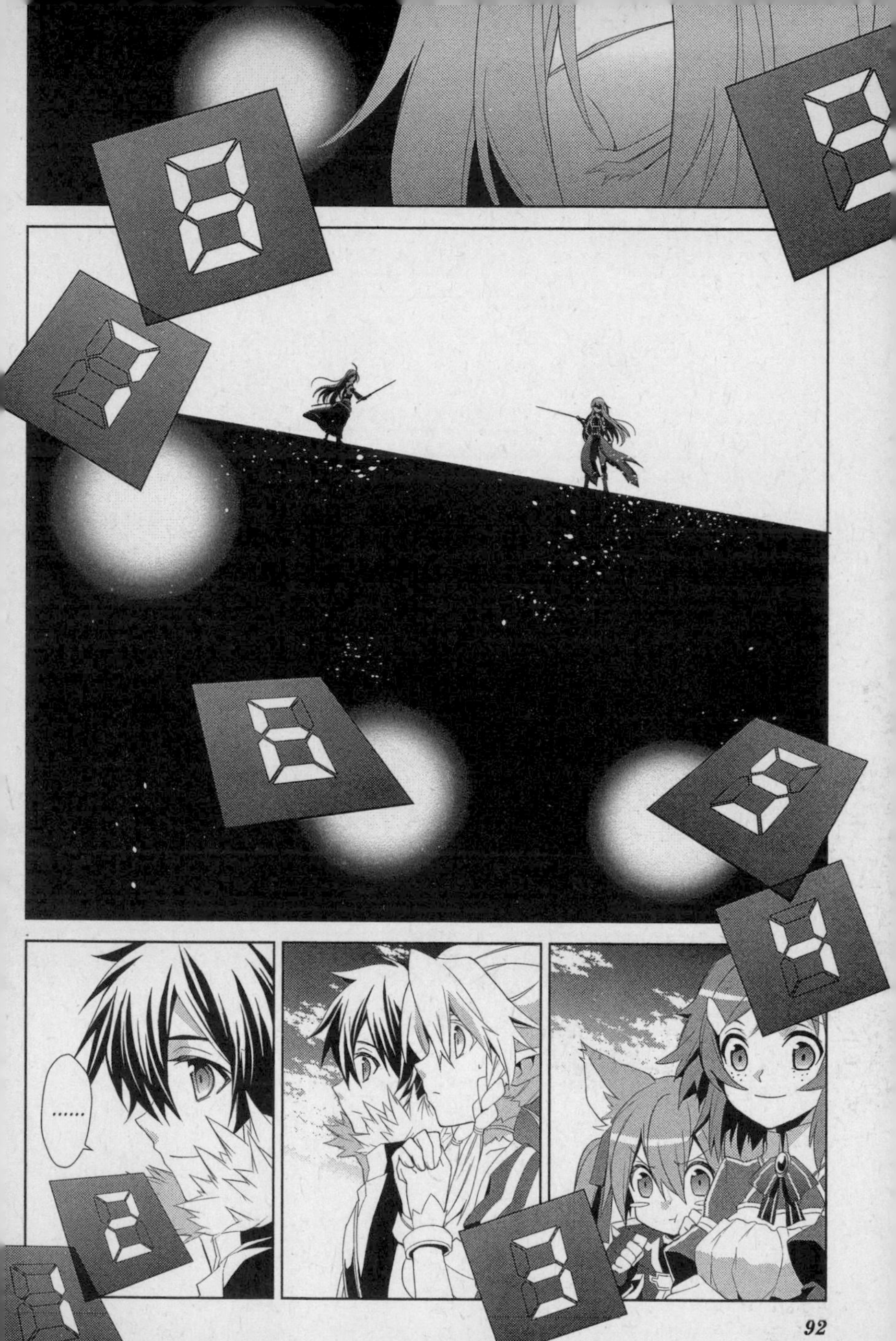
......

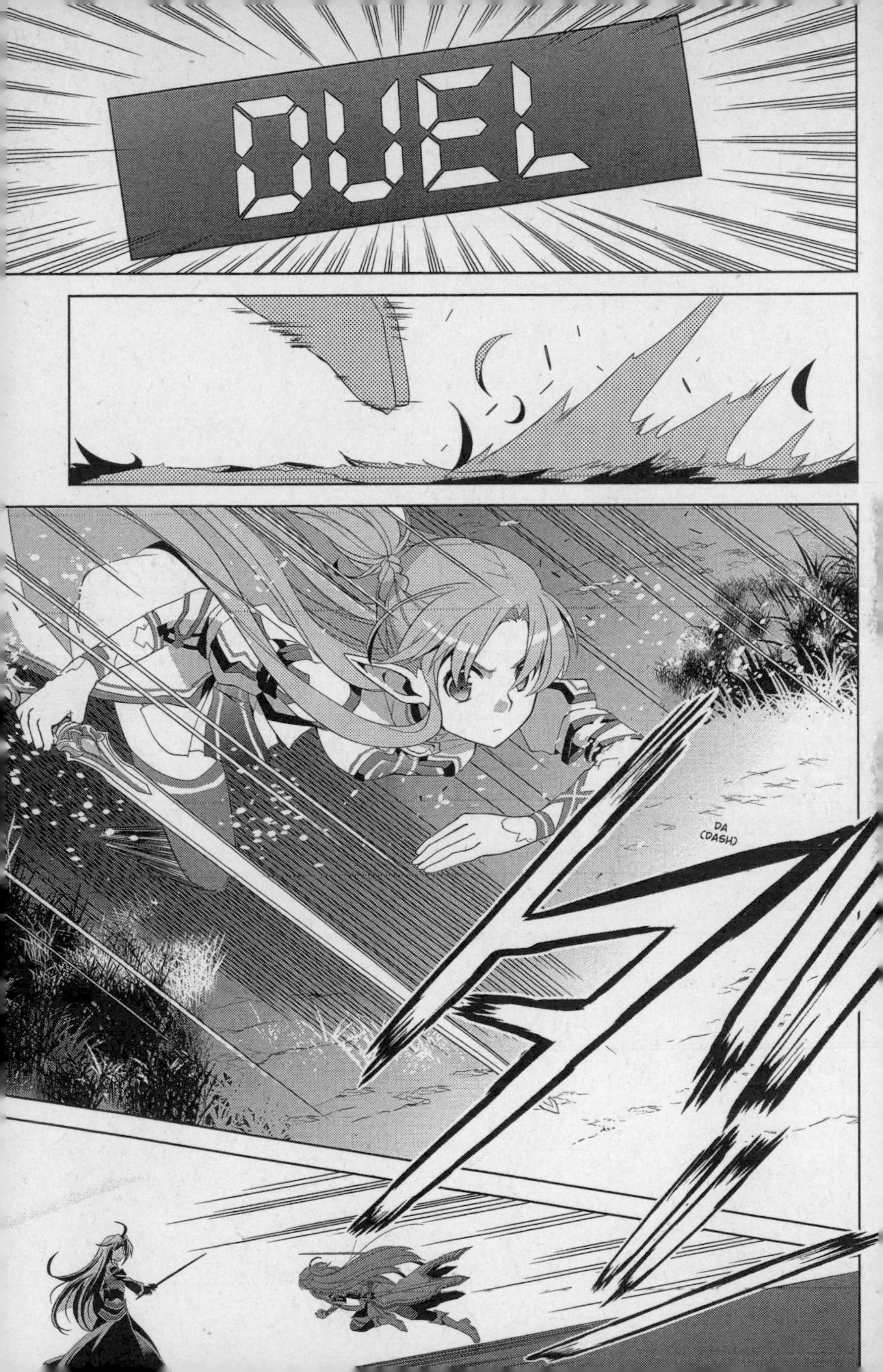
DUEL
DA
(DASH)

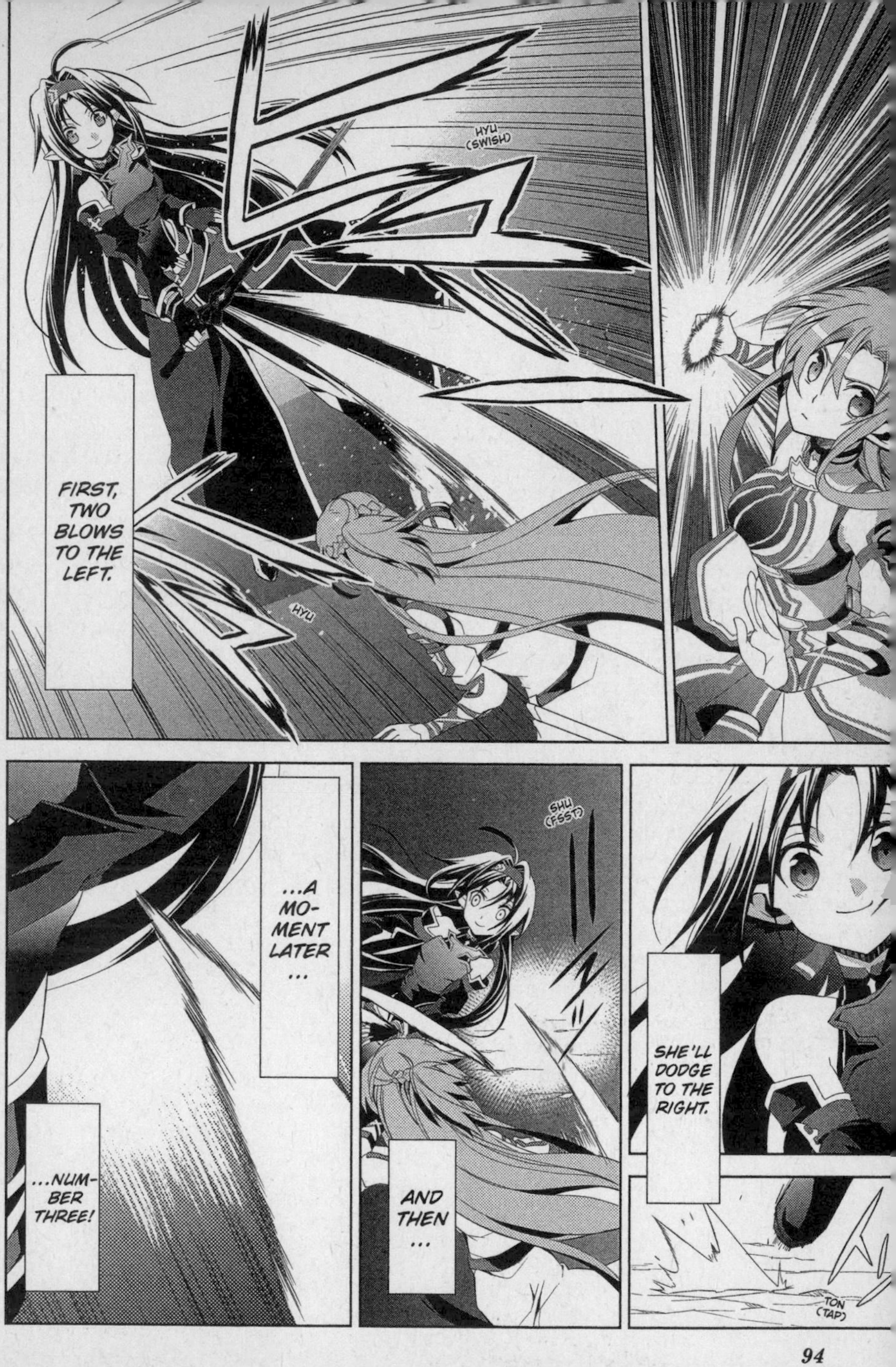
HYU (SWISH)
FIRST, TWO BLOWS TO THE LEFT.
HYU
SHE'LL DODGE TO THE RIGHT.
TON (TAP)
SHU (FSST)
...A MOMENT LATER...
AND THEN...
...NUMBER THREE!

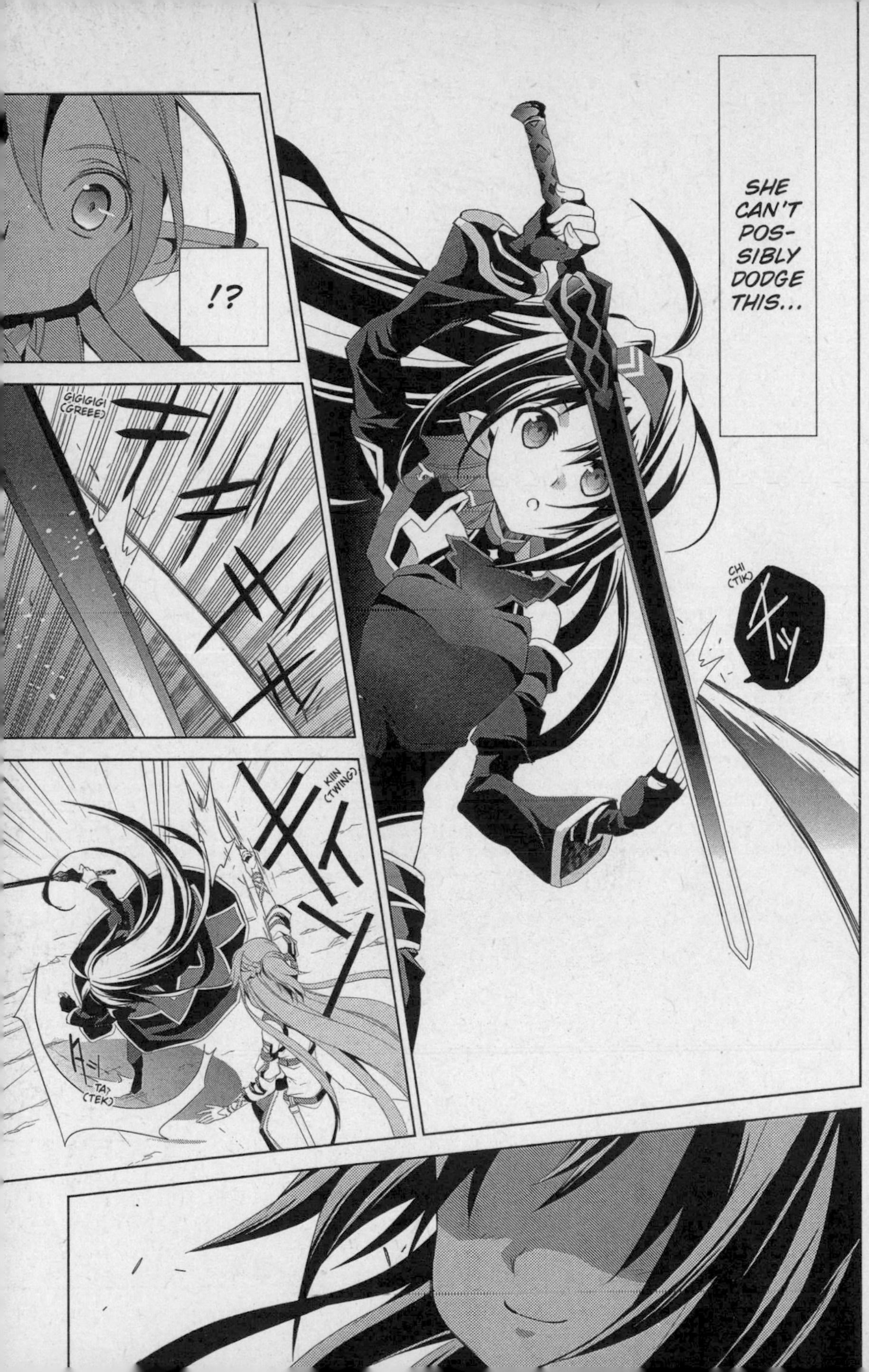
SHE CAN'T POS-SIBLY DODGE THIS...
CHI (TIK)
!?
GIGIGIGI (GREEE)
KIIN (TWING)
TA (TEK)

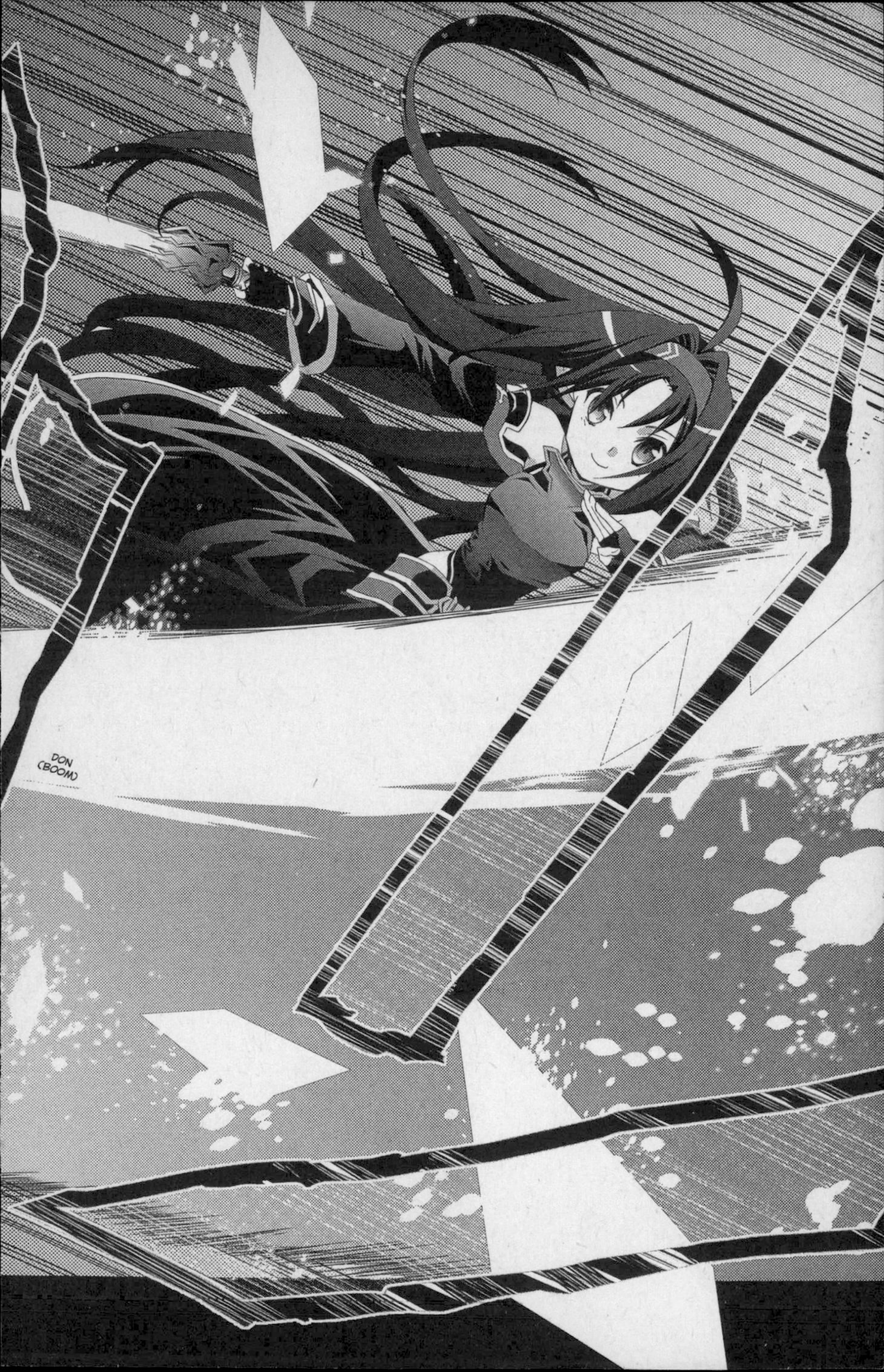
DON
(BOOM)

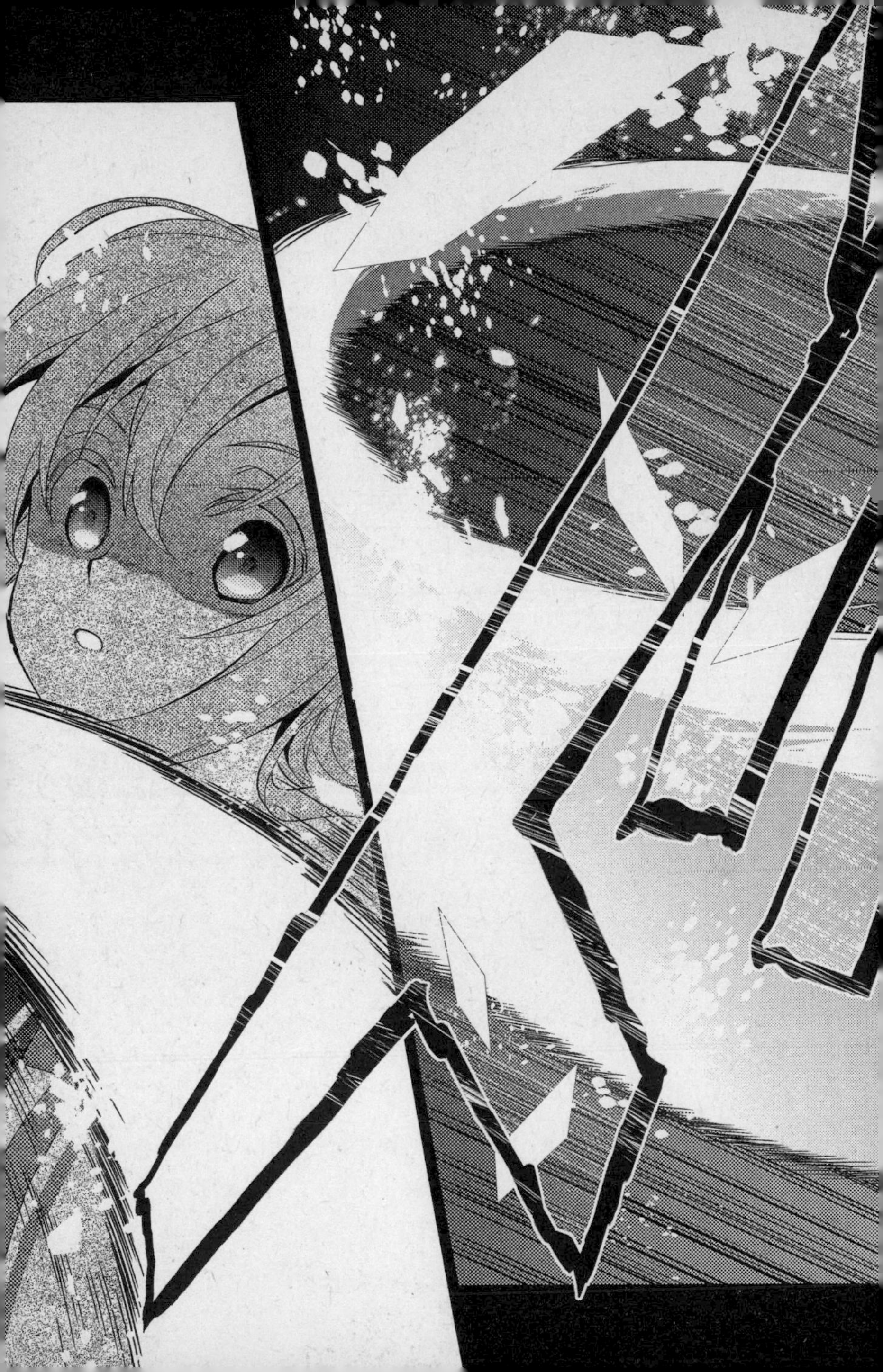

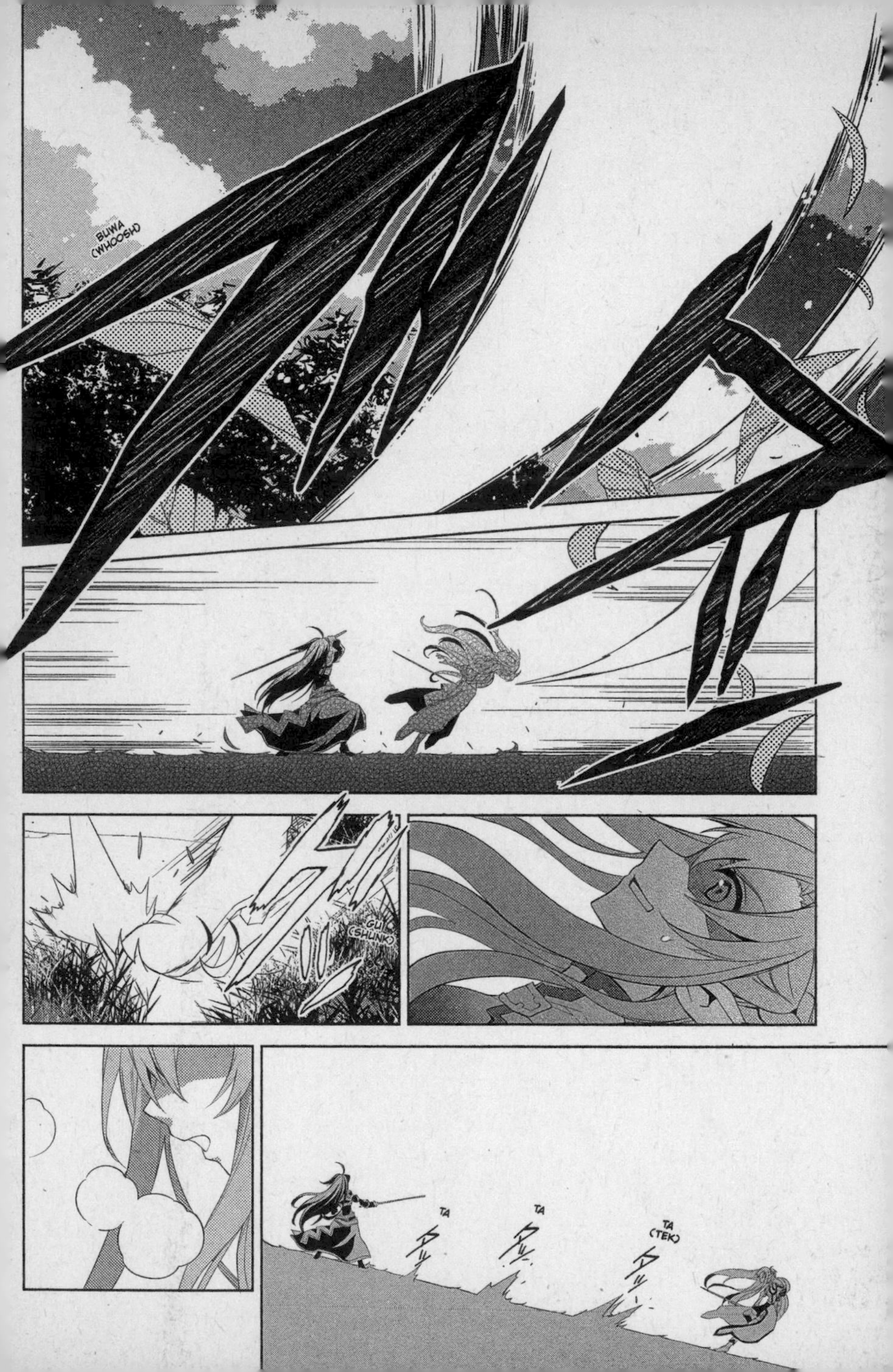
BUWA
(WHOOSH)
GU
(SHLINK)
TA
(TEK)
TA
TA

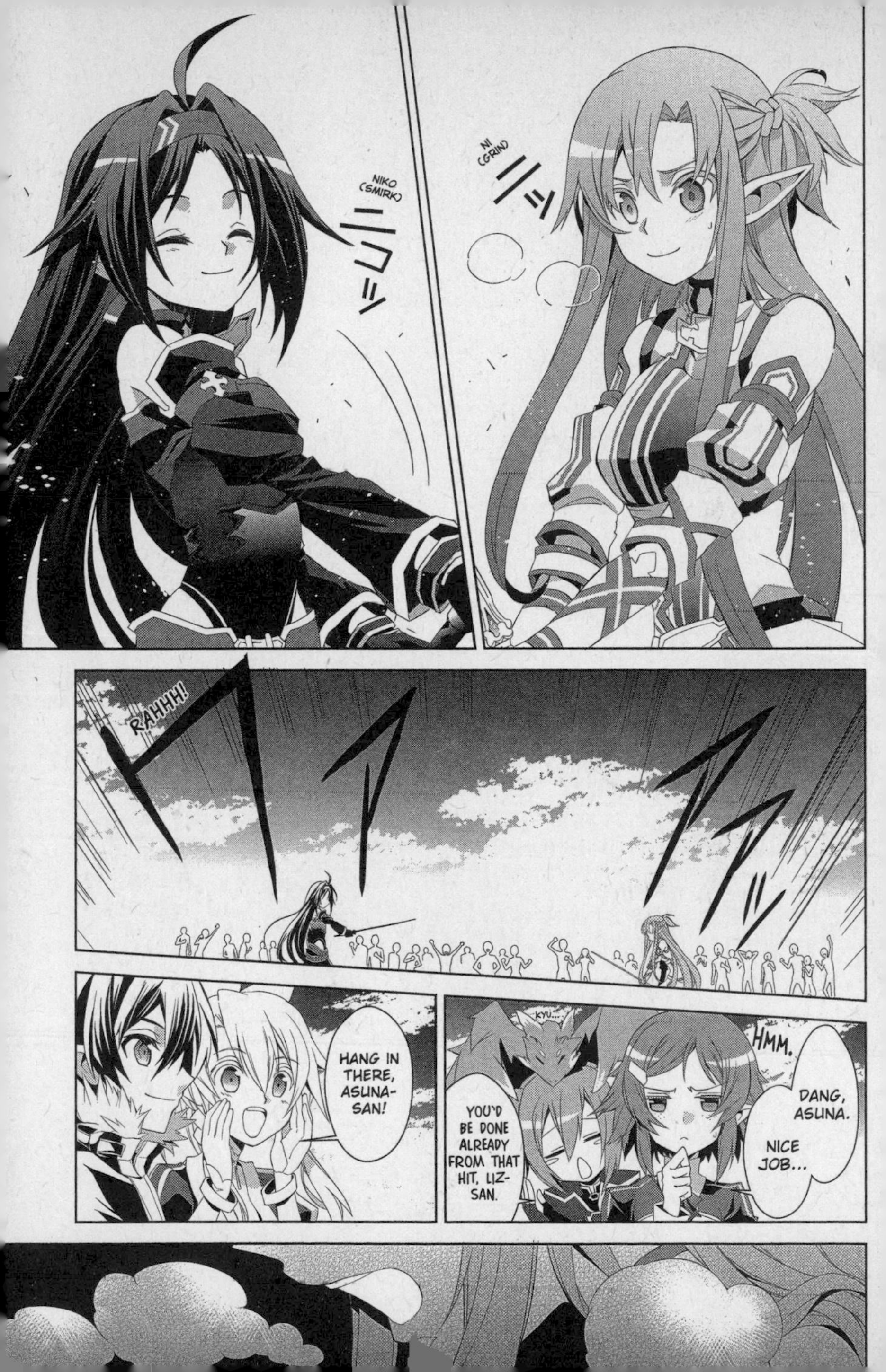
NI (GRIN)
NIKO (SMIRK)
RAHHH!
HMM.
KYU...
DANG, ASUNA.
NICE JOB...
YOU'D BE DONE ALREADY FROM THAT HIT, LIZ-SAN.
HANG IN THERE, ASUNA-SAN!

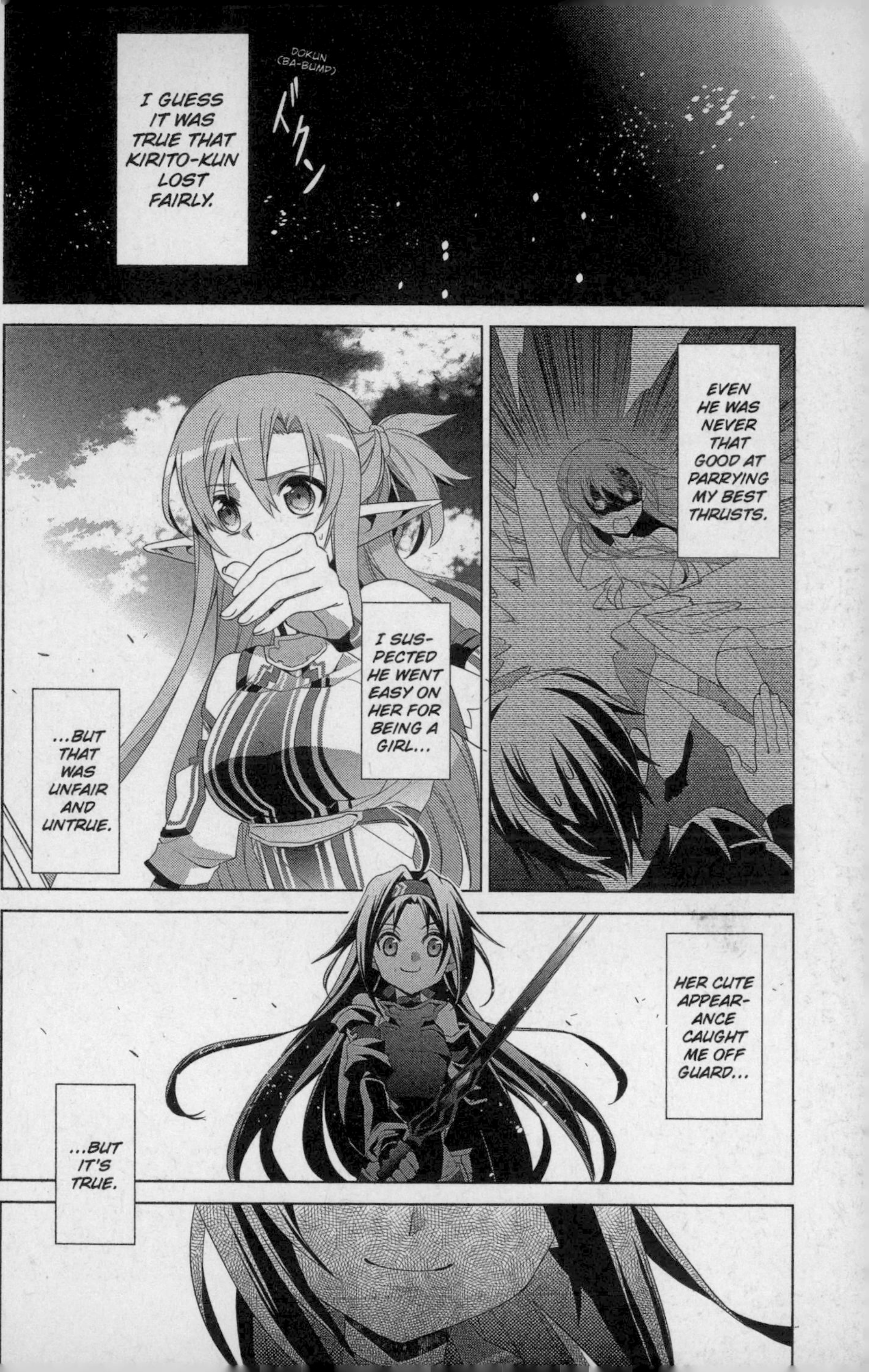
DOKUN (BA-BUMP)
I GUESS IT WAS TRUE THAT KIRITO-KUN LOST FAIRLY.
EVEN HE WAS NEVER THAT GOOD AT PARRYING MY BEST THRUSTS.
I SUS-PECTED HE WENT EASY ON HER FOR BEING A GIRL...
...BUT THAT WAS UNFAIR AND UNTRUE.
HER CUTE APPEAR-ANCE CAUGHT ME OFF GUARD...
...BUT IT'S TRUE.

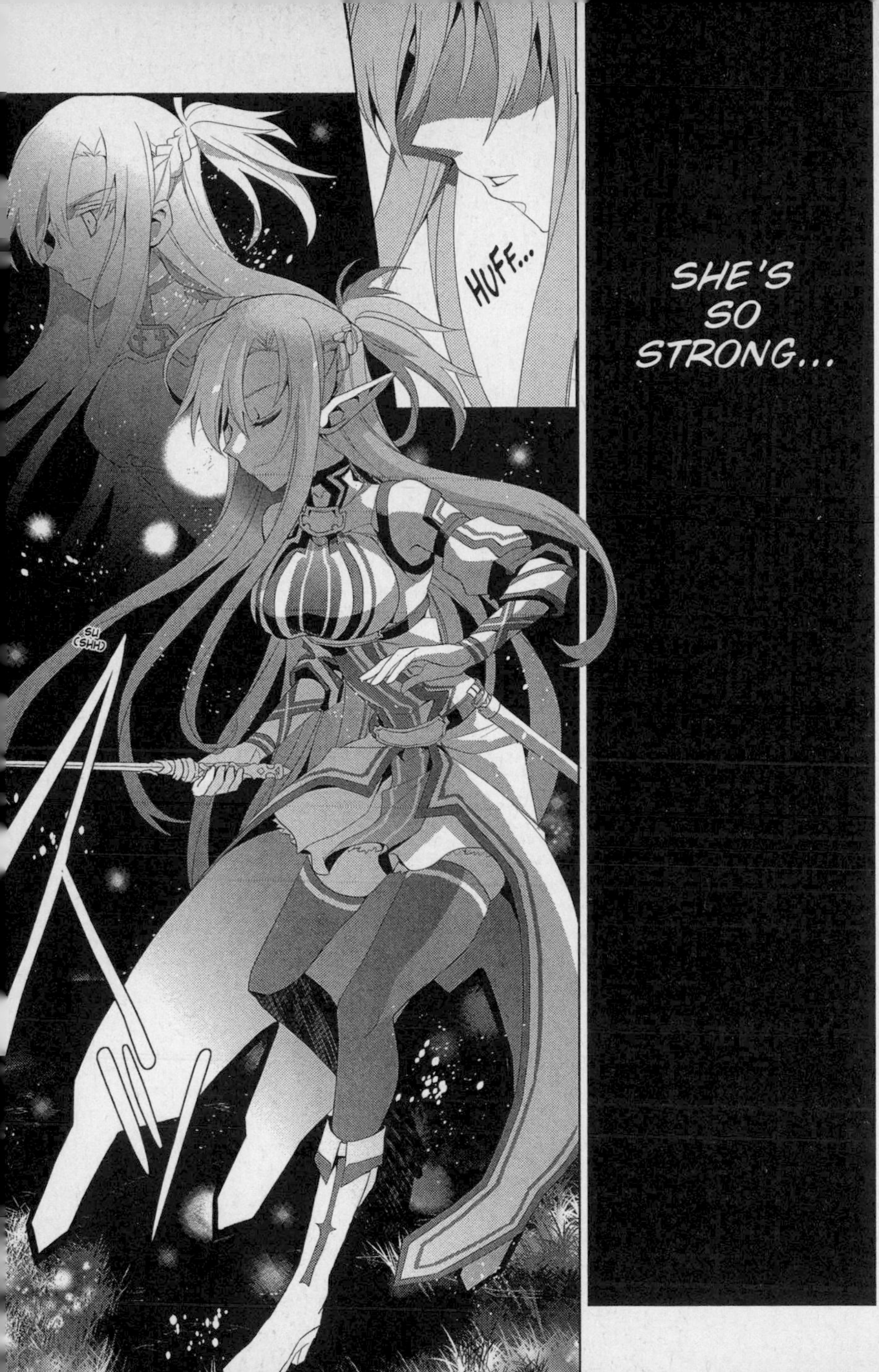
SHE'S SO STRONG...
HUFF...
SU
(SHH)

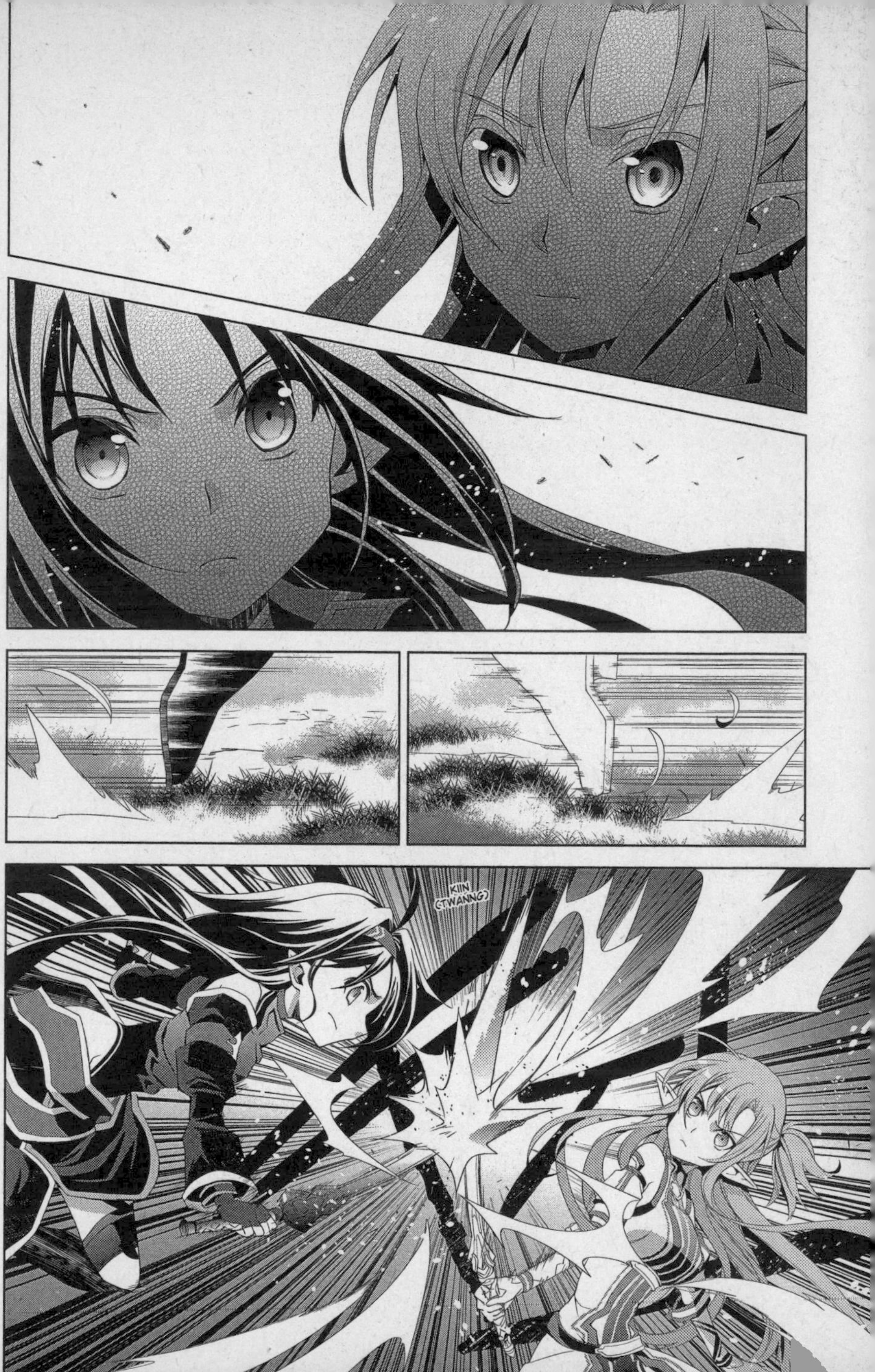
KIIN (TWANNG)

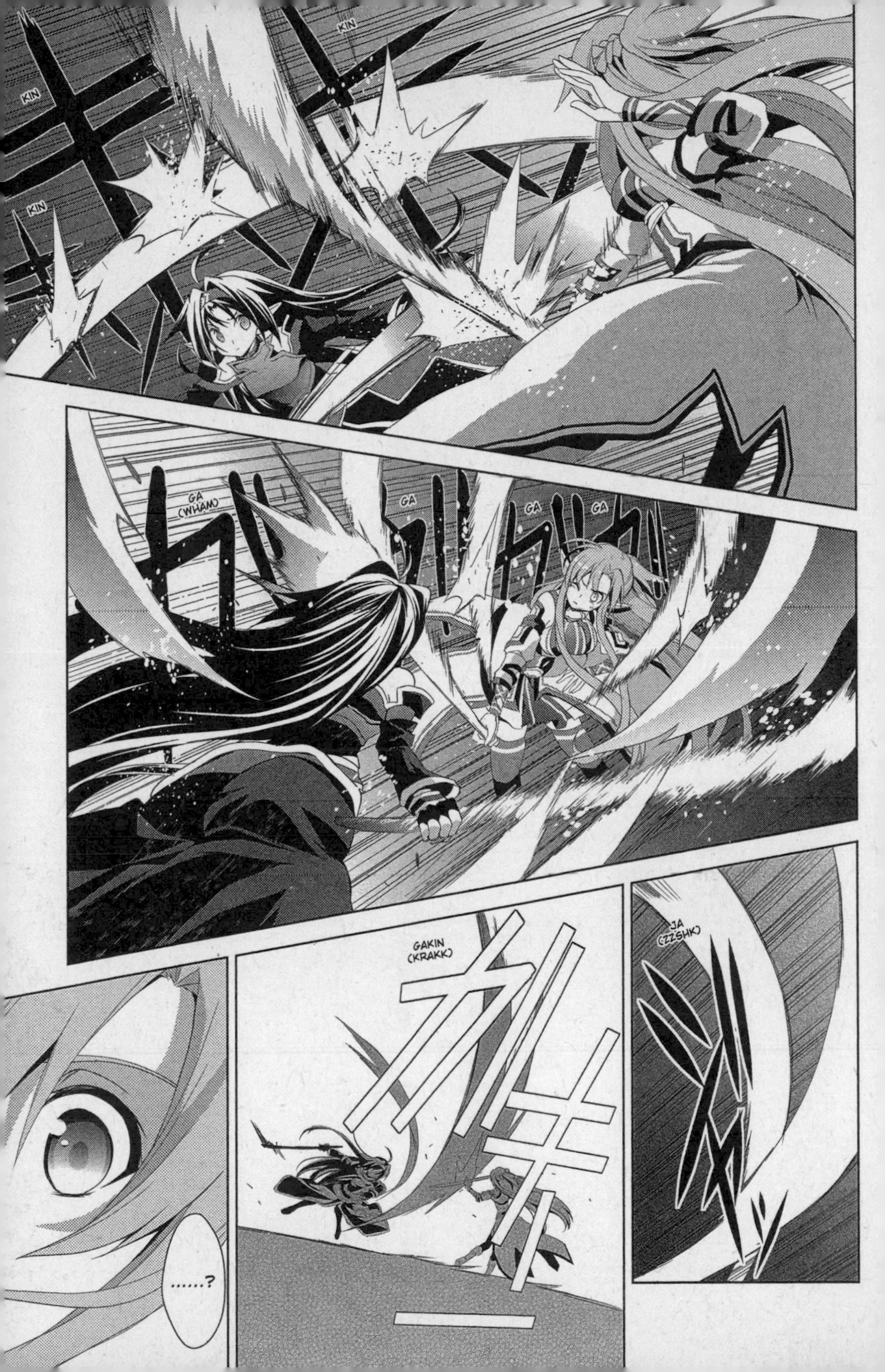
KIN
KIN
KIN
GA
GA
GA
GA (WHAM)
JA (ZZSHK)
GAKIN (KRAKK)
......?

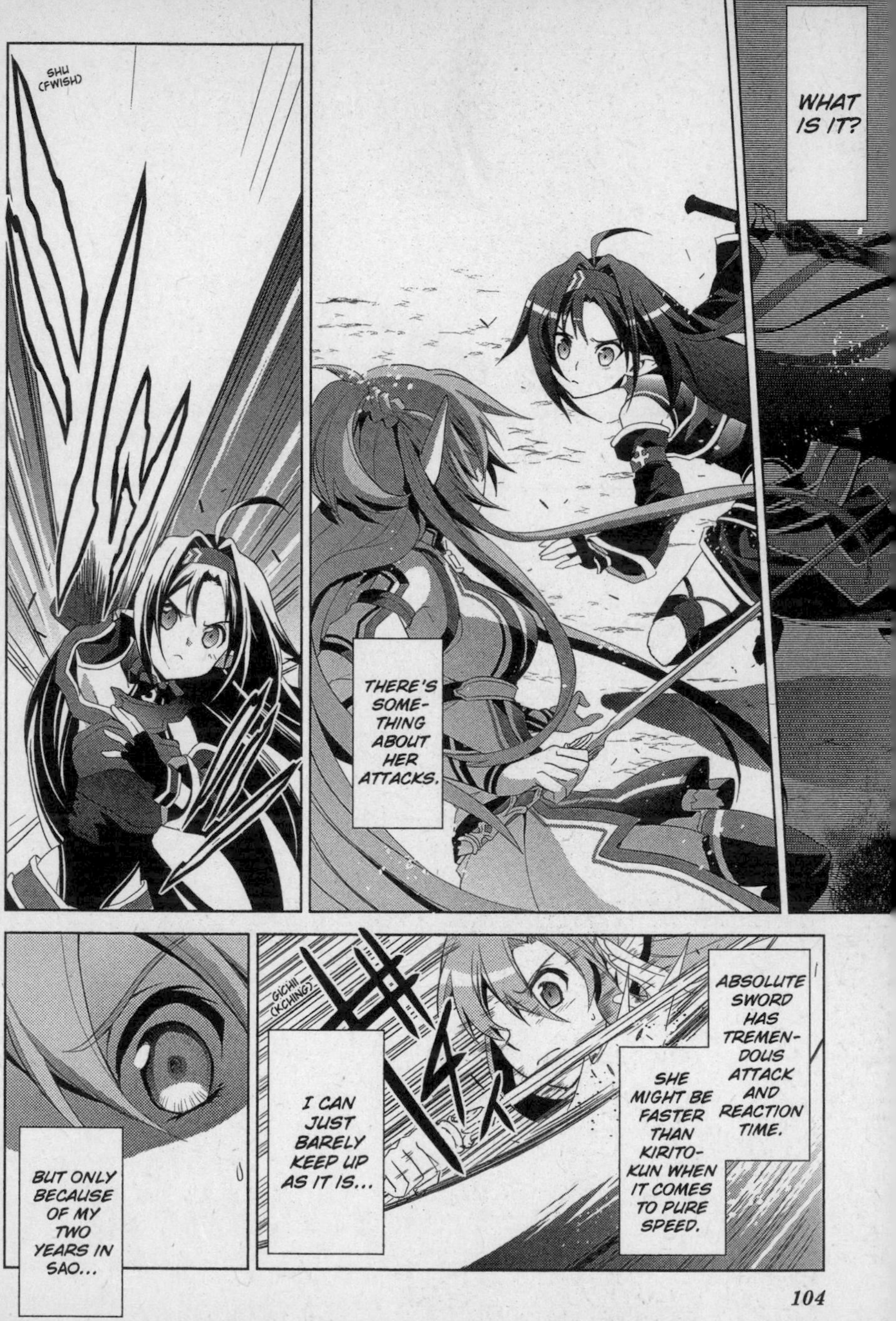
WHAT IS IT?
THERE'S SOME-THING ABOUT HER ATTACKS.
SHU (FWISH)
ABSOLUTE SWORD HAS TREMEN-DOUS ATTACK AND REACTION TIME.
SHE MIGHT BE FASTER THAN KIRITO-KUN WHEN IT COMES TO PURE SPEED.
GICHI (KCHING)
I CAN JUST BARELY KEEP UP AS IT IS...
BUT ONLY BECAUSE OF MY TWO YEARS IN SAO...

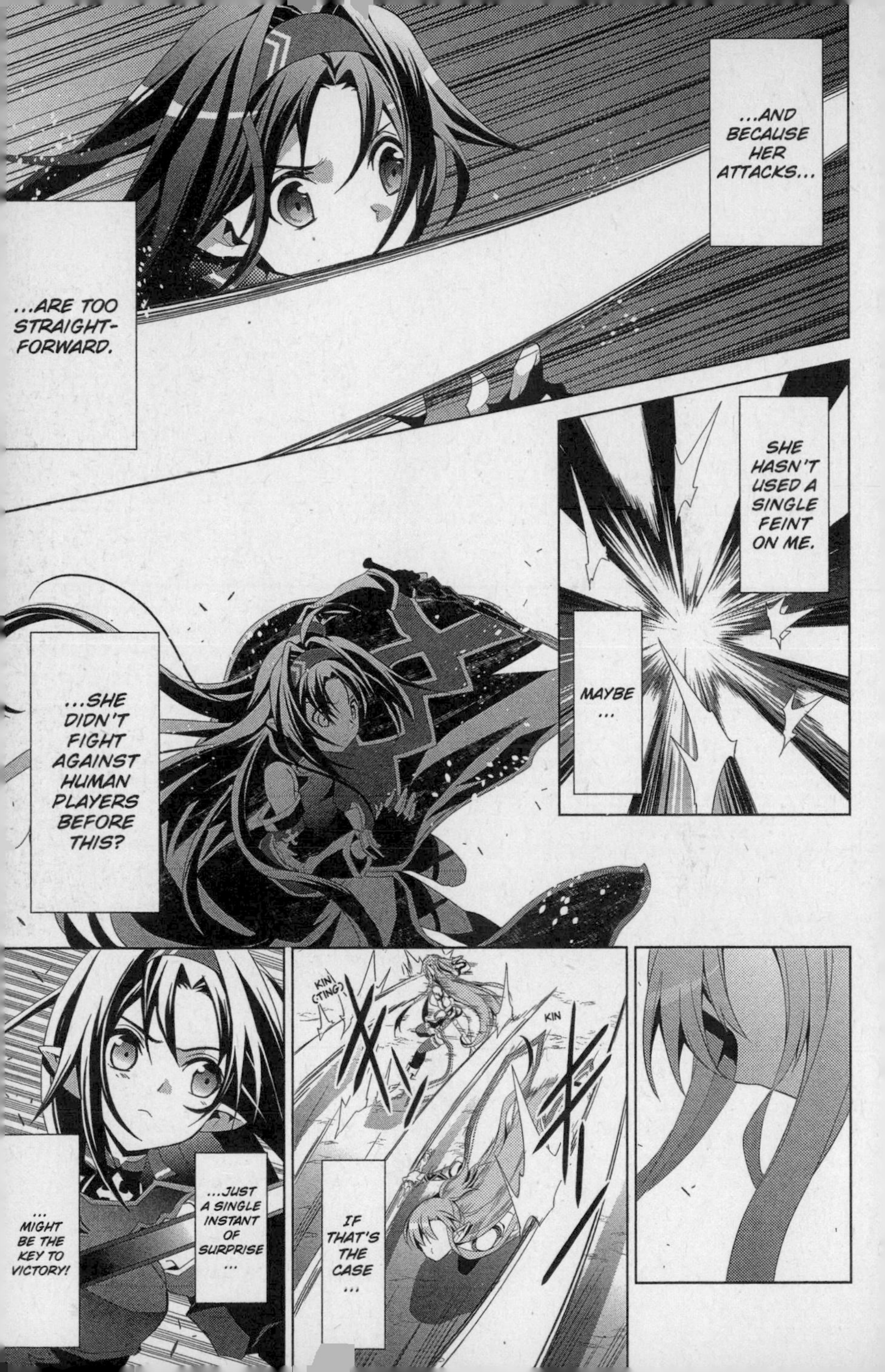
...AND BECAUSE HER ATTACKS...
...ARE TOO STRAIGHT-FORWARD.
SHE HASN'T USED A SINGLE FEINT ON ME.
MAYBE ...
...SHE DIDN'T FIGHT AGAINST HUMAN PLAYERS BEFORE THIS?
KIN (TING)
KIN
IF THAT'S THE CASE ...
...JUST A SINGLE INSTANT OF SURPRISE ...
... MIGHT BE THE KEY TO VICTORY!

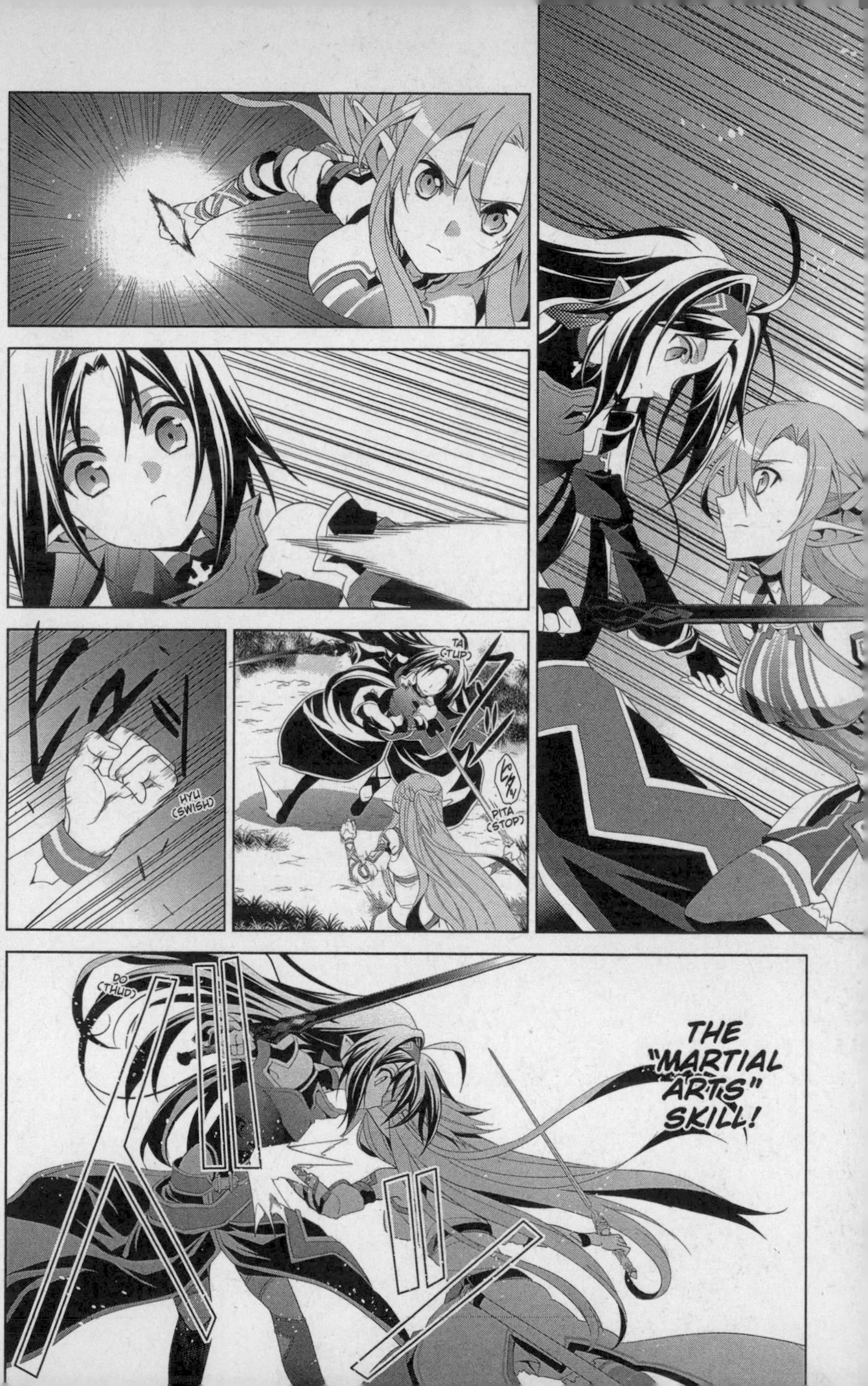
TA
(TUP)
PITA
(STOP)
HYU
(SWISH)
DO
(THUD)
THE "MARTIAL ARTS" SKILL!

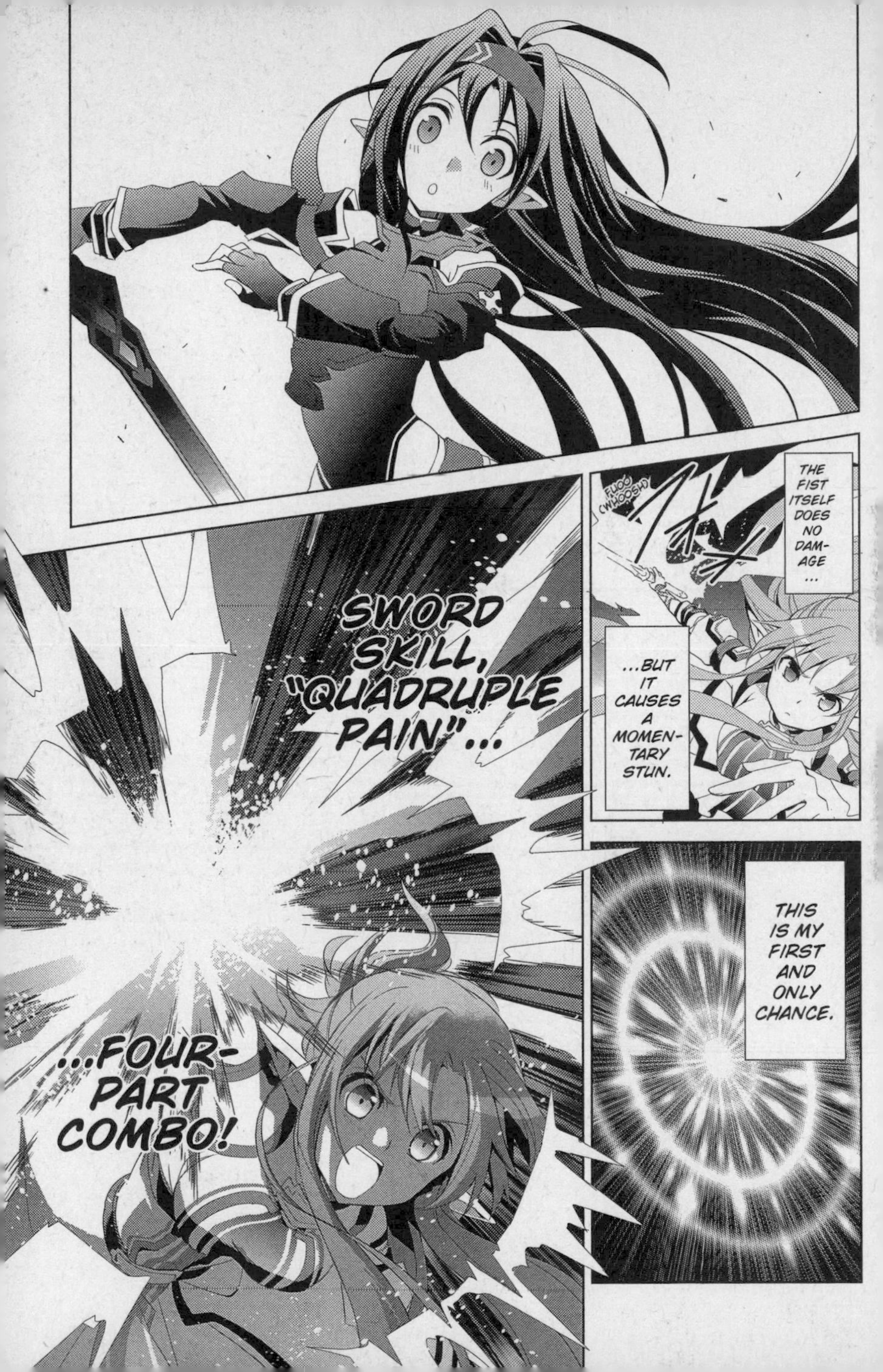
FUOO (WHOOSH)
THE FIST ITSELF DOES NO DAM-AGE...
...BUT IT CAUSES A MOMEN-TARY STUN.
THIS IS MY FIRST AND ONLY CHANCE.
SWORD SKILL, "QUADRUPLE PAIN"...
...FOUR-PART COMBO!

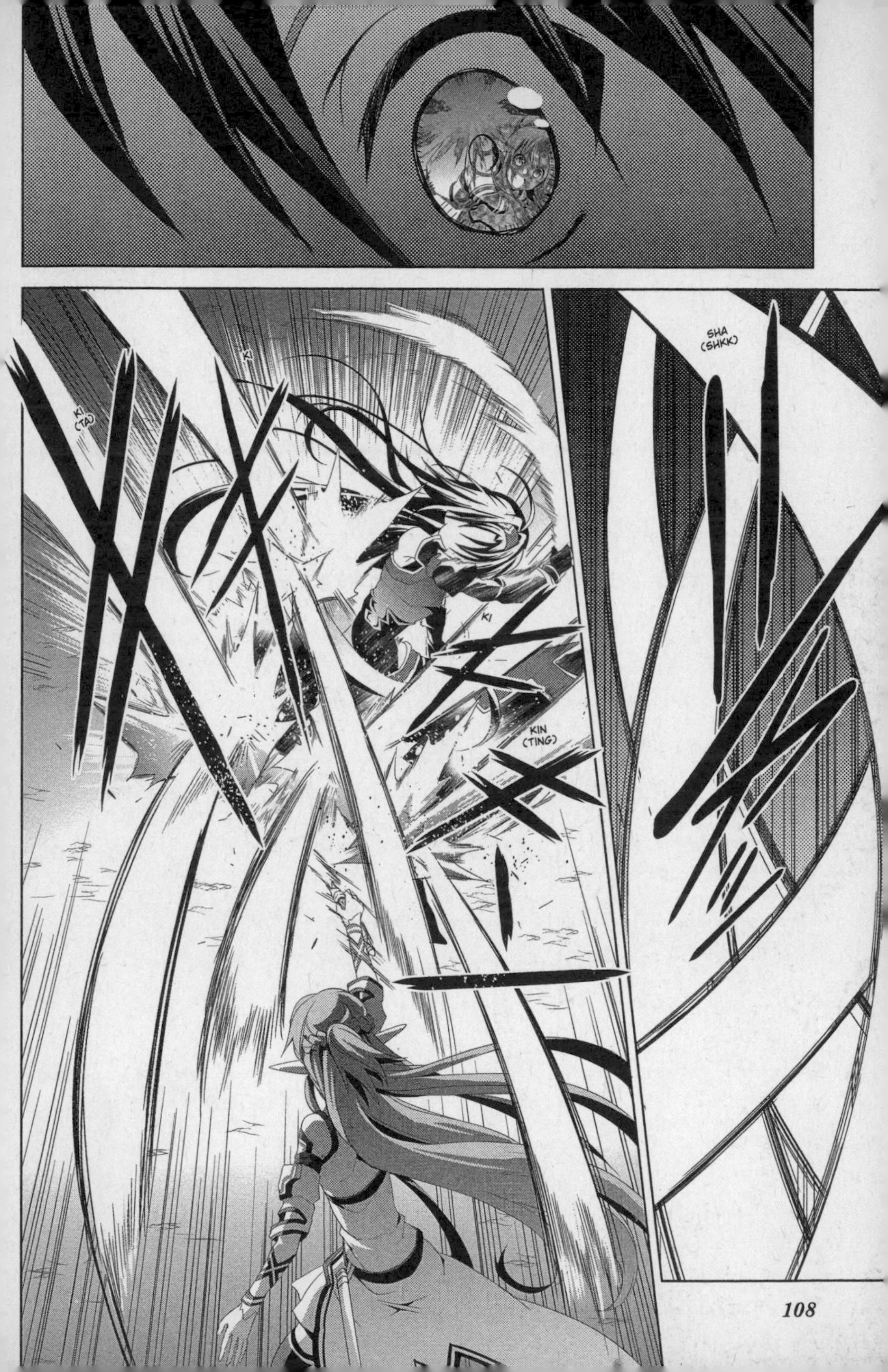
SHA (SHKK)
KI
KI (TA)
KI
KIN (TING)

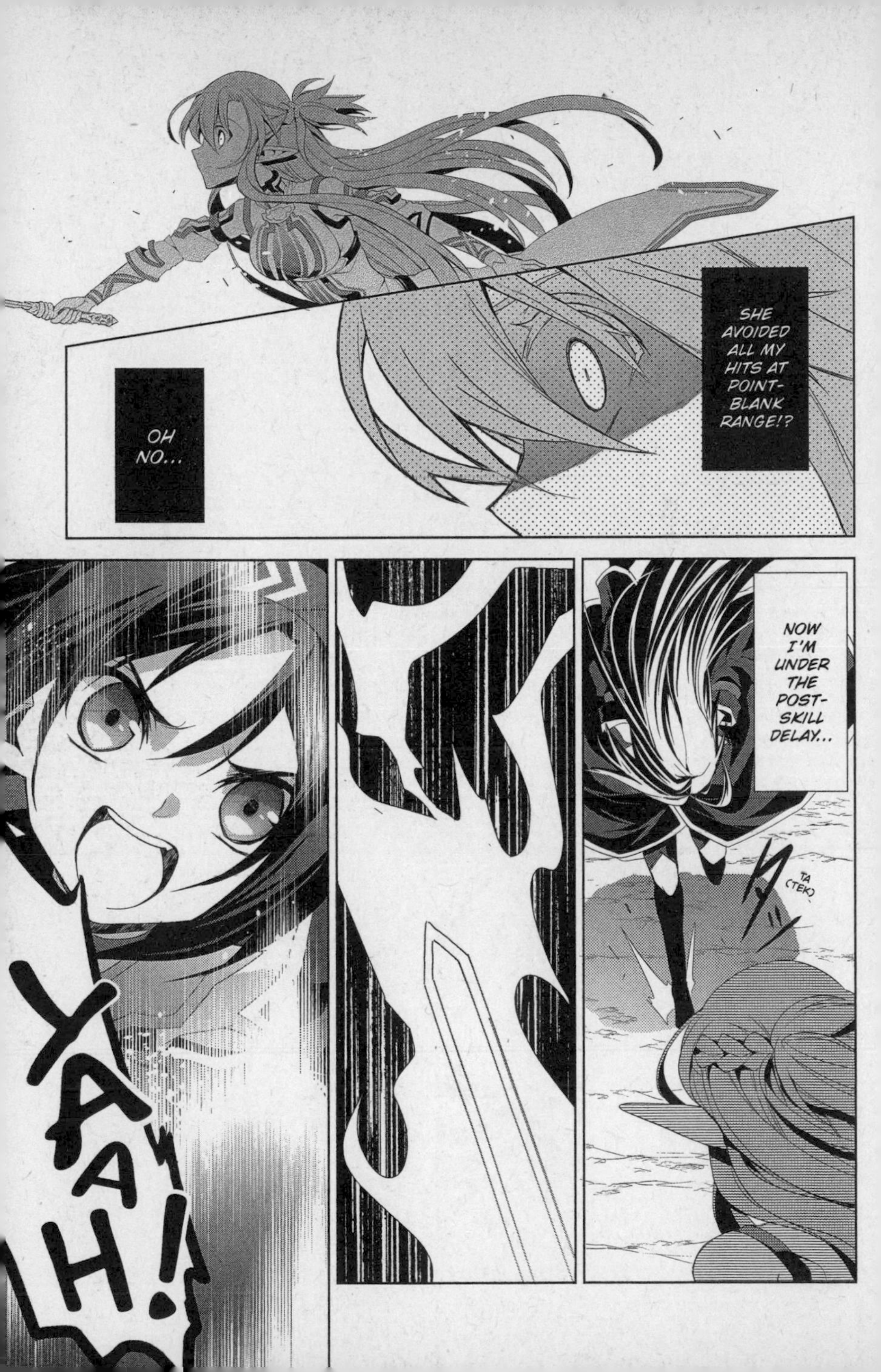
SHE AVOIDED ALL MY HITS AT POINT-BLANK RANGE!?
OH NO...
NOW I'M UNDER THE POST-SKILL DELAY...
TA (TEK)
YAAAH!

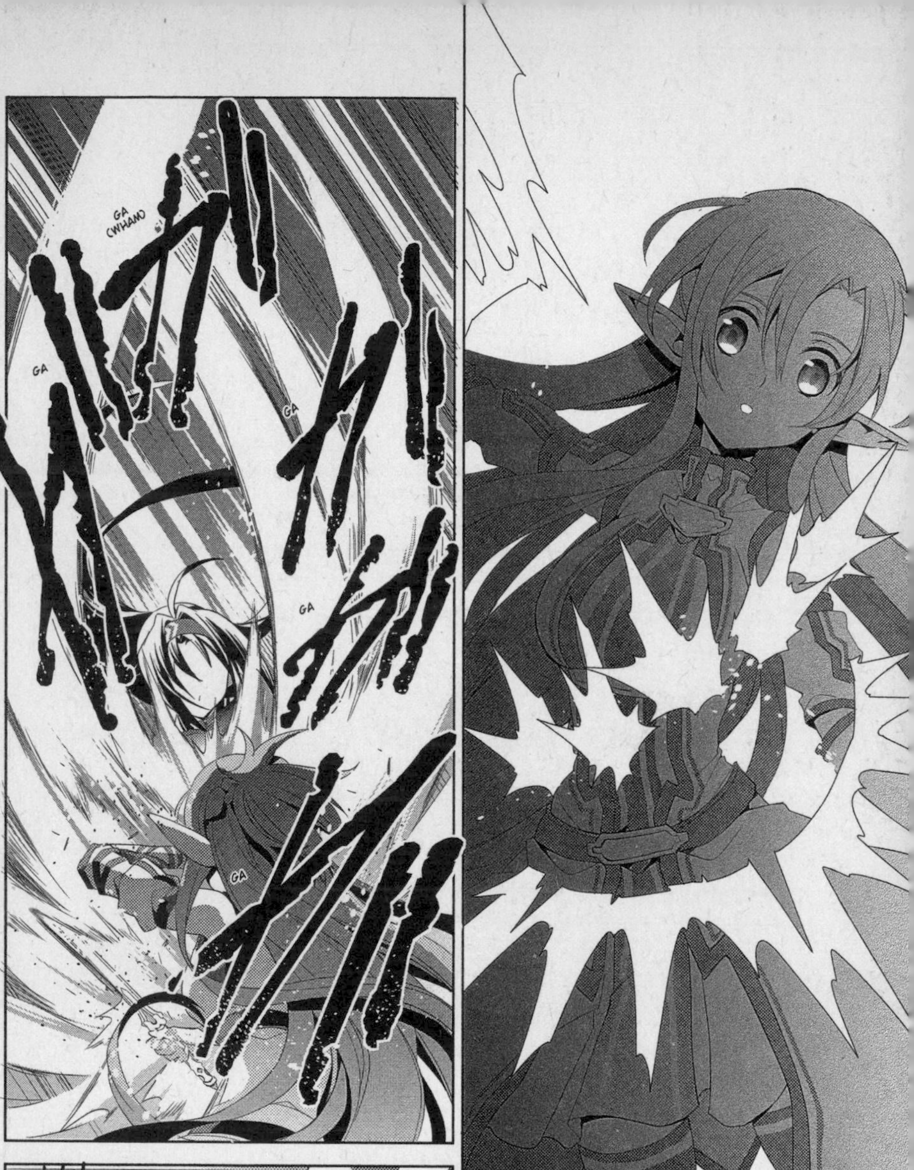
GA (WHAM)
GA
GA
GA
GA
ZA (ZZZSHH)
ZA
ZA
ZA

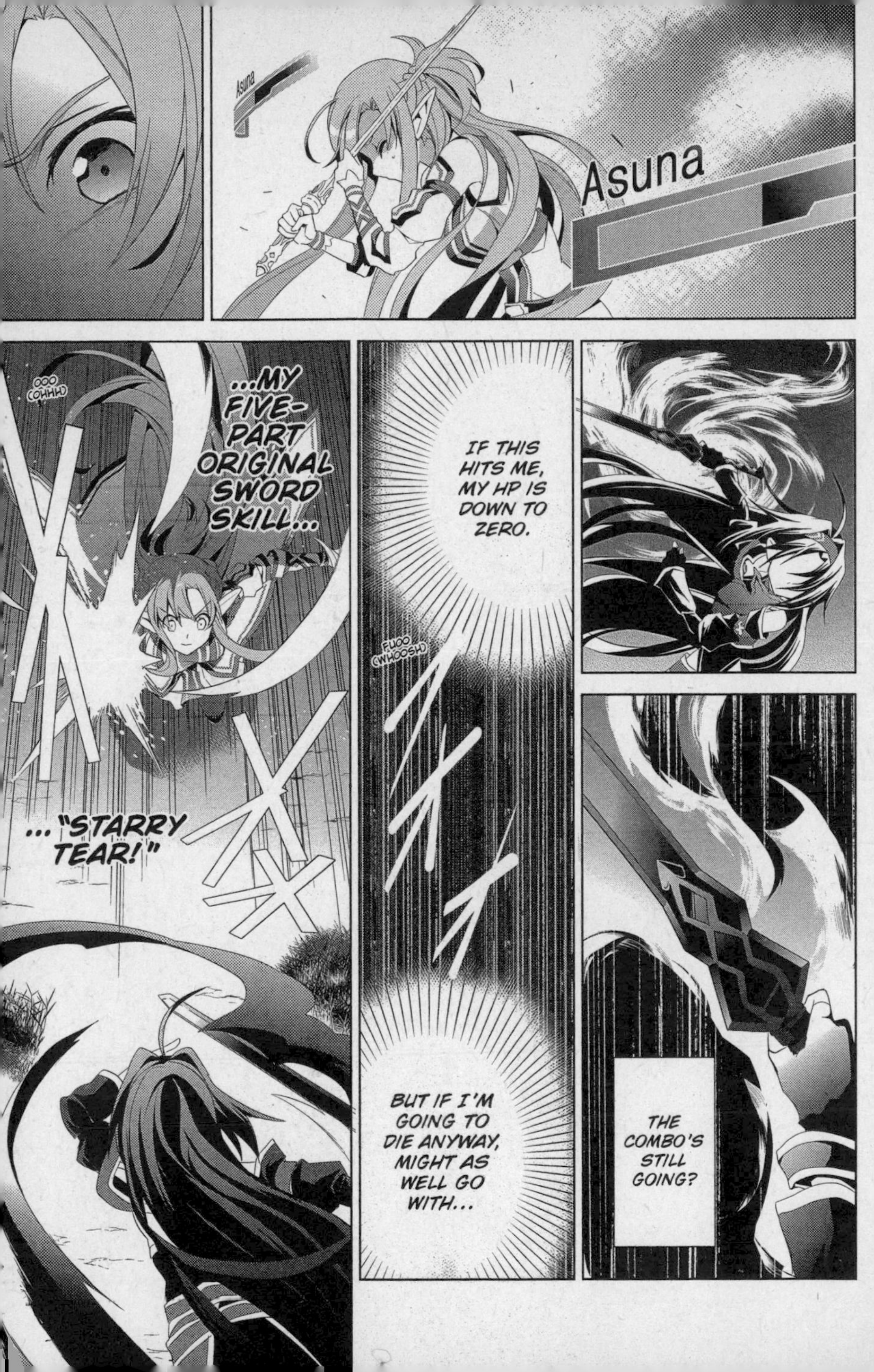
Asuna
Asuna
THE COMBO'S STILL GOING?
IF THIS HITS ME, MY HP IS DOWN TO ZERO.
FUOO (WHOOSH)
BUT IF I'M GOING TO DIE ANYWAY, MIGHT AS WELL GO WITH...
OOO (OHHH)
...MY FIVE-PART ORIGINAL SWORD SKILL...
... "STARRY TEAR!"

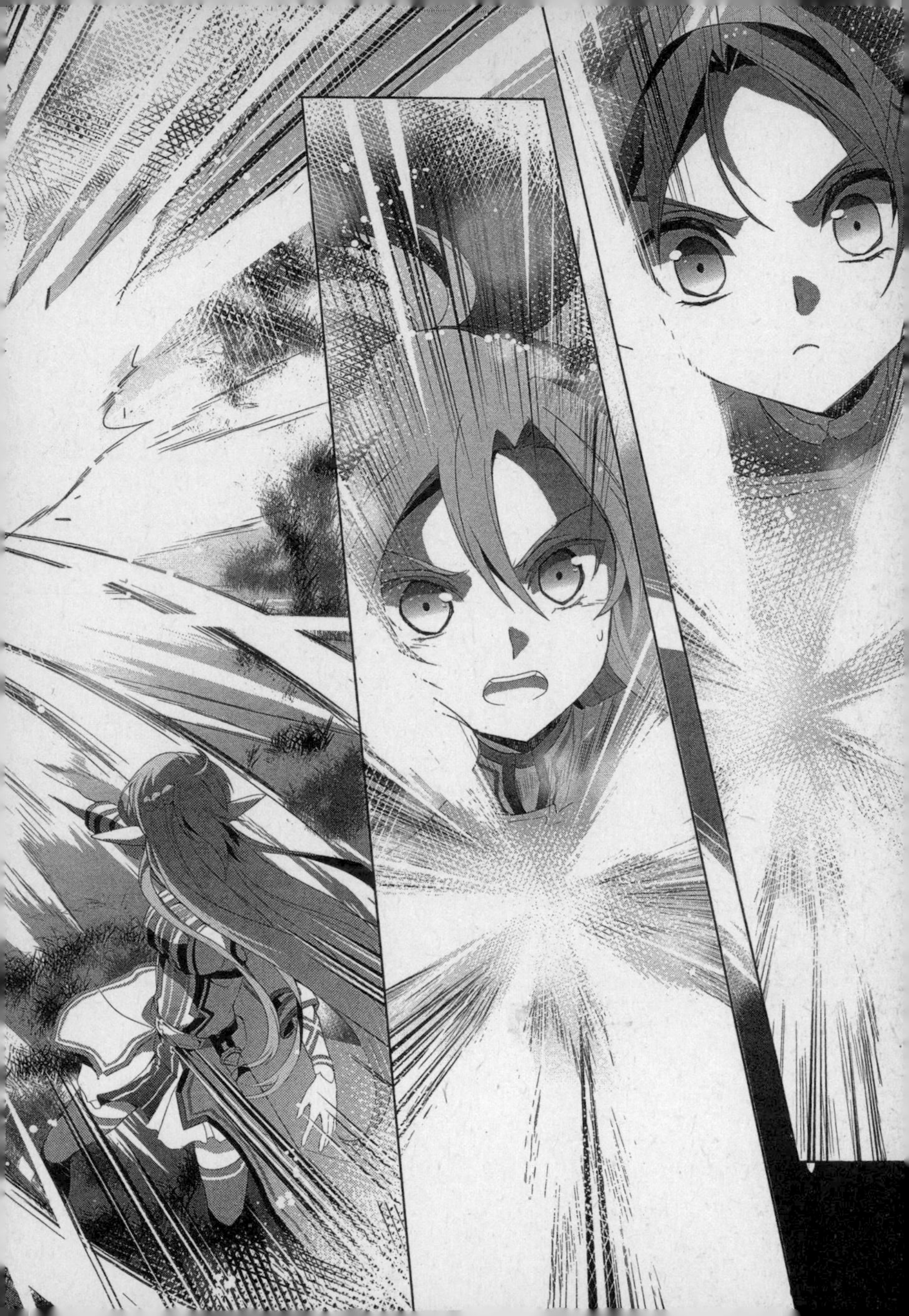

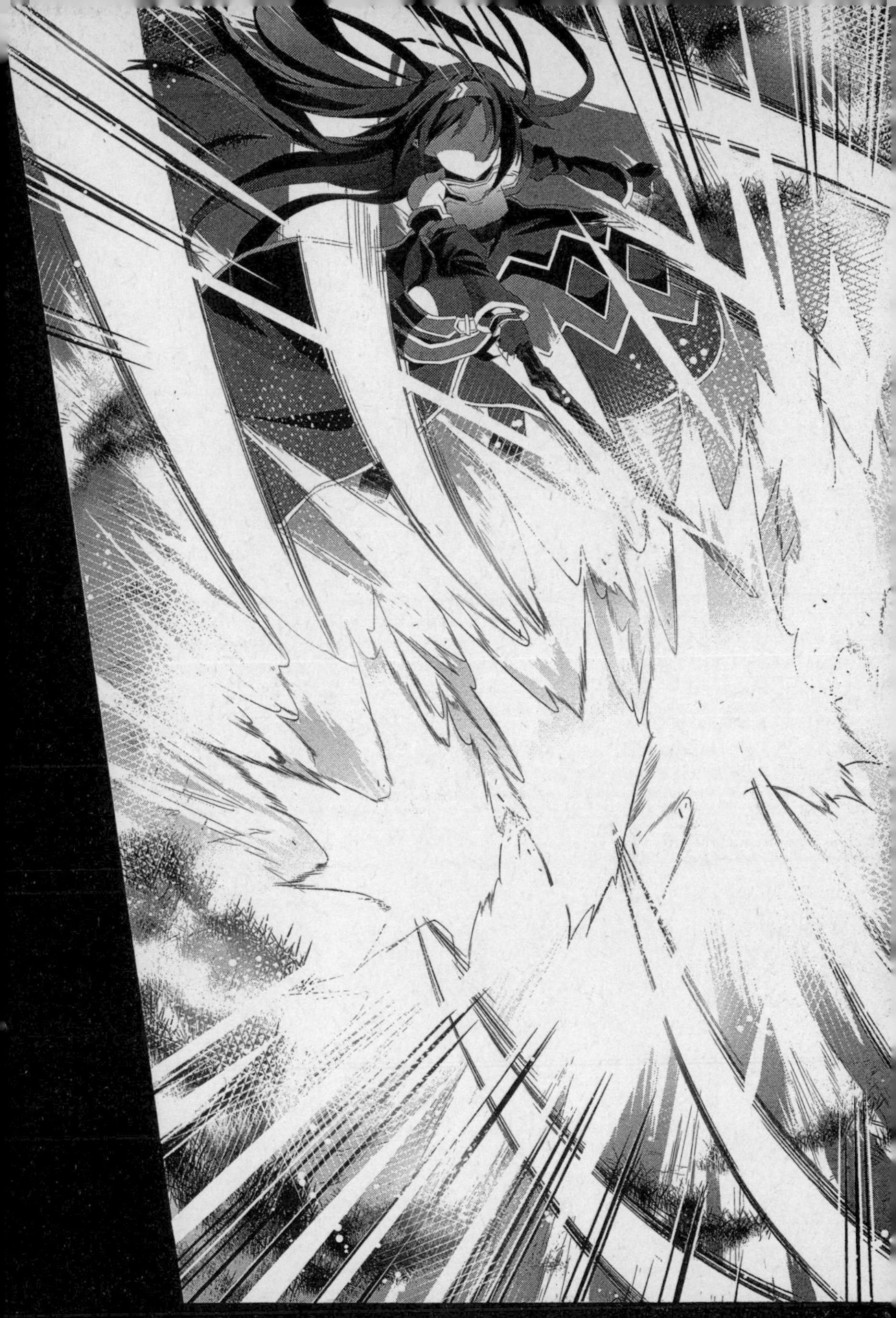

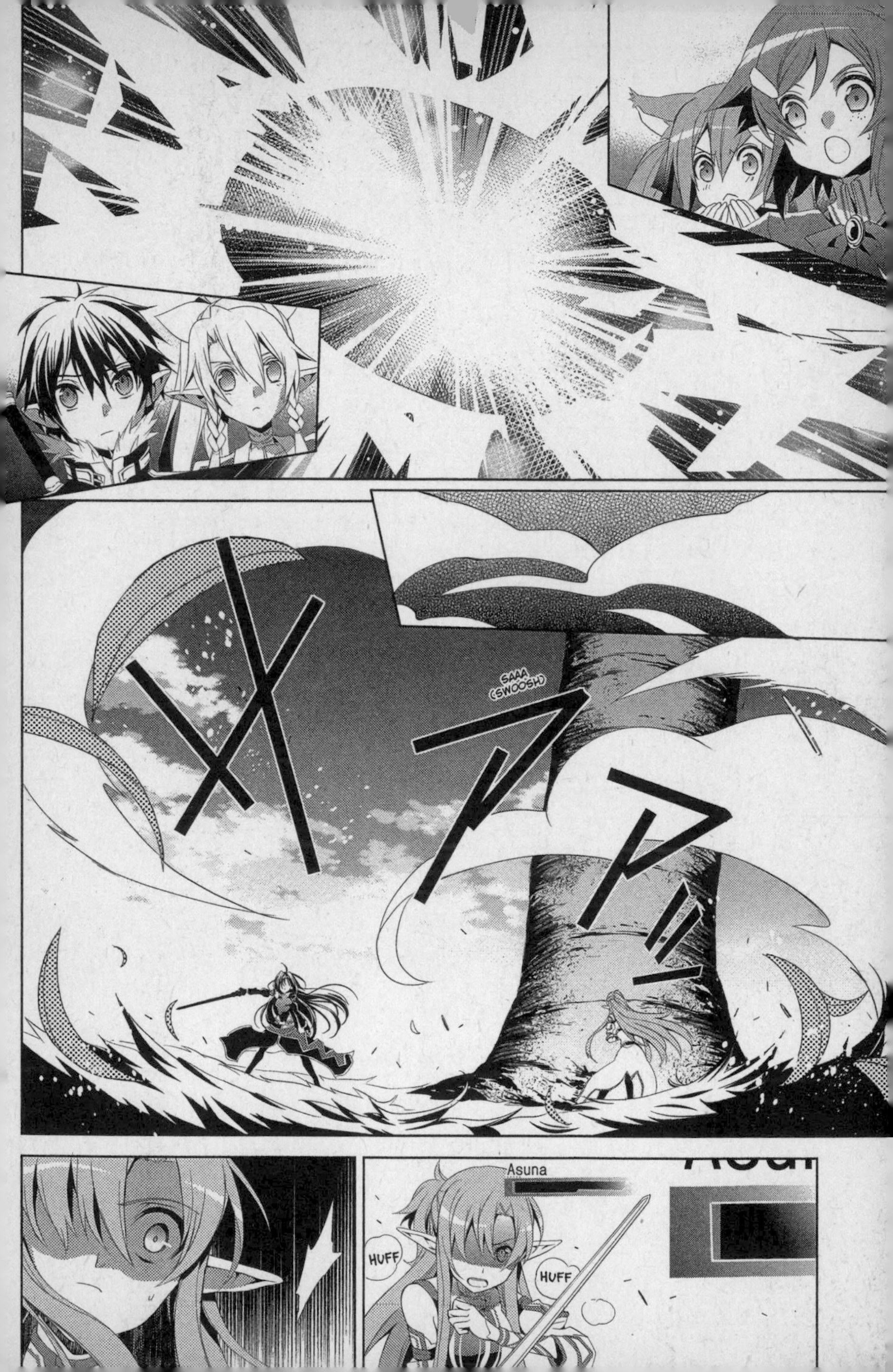
SAAA (SWOOSH)
Asuna
HUFF
HUFF

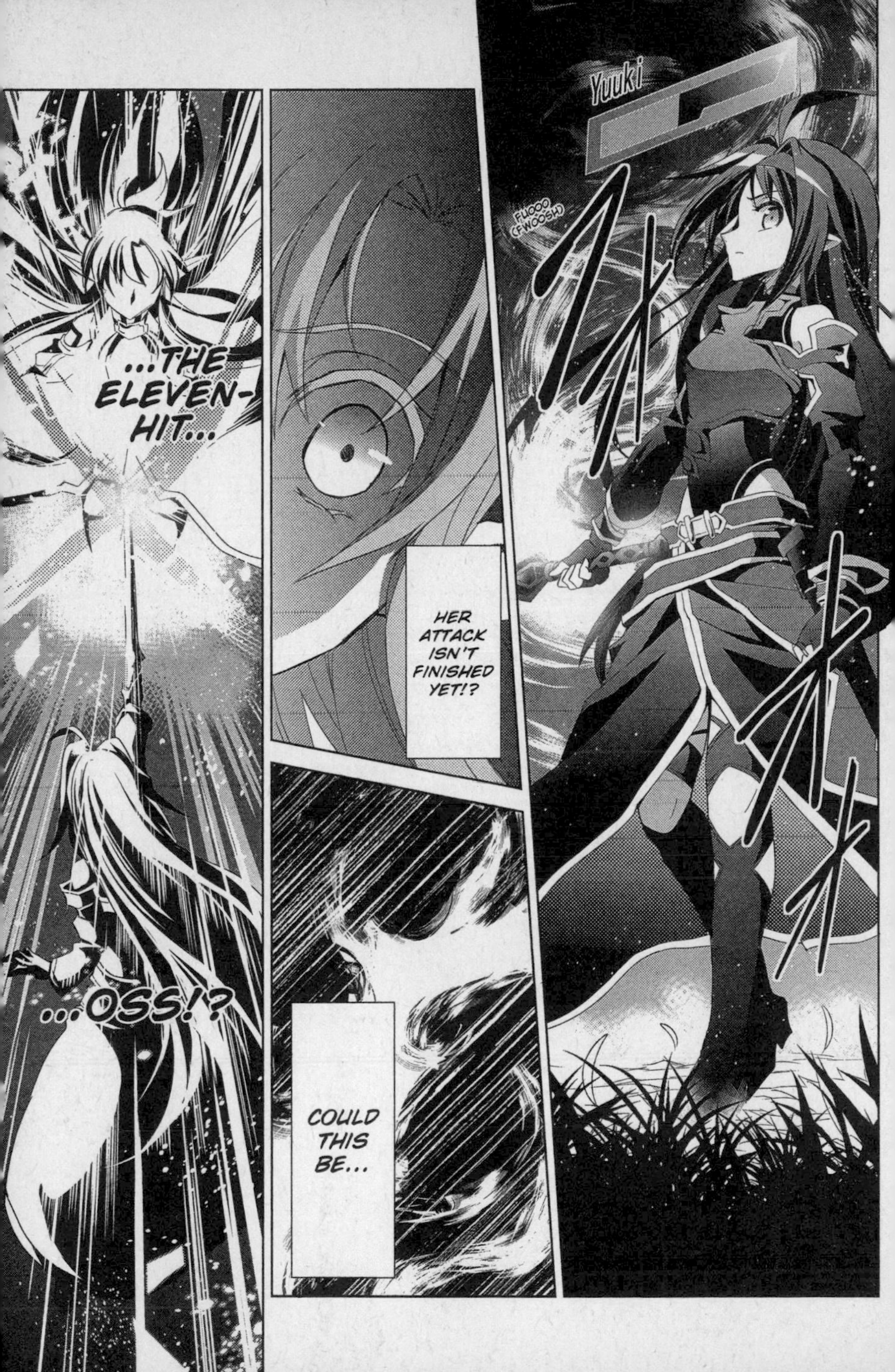
Yuuki
FUOOO
(FWOOSH)
HER ATTACK ISN'T FINISHED YET!?
COULD THIS BE...
...THE ELEVEN-HIT...
...OSS!?

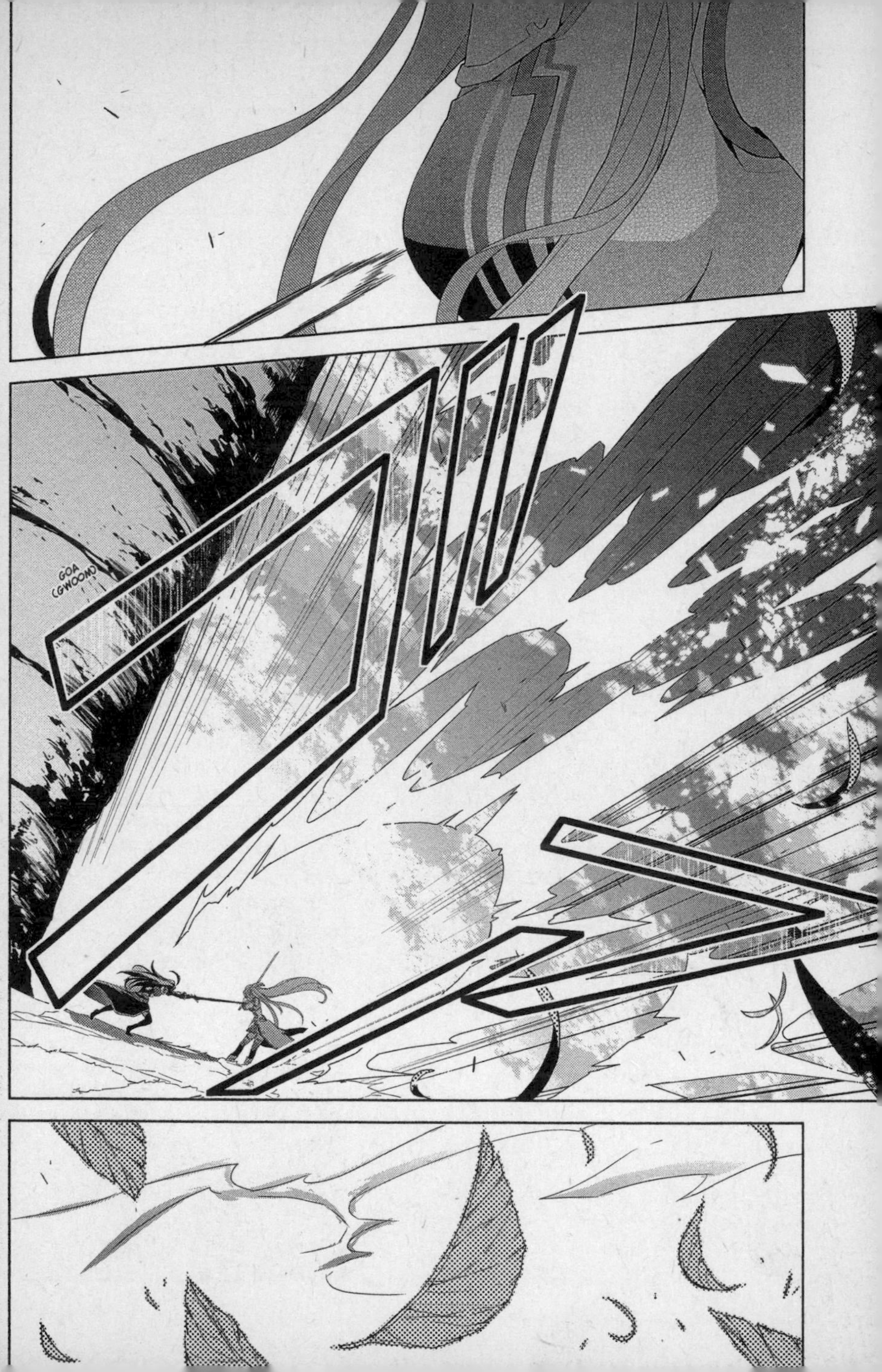
GOA
(GWOOM)

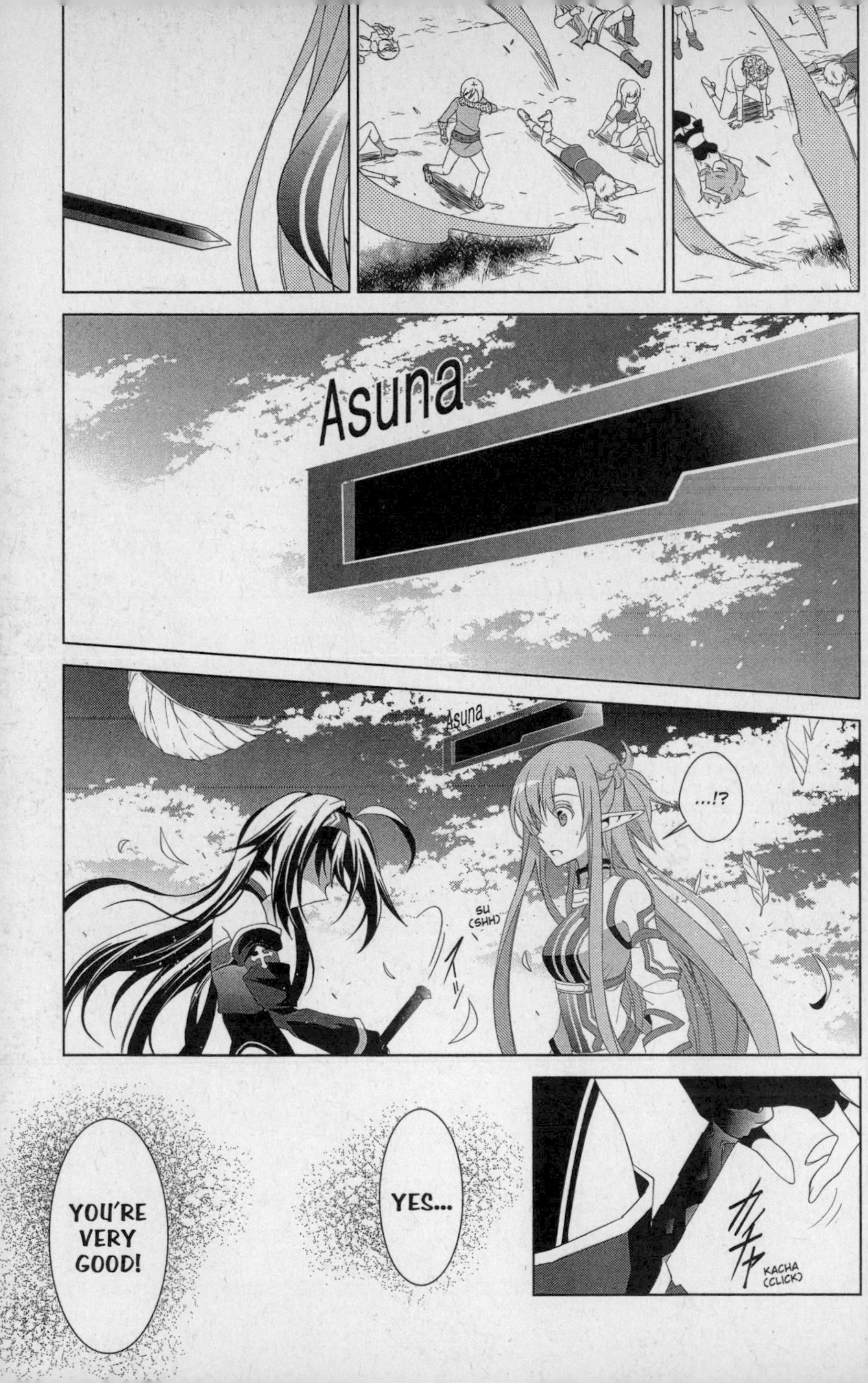
Asuna
Asuna
...!?
SU (SHH)
KACHA (CLICK)
YES...
YOU'RE VERY GOOD!

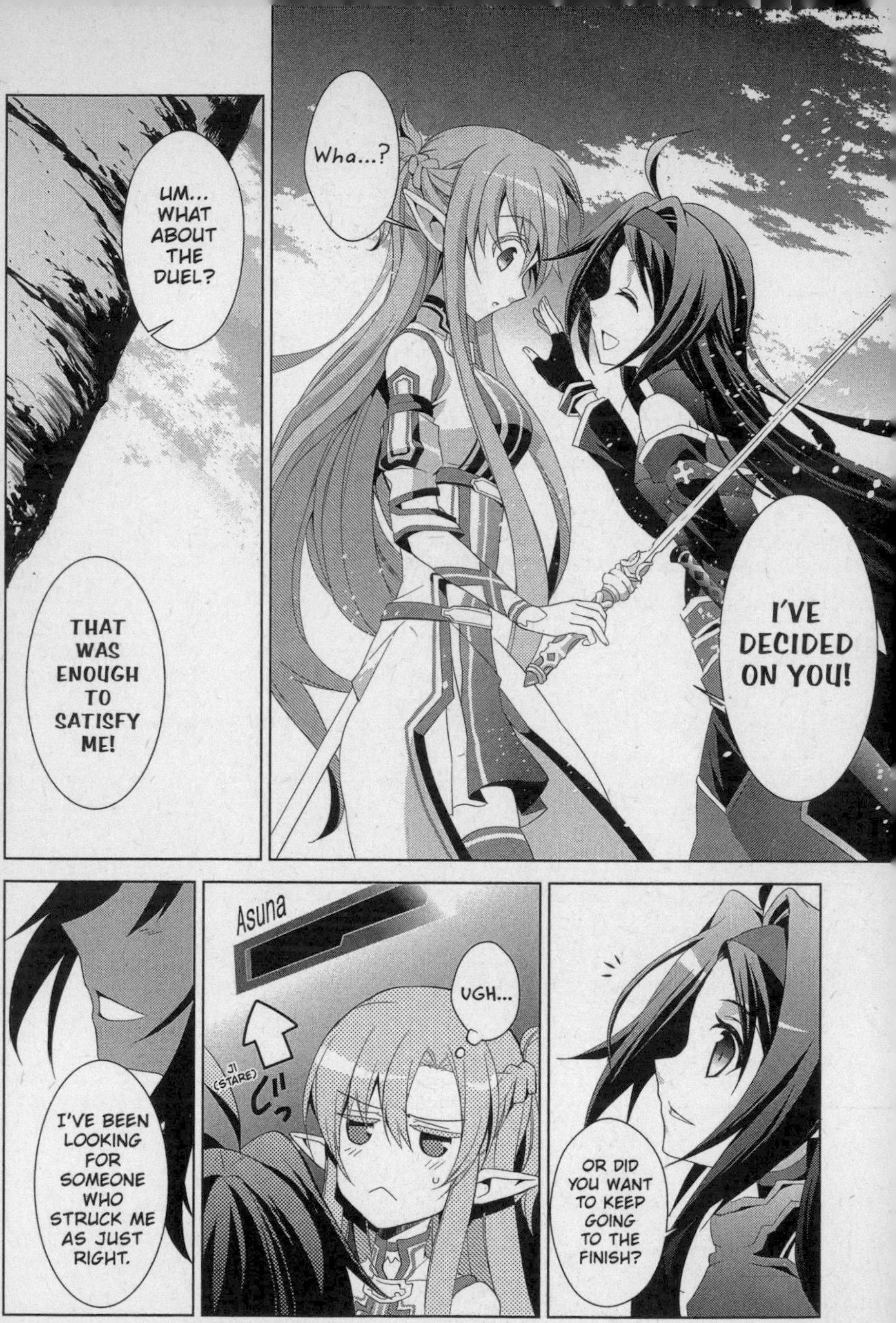
Wha...?
I'VE DECIDED ON YOU!
UM... WHAT ABOUT THE DUEL?
THAT WAS ENOUGH TO SATISFY ME!
OR DID YOU WANT TO KEEP GOING TO THE FINISH?
Asuna
UGH...
JI (STARE)
じっ
I'VE BEEN LOOKING FOR SOMEONE WHO STRUCK ME AS JUST RIGHT.

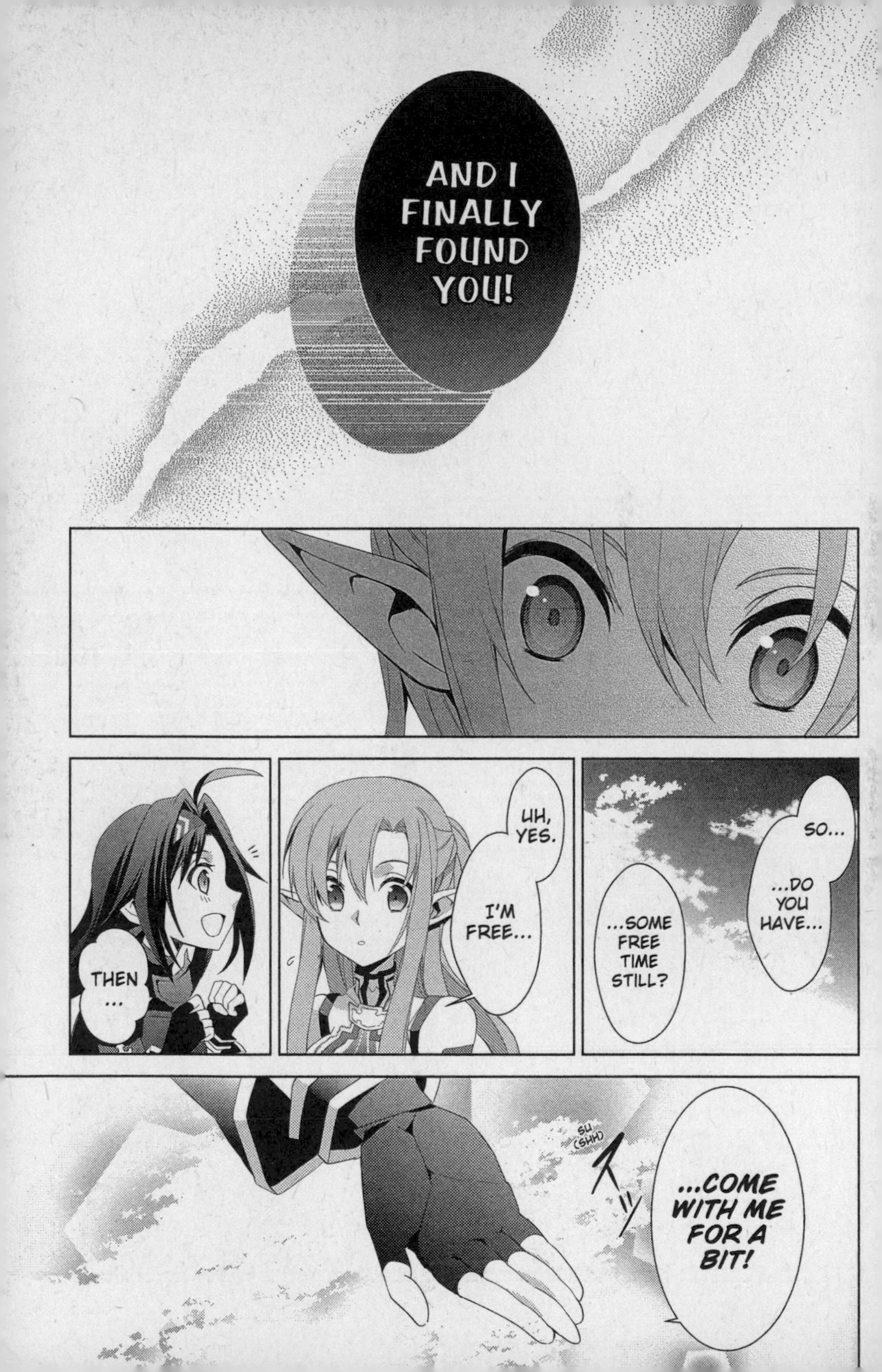
AND I FINALLY FOUND YOU!
SO...
...DO YOU HAVE...
...SOME FREE TIME STILL?
UH, YES.
I'M FREE...
THEN ...
...COME WITH ME FOR A BIT!
SU (SHH)

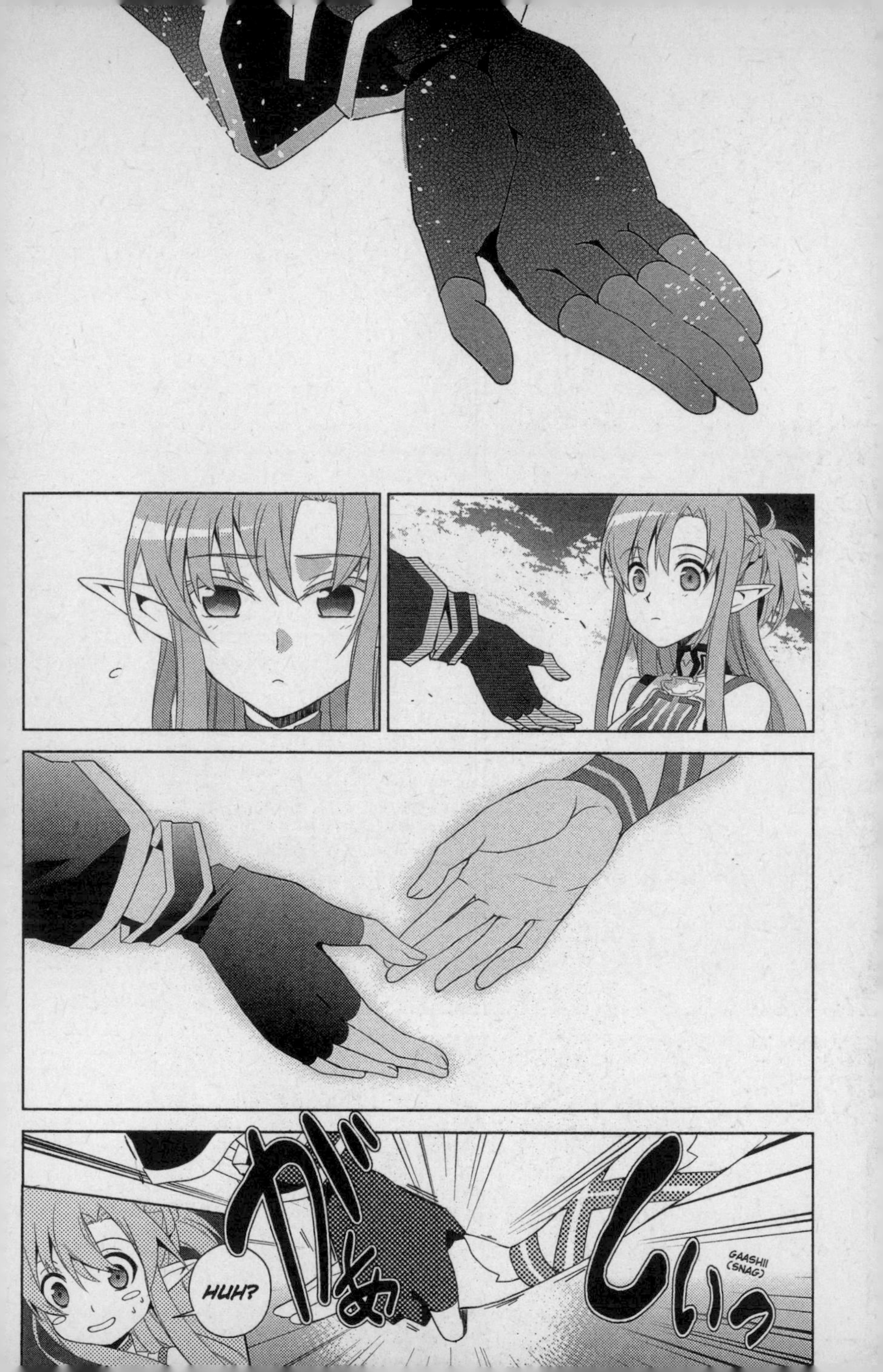
GAASHII
(SNAG)
がしぃっ
HUH?

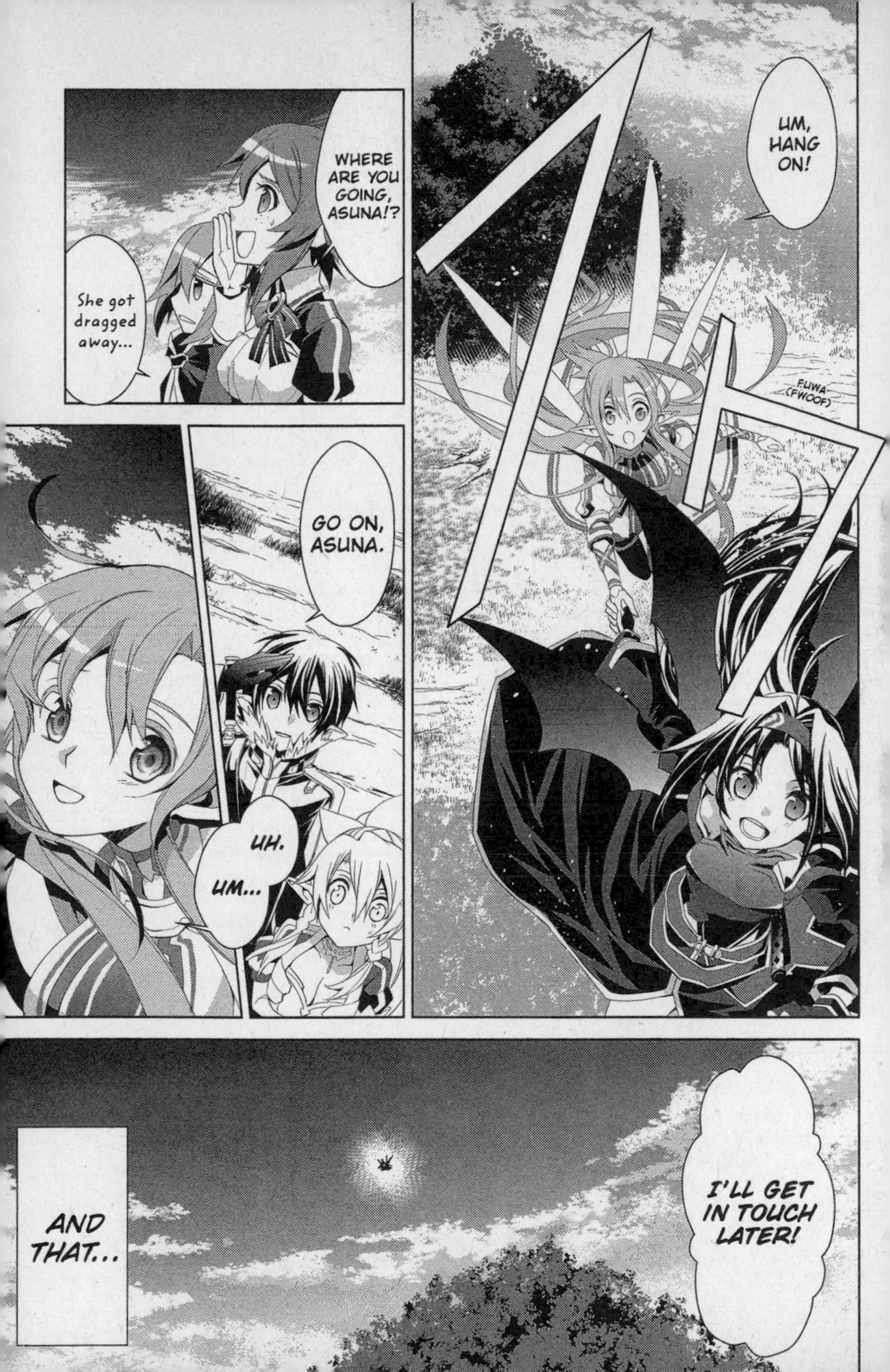
UM, HANG ON!
FUWA (FWOOF)
WHERE ARE YOU GOING, ASUNA!?
She got dragged away...
GO ON, ASUNA.
UH.
UM...
I'LL GET IN TOUCH LATER!
AND THAT...

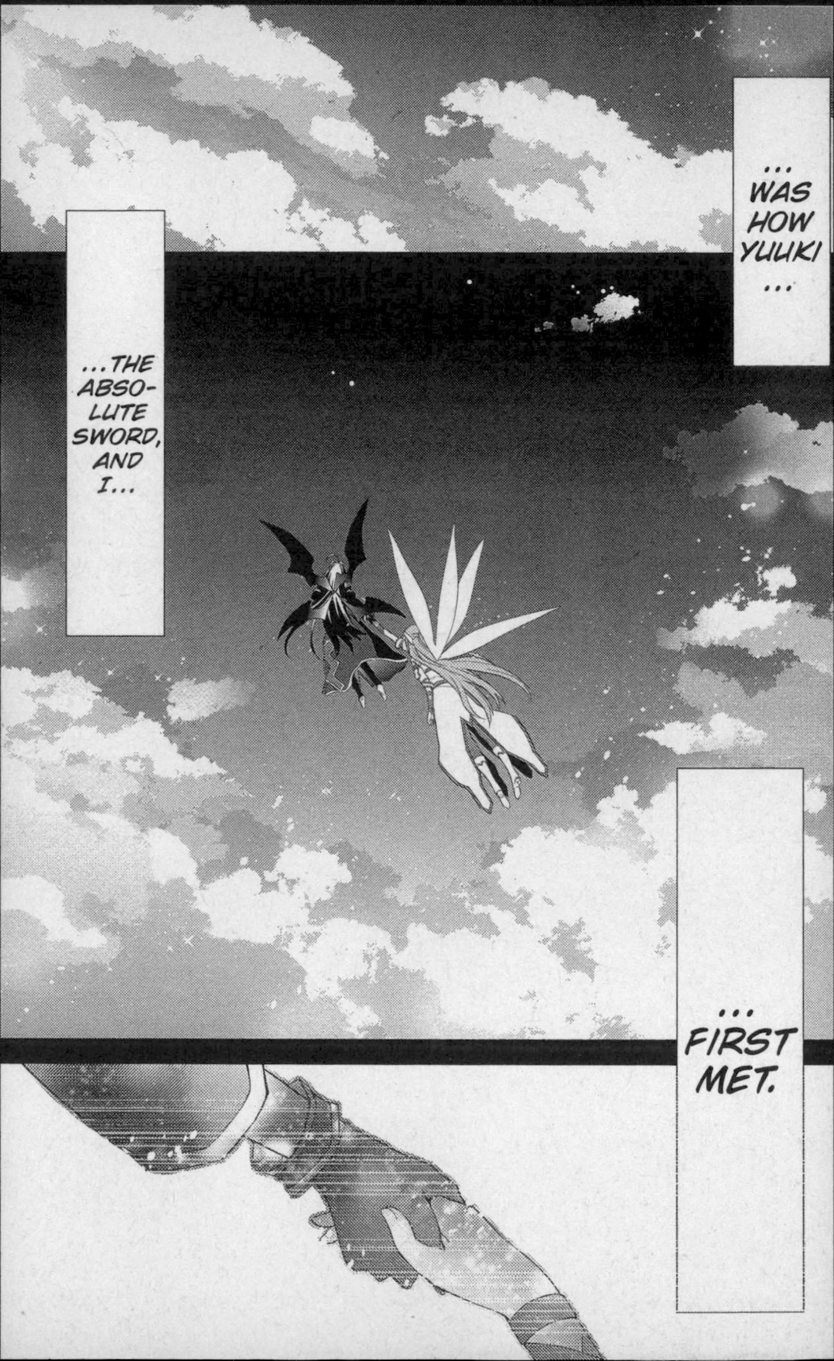
...WAS HOW YUUKI...
...THE ABSO-LUTE SWORD, AND I...
...FIRST MET.

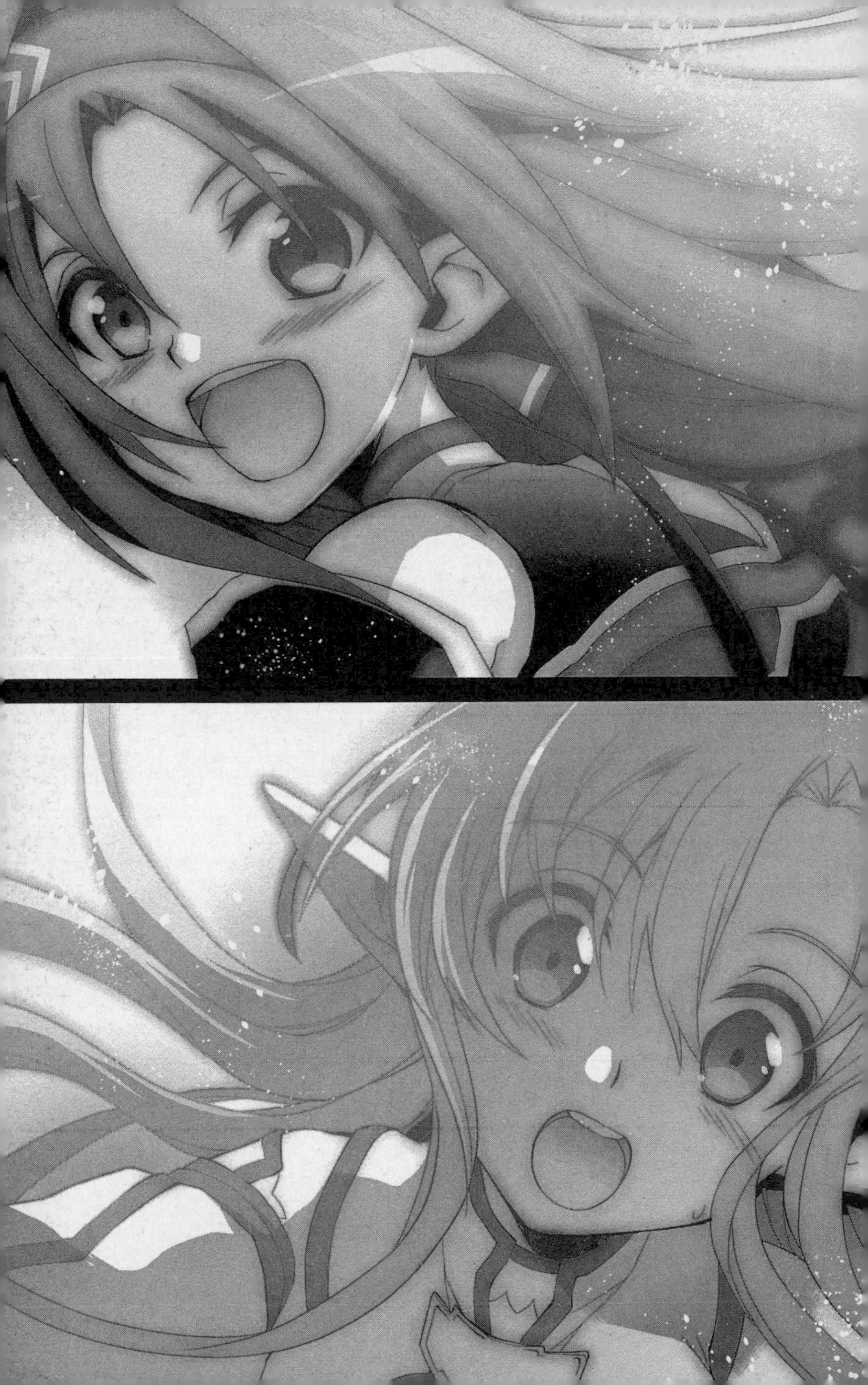

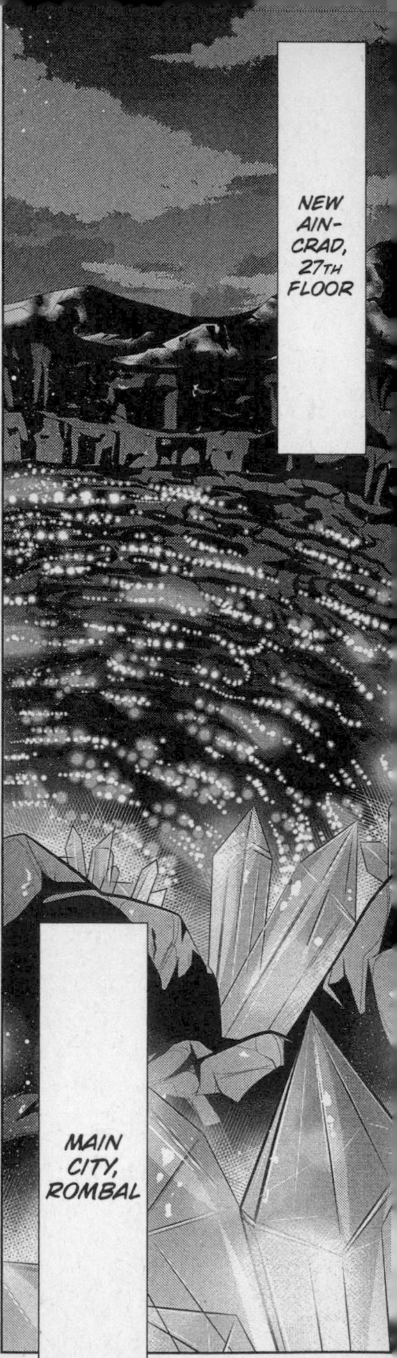
NEW AIN-CRAD, 27TH FLOOR
MAIN CITY, ROMBAL
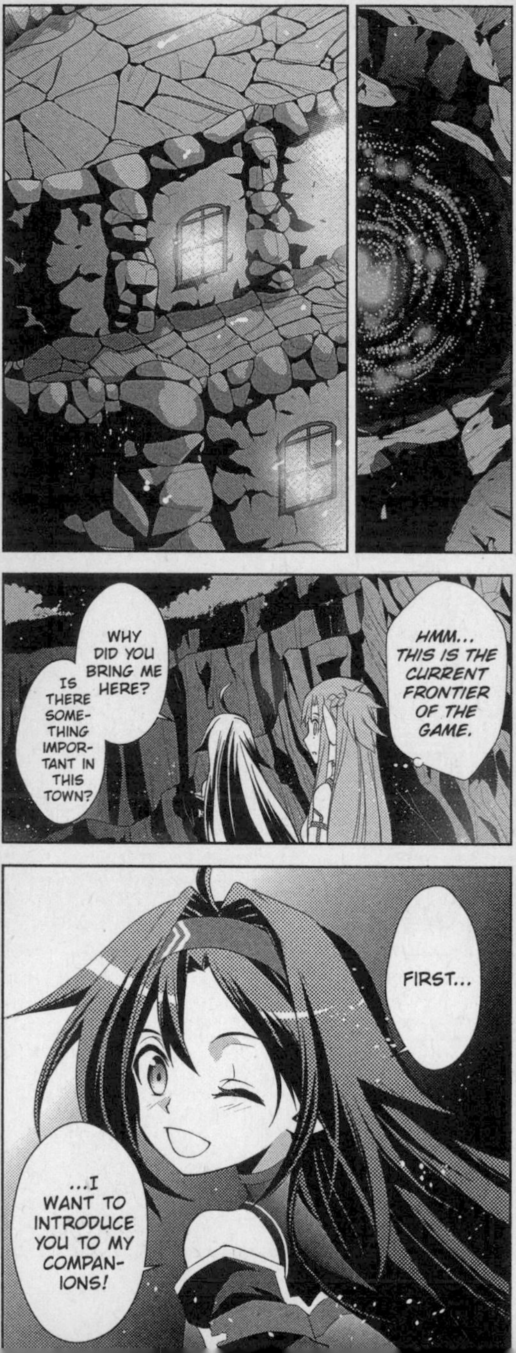
HMM... THIS IS THE CURRENT FRONTIER OF THE GAME.
WHY DID YOU BRING ME HERE?
IS THERE SOME-THING IMPOR-TANT IN THIS TOWN?
FIRST...
...I WANT TO INTRODUCE YOU TO MY COMPAN-IONS!

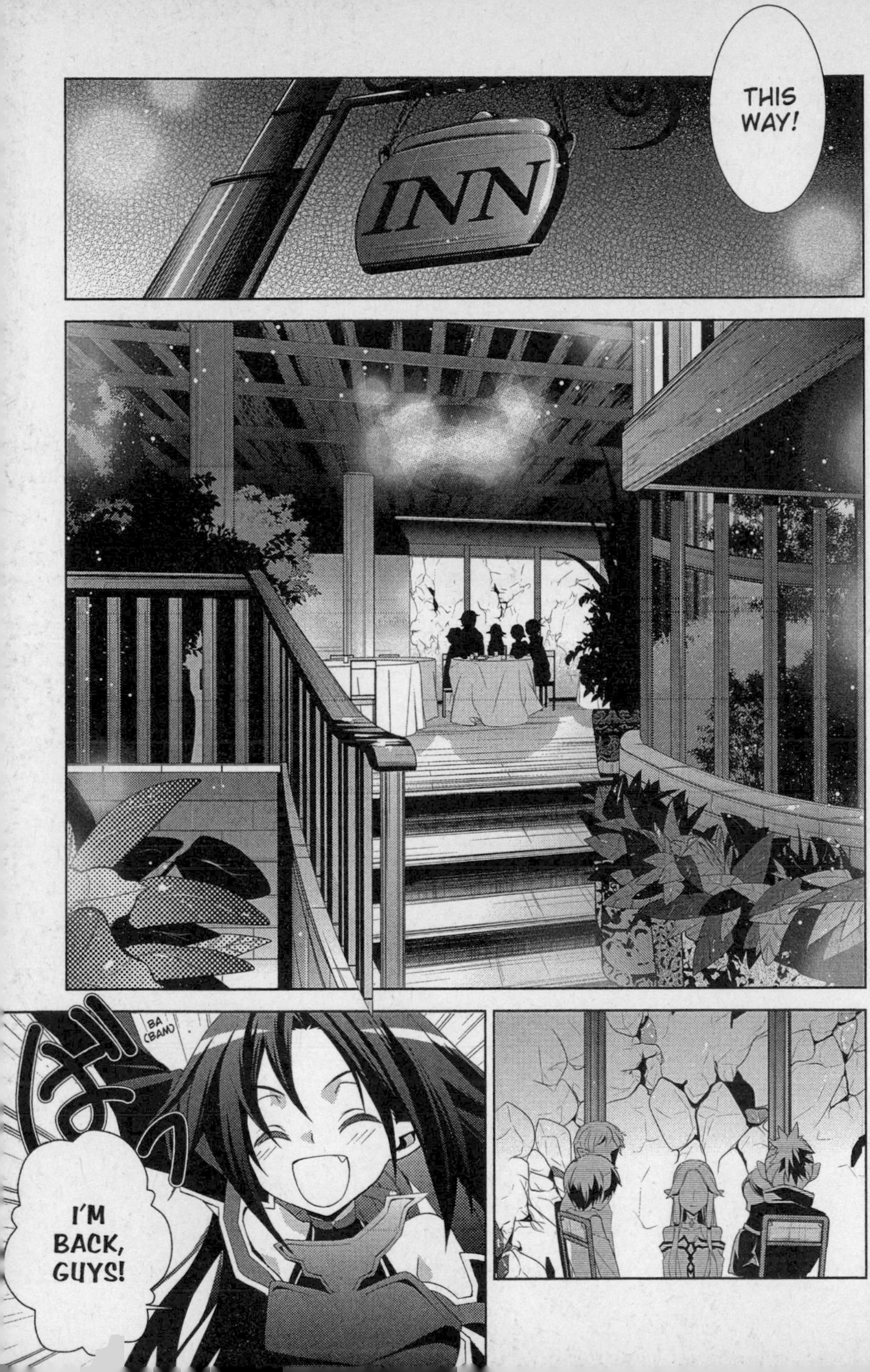
THIS WAY!
INN
BA (BAM)
I'M BACK, GUYS!

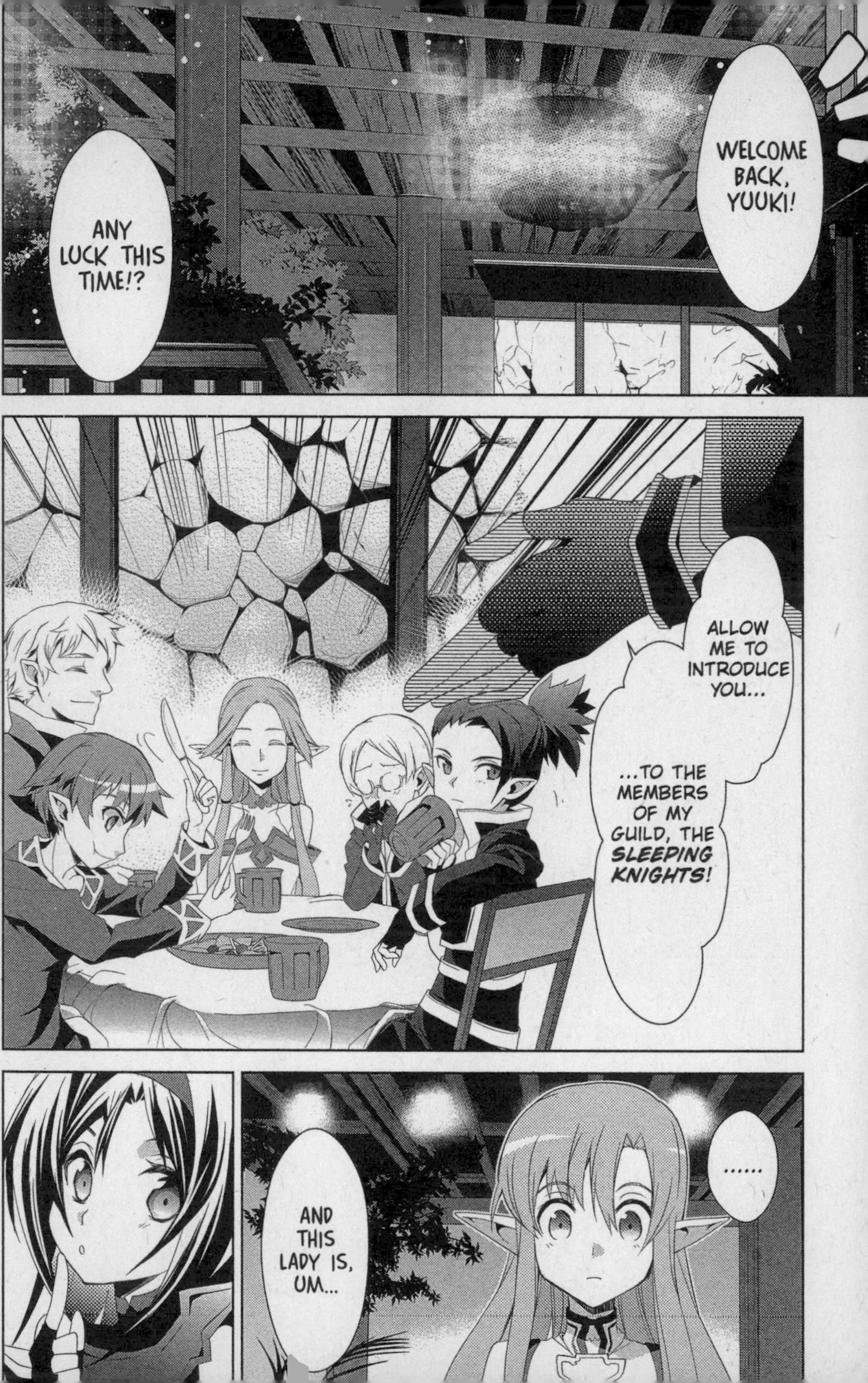
WELCOME BACK, YUUKI!
ANY LUCK THIS TIME!?
ALLOW ME TO INTRODUCE YOU...
...TO THE MEMBERS OF MY GUILD, THE *SLEEPING KNIGHTS*!
......
AND THIS LADY IS, UM...

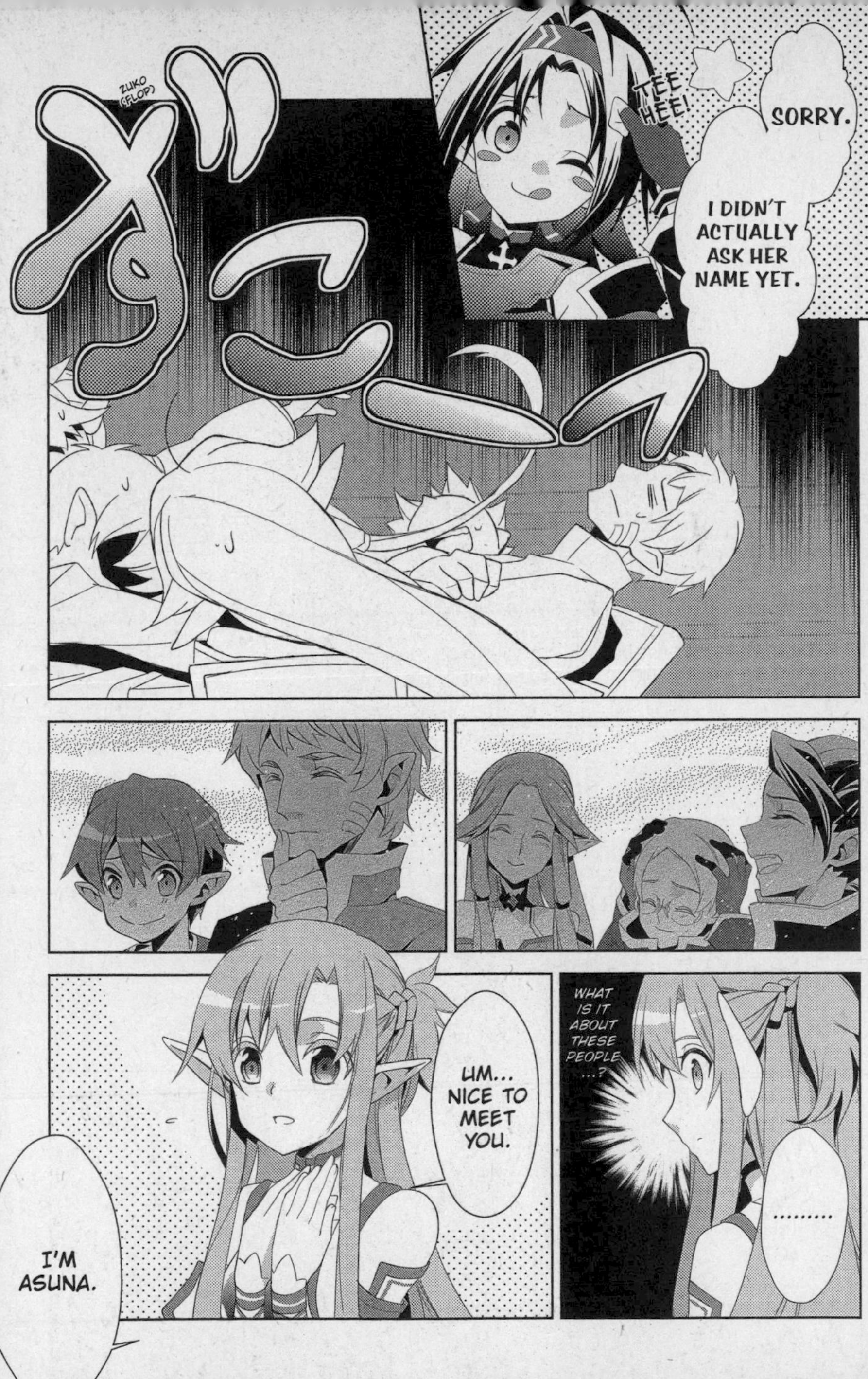
TEE HEE!
SORRY.
I DIDN'T ACTUALLY ASK HER NAME YET.
ZUKO (FLOP)
WHAT IS IT ABOUT THESE PEOPLE ...?
....
UM... NICE TO MEET YOU.
I'M ASUNA.

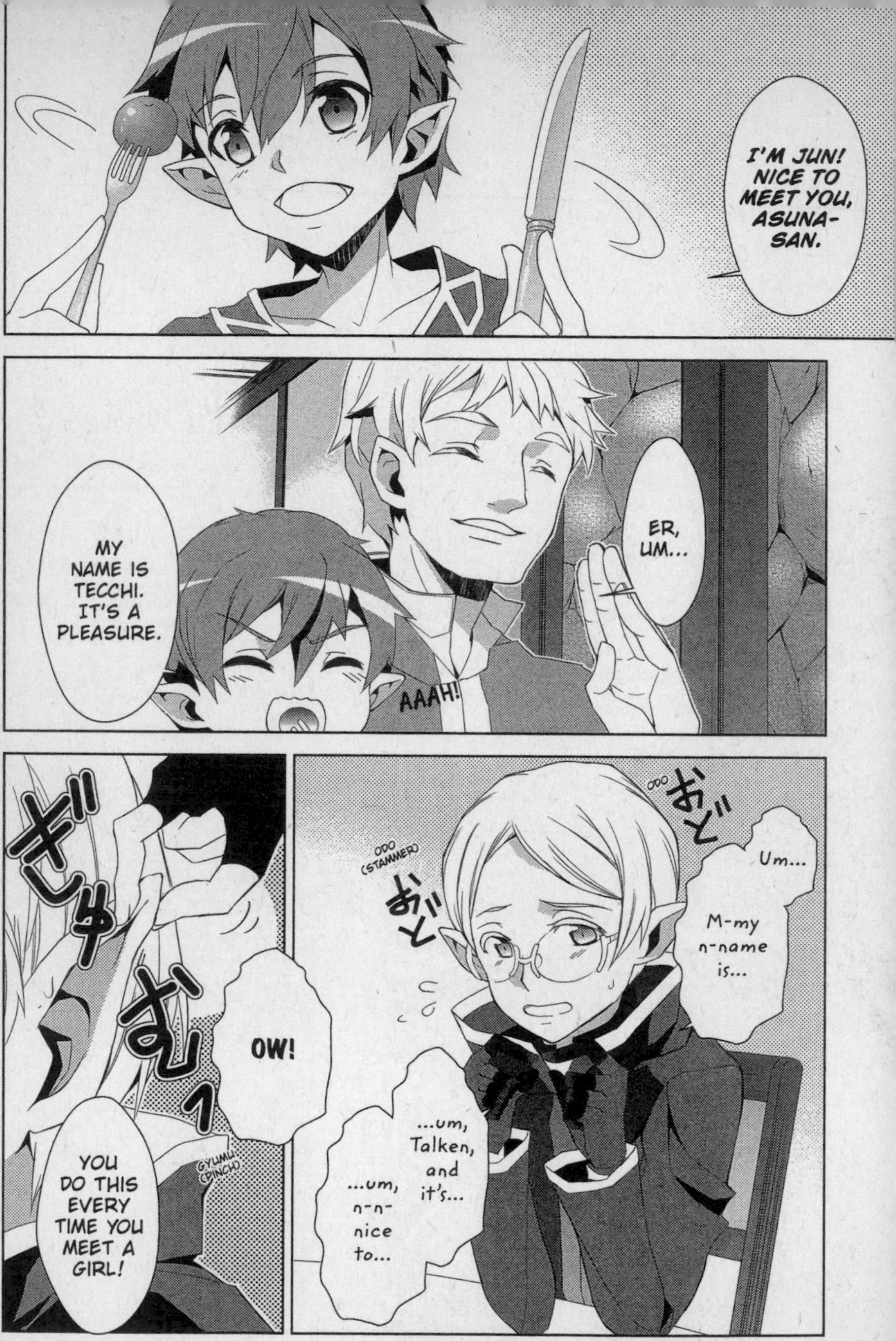
I'M JUN! NICE TO MEET YOU, ASUNA-SAN.
ER, UM...
AAAH!
MY NAME IS TECCHI. IT'S A PLEASURE.
ODO おど
Um...
M-my n-name is...
ODO (STAMMER) おど
...um, Talken, and it's...
...um, n-n- nice to...
ぎゅむっ
OW!
GYUMU (PINCH)
YOU DO THIS EVERY TIME YOU MEET A GIRL!

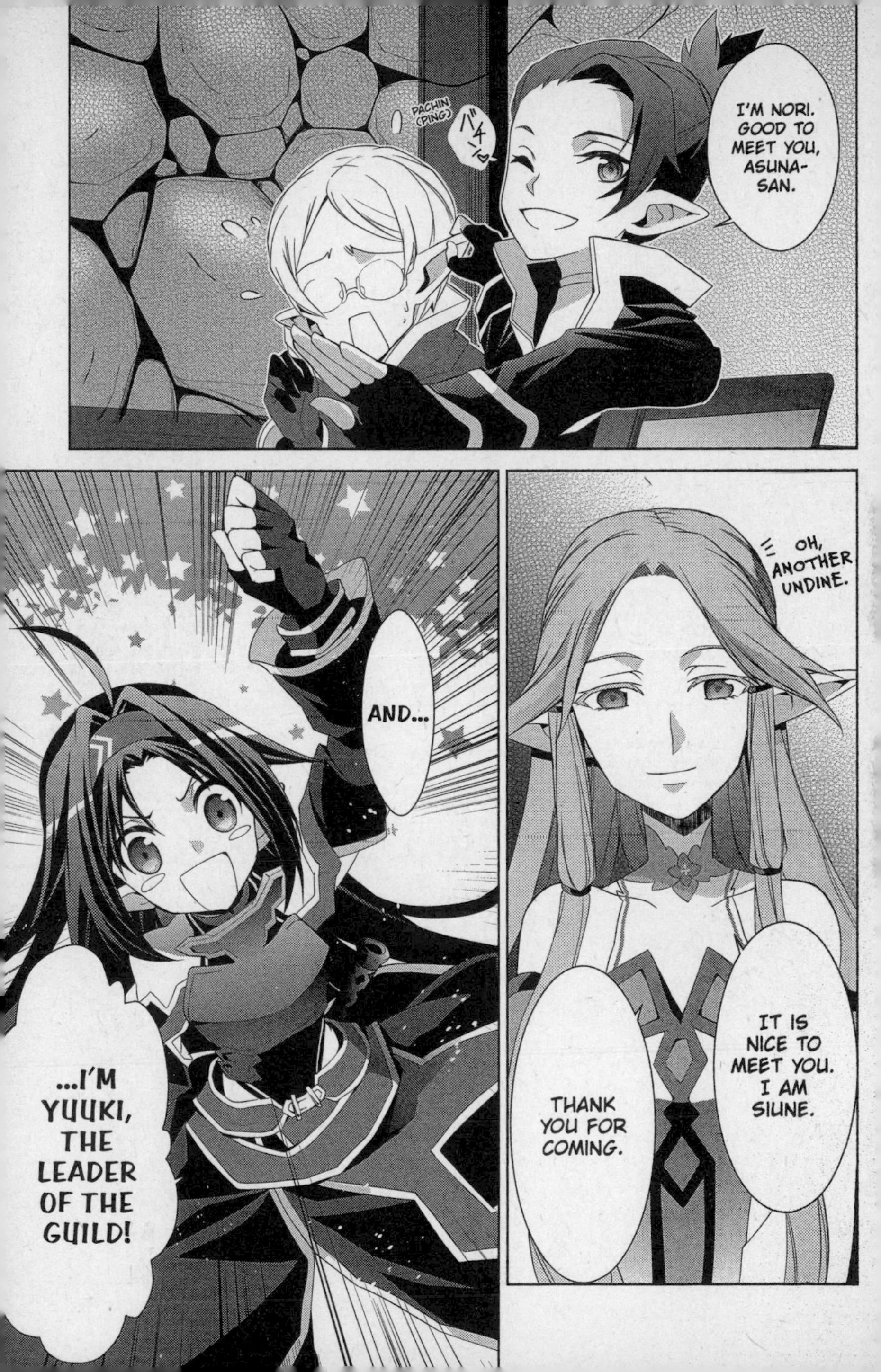
I'M NORI. GOOD TO MEET YOU, ASUNA-SAN.
PACHIN (PING)
OH, ANOTHER UNDINE.
IT IS NICE TO MEET YOU. I AM SIUNE.
THANK YOU FOR COMING.
AND...
...I'M YUUKI, THE LEADER OF THE GUILD!

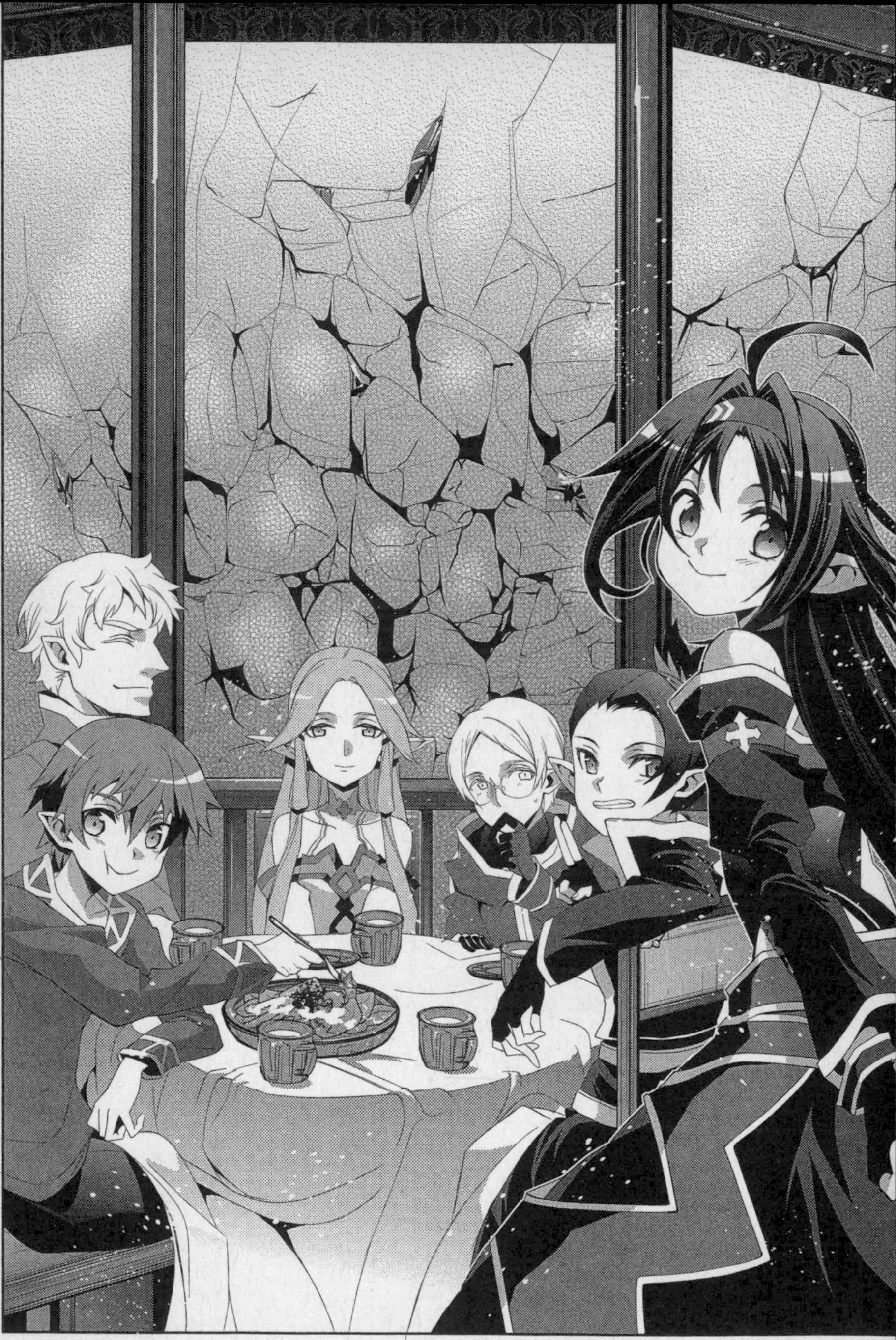

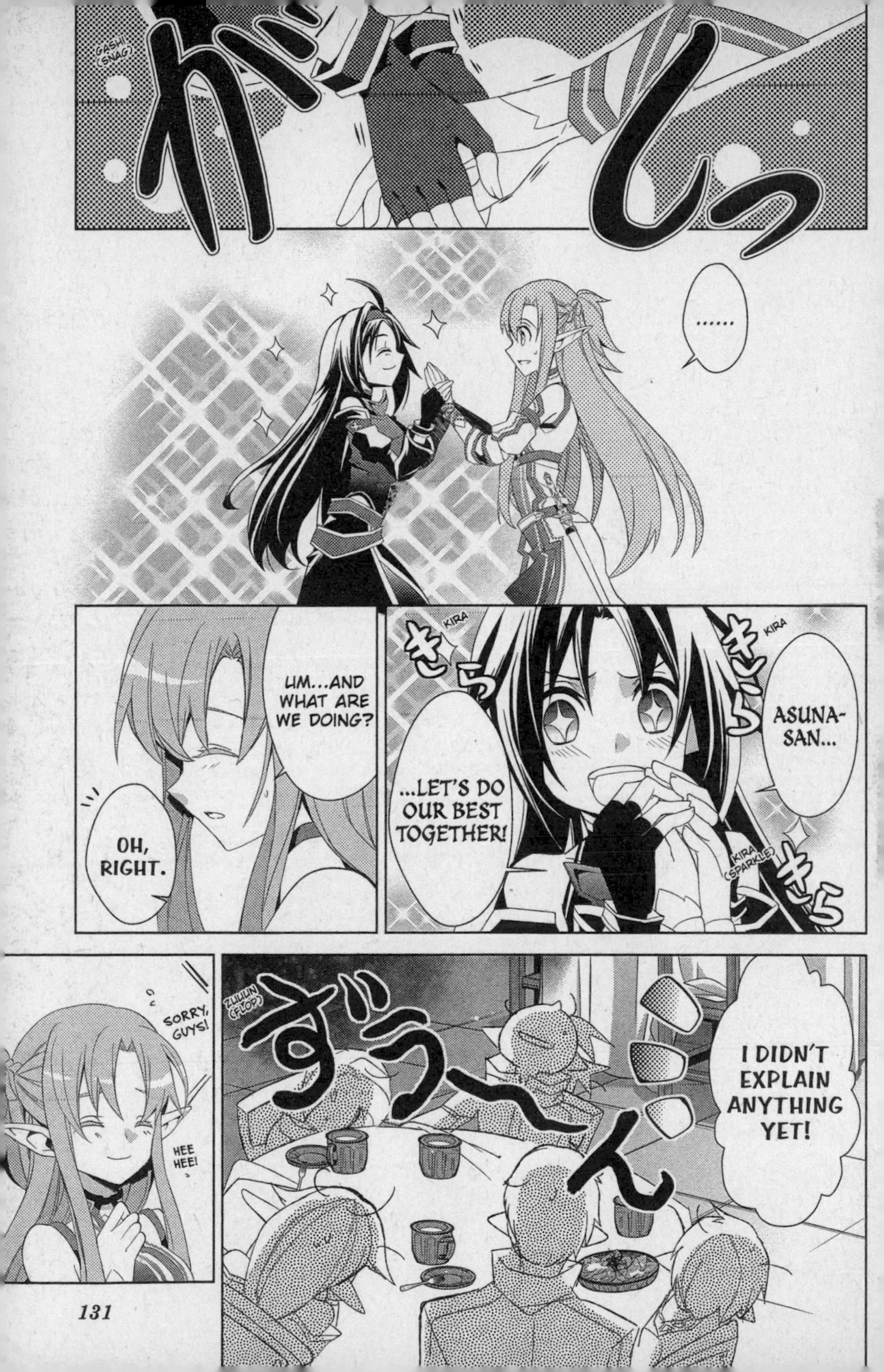
GASHI (SNAG)
......
KIRA
KIRA
ASUNA-SAN...
...LET'S DO OUR BEST TOGETHER!
KIRA (SPARKLE)
UM...AND WHAT ARE WE DOING?
OH, RIGHT.
I DIDN'T EXPLAIN ANYTHING YET!
ZUUUN (FLOP)
SORRY, GUYS!
HEE HEE!

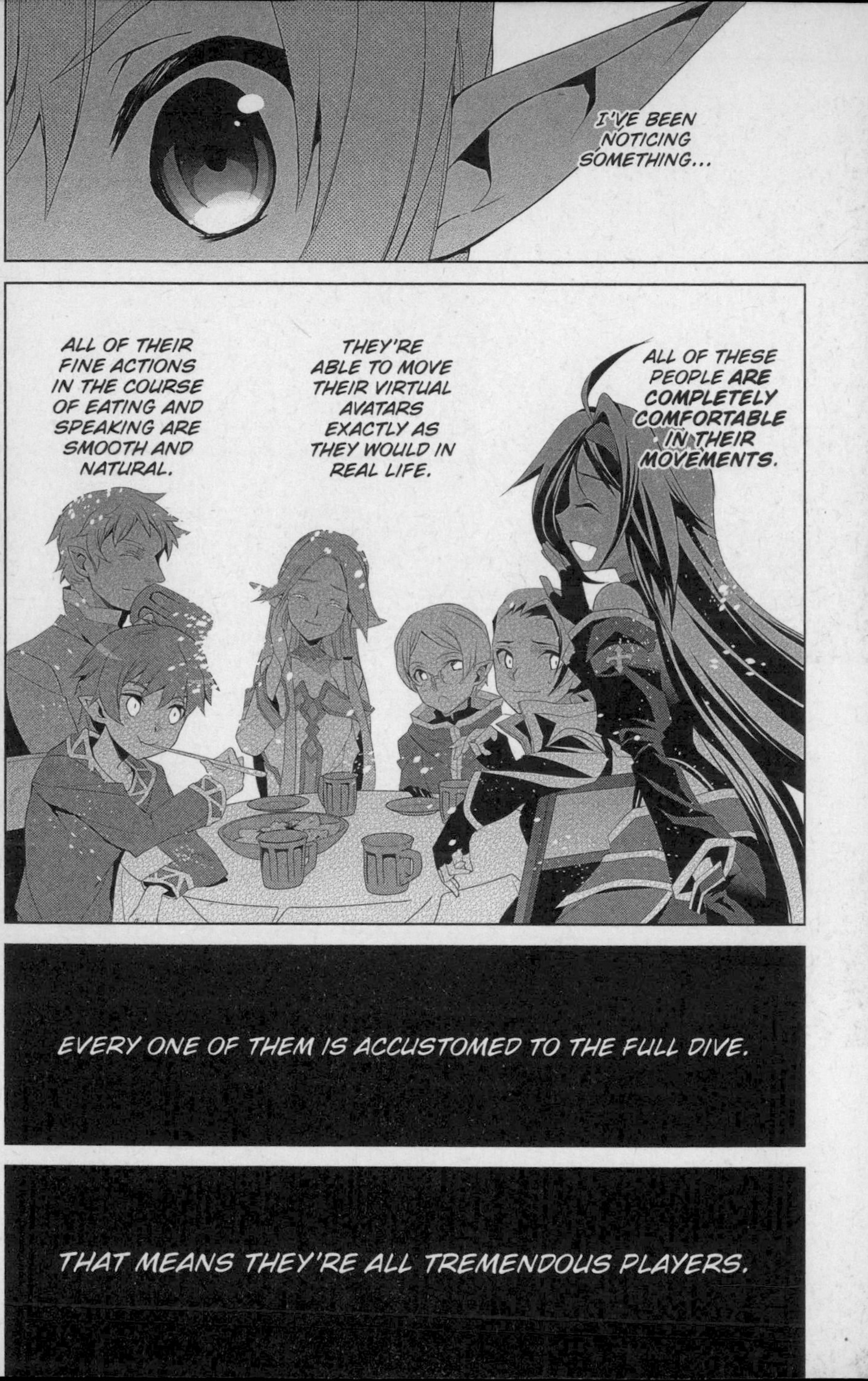
I'VE BEEN NOTICING SOMETHING...
ALL OF THESE PEOPLE ARE COMPLETELY COMFORTABLE IN THEIR MOVEMENTS.
THEY'RE ABLE TO MOVE THEIR VIRTUAL AVATARS EXACTLY AS THEY WOULD IN REAL LIFE.
ALL OF THEIR FINE ACTIONS IN THE COURSE OF EATING AND SPEAKING ARE SMOOTH AND NATURAL.
EVERY ONE OF THEM IS ACCUSTOMED TO THE FULL DIVE.
THAT MEANS THEY'RE ALL TREMENDOUS PLAYERS.

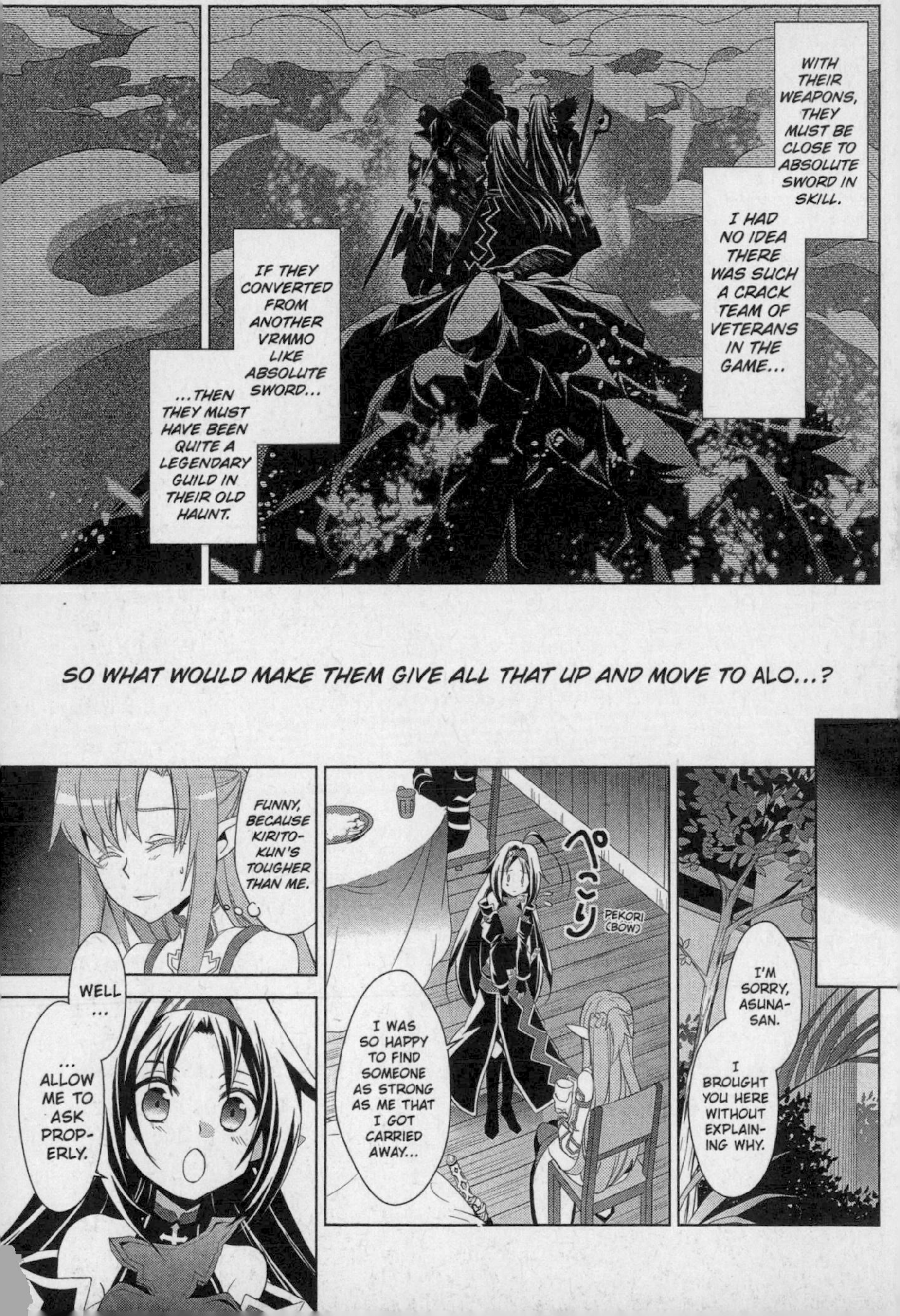
WITH THEIR WEAPONS, THEY MUST BE CLOSE TO ABSOLUTE SWORD IN SKILL.
I HAD NO IDEA THERE WAS SUCH A CRACK TEAM OF VETERANS IN THE GAME...
IF THEY CONVERTED FROM ANOTHER VRMMO LIKE ABSOLUTE SWORD...
...THEN THEY MUST HAVE BEEN QUITE A LEGENDARY GUILD IN THEIR OLD HAUNT.
SO WHAT WOULD MAKE THEM GIVE ALL THAT UP AND MOVE TO ALO...?
I'M SORRY, ASUNA-SAN.
I BROUGHT YOU HERE WITHOUT EXPLAINING WHY.
PEKORI (BOW)
I WAS SO HAPPY TO FIND SOMEONE AS STRONG AS ME THAT I GOT CARRIED AWAY...
FUNNY, BECAUSE KIRITO-KUN'S TOUGHER THAN ME.
WELL...
...ALLOW ME TO ASK PROPERLY.

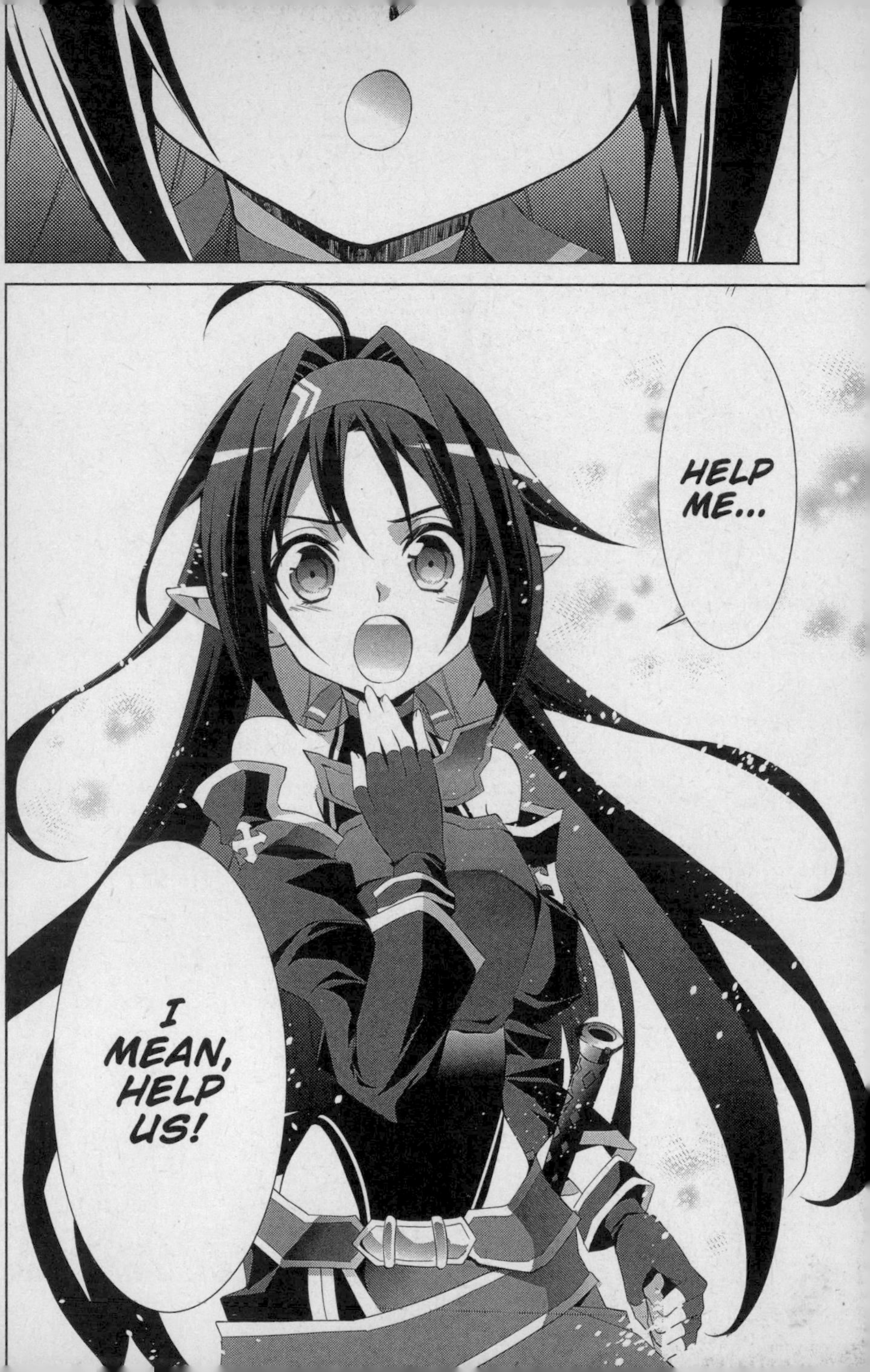
HELP ME...
I MEAN, HELP US!

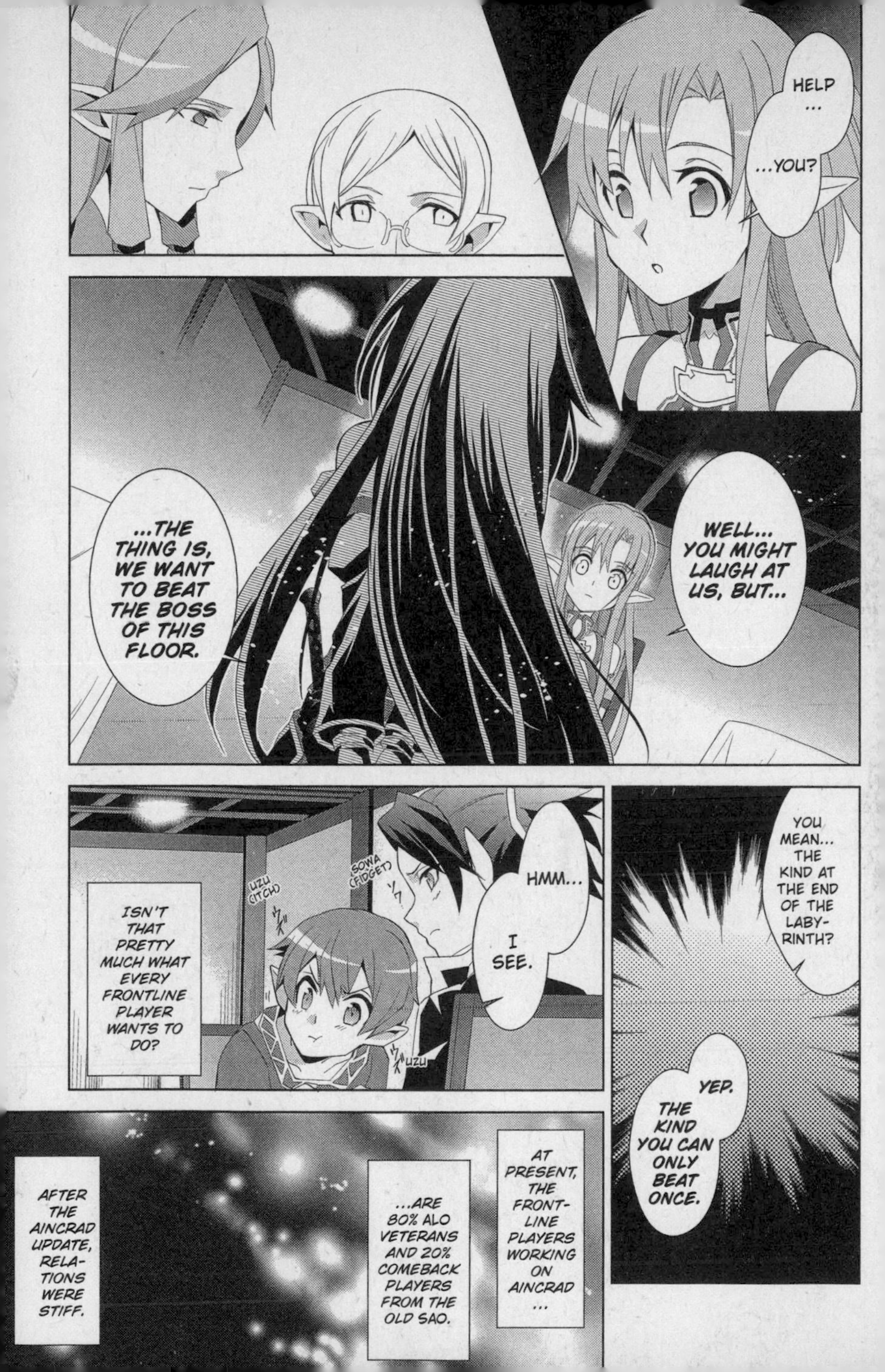
HELP ...
...YOU?
WELL... YOU MIGHT LAUGH AT US, BUT...
...THE THING IS, WE WANT TO BEAT THE BOSS OF THIS FLOOR.
YOU MEAN... THE KIND AT THE END OF THE LABY-RINTH?
YEP. THE KIND YOU CAN ONLY BEAT ONCE.
HMM...
I SEE.
SOWA (FIDGET)
UZU (ITCH)
ISN'T THAT PRETTY MUCH WHAT EVERY FRONTLINE PLAYER WANTS TO DO?
UZU
AT PRESENT, THE FRONT-LINE PLAYERS WORKING ON AINCRAD ...
...ARE 80% ALO VETERANS AND 20% COMEBACK PLAYERS FROM THE OLD SAO.
AFTER THE AINCRAD UPDATE, RELA-TIONS WERE STIFF.

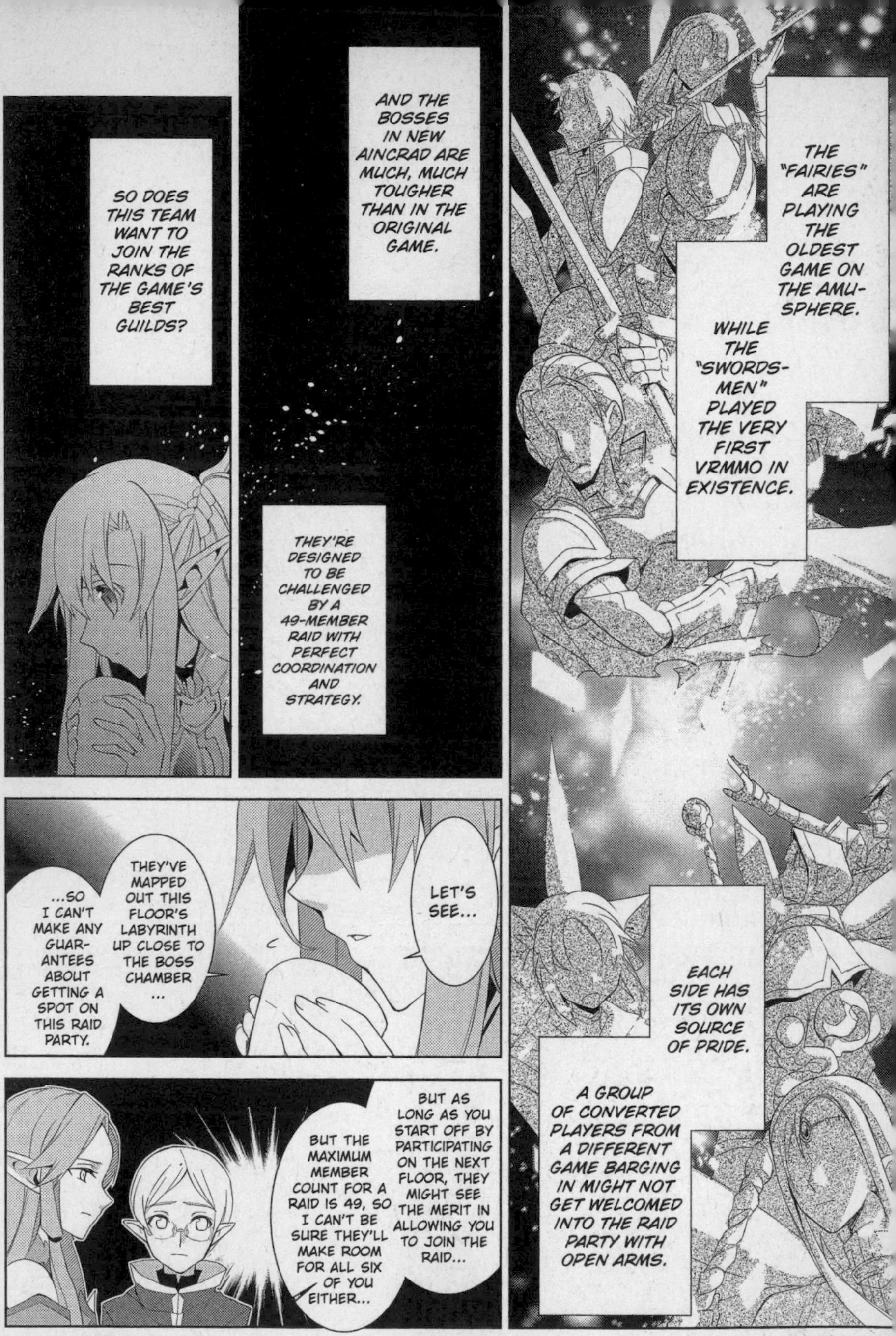
THE "FAIRIES" ARE PLAYING THE OLDEST GAME ON THE AMUSPHERE.
WHILE THE "SWORDSMEN" PLAYED THE VERY FIRST VRMMO IN EXISTENCE.
EACH SIDE HAS ITS OWN SOURCE OF PRIDE.
A GROUP OF CONVERTED PLAYERS FROM A DIFFERENT GAME BARGING IN MIGHT NOT GET WELCOMED INTO THE RAID PARTY WITH OPEN ARMS.
AND THE BOSSES IN NEW AINCRAD ARE MUCH, MUCH TOUGHER THAN IN THE ORIGINAL GAME.
THEY'RE DESIGNED TO BE CHALLENGED BY A 49-MEMBER RAID WITH PERFECT COORDINATION AND STRATEGY.
SO DOES THIS TEAM WANT TO JOIN THE RANKS OF THE GAME'S BEST GUILDS?
LET'S SEE...
THEY'VE MAPPED OUT THIS FLOOR'S LABYRINTH UP CLOSE TO THE BOSS CHAMBER...
...SO I CAN'T MAKE ANY GUARANTEES ABOUT GETTING A SPOT ON THIS RAID PARTY.
BUT AS LONG AS YOU START OFF BY PARTICIPATING ON THE NEXT FLOOR, THEY MIGHT SEE THE MERIT IN ALLOWING YOU TO JOIN THE RAID...
BUT THE MAXIMUM MEMBER COUNT FOR A RAID IS 49, SO I CAN'T BE SURE THEY'LL MAKE ROOM FOR ALL SIX OF YOU EITHER...

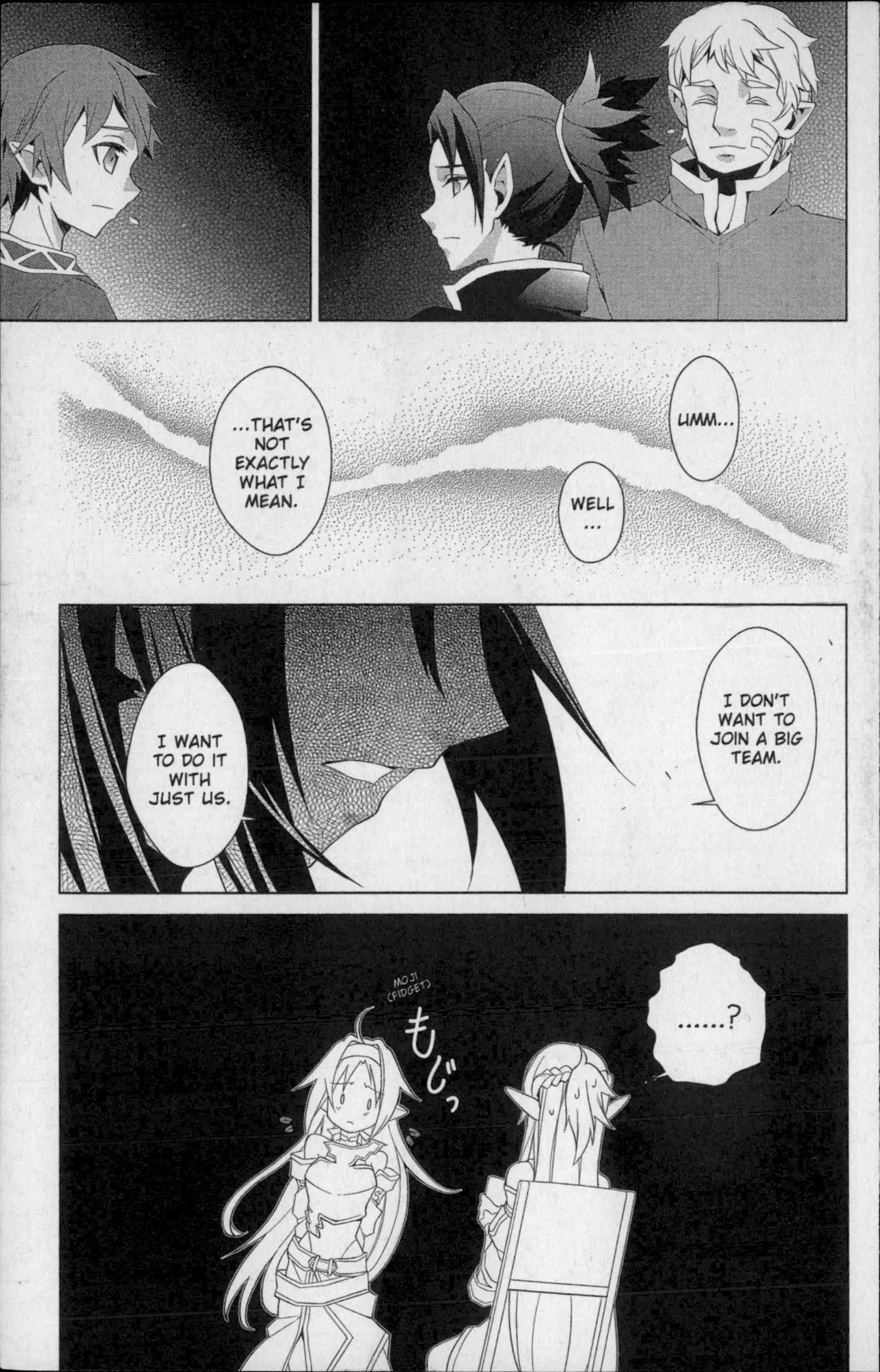
UMM...
WELL ...
...THAT'S NOT EXACTLY WHAT I MEAN.
I DON'T WANT TO JOIN A BIG TEAM.
I WANT TO DO IT WITH JUST US.
......?
MOJI (FIDGET)
もじっ

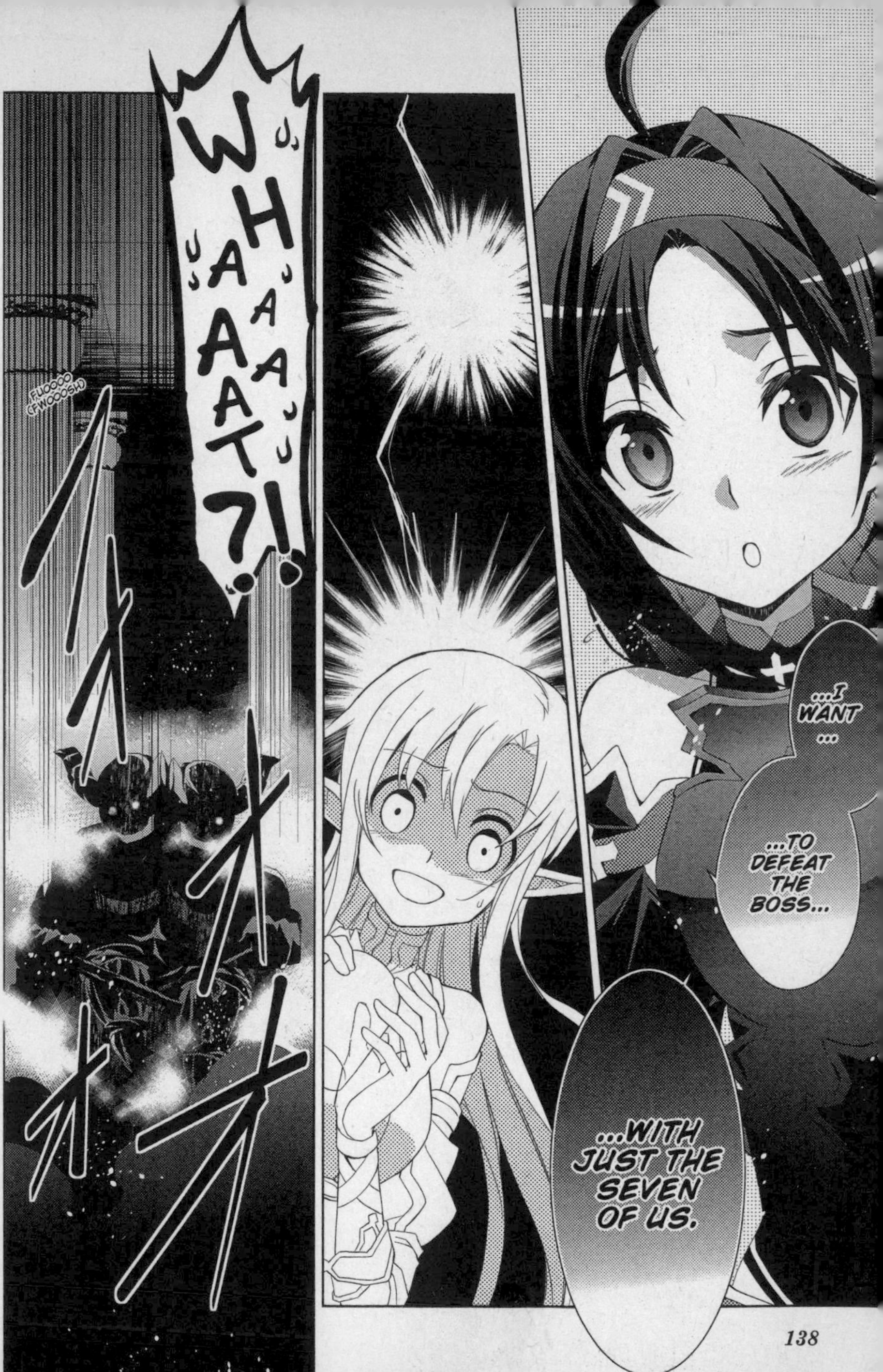
...I WANT...
...TO DEFEAT THE BOSS...
...WITH JUST THE SEVEN OF US.
WHAAAAAT?!
FUOOOO (FWOOOSH)

TRANSLATION NOTES

COMMON HONORIFICS

no honorific: Indicates familiarity or closeness; if used without permission or reason, addressing someone in this manner would constitute an insult.

-san: The Japanese equivalent of Mr./Mrs./Miss. If a situation calls for politeness, this is the fail-safe honorific.

-kun: Used most often when referring to boys, this indicates affection or familiarity. Occasionally used by older men among their peers, but it may also be used by anyone referring to a person of lower standing.

-chan: An affectionate honorific indicating familiarity used mostly in reference to girls; also used in reference to cute persons or animals of either gender.

Onii-chan: An affectionate term for "older brother."

PAGE 17

Absolute Sword: The original term used in Japanese is *zekken*, written with the kanji for "end/sever" and "sword"—the first character is included in longer words like "ultimate" or "absolute." While that term is made-up and doesn't exist in Japanese, there is a loanword *zekken* from the German "*decken*" that refers to the numbered bibs that athletes wear over their shirts in a race or marathon, hence Asuna's confusion.

SWORD ART ONLINE
MOTHER'S ROSARY

To Be Continued in the Next Stage...!!

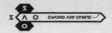

SWORD ART ONLINE mother's rosary
BACKGROUND GUIDE 03

DUELS IN *ALO*

BECAUSE OF THE DANGER OF DEATH IN *SAO*, DUELS WERE ALMOST ALWAYS SETTLED WITH THE "FIRST-STRIKE MODE," WHERE THE FIRST CLEAN HIT BROUGHT AN END TO THE BATTLE. BUT IN *ALO*, WHERE THERE'S NO DANGER OF DYING, THE "FULL-FINISH MODE," WHERE ONE CONTESTANT HAS TO BE TAKEN ALL THE WAY DOWN TO ZERO HP, IS THE STANDARD CHOICE. BUT THERE IS A HEAVY DEATH PENALTY IN *ALO*, INCLUDING THE LOSS OF SKILL EXPERIENCE, AND RESURRECTION ITEMS ARE EXPENSIVE. SO IT'S COMMON FOR THE LOSING PLAYER TO RESIGN AND END THE DUEL BEFORE IT GOES ALL THE WAY.

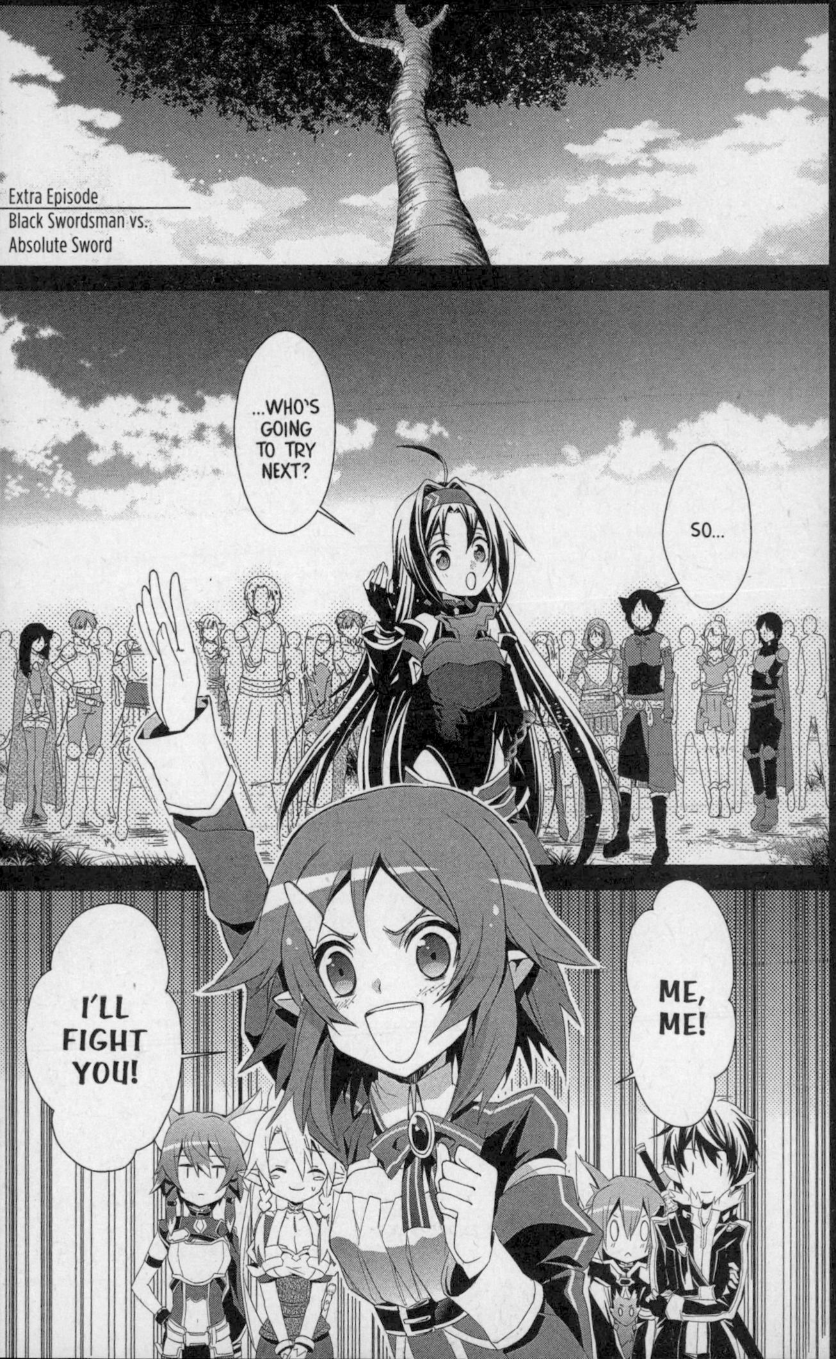
Extra Episode
Black Swordsman vs. Absolute Sword
SO...
...WHO'S GOING TO TRY NEXT?
ME, ME!
I'LL FIGHT YOU!

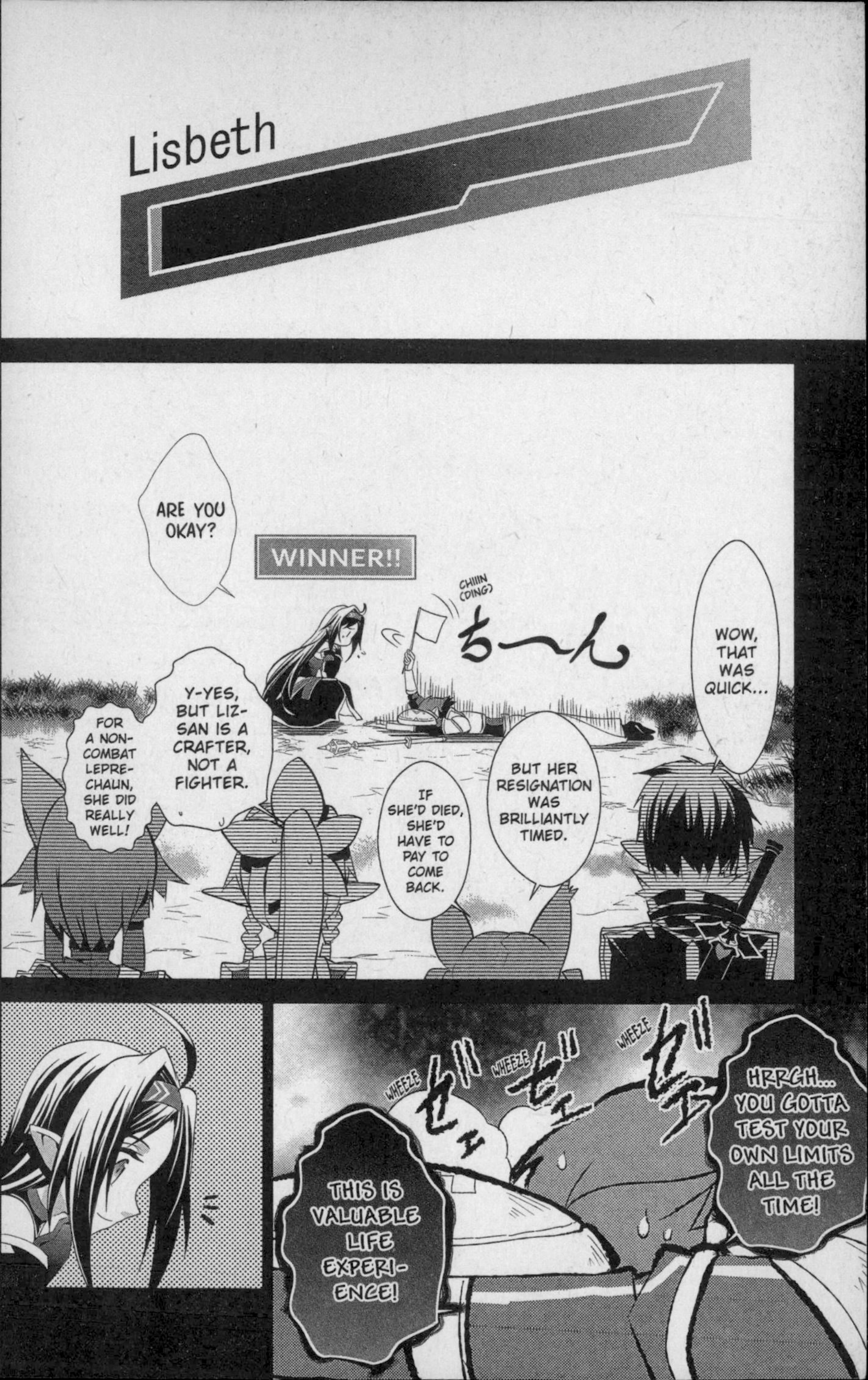
Lisbeth
WOW, THAT WAS QUICK...
CHIIIN (DING)
ち〜ん
WINNER!!
ARE YOU OKAY?
BUT HER RESIGNATION WAS BRILLIANTLY TIMED.
IF SHE'D DIED, SHE'D HAVE TO PAY TO COME BACK.
Y-YES, BUT LIZ-SAN IS A CRAFTER, NOT A FIGHTER.
FOR A NON-COMBAT LEPRE-CHAUN, SHE DID REALLY WELL!
HRRGH... YOU GOTTA TEST YOUR OWN LIMITS ALL THE TIME!
WHEEZE
WHEEZE
WHEEZE
THIS IS VALUABLE LIFE EXPERI-ENCE!

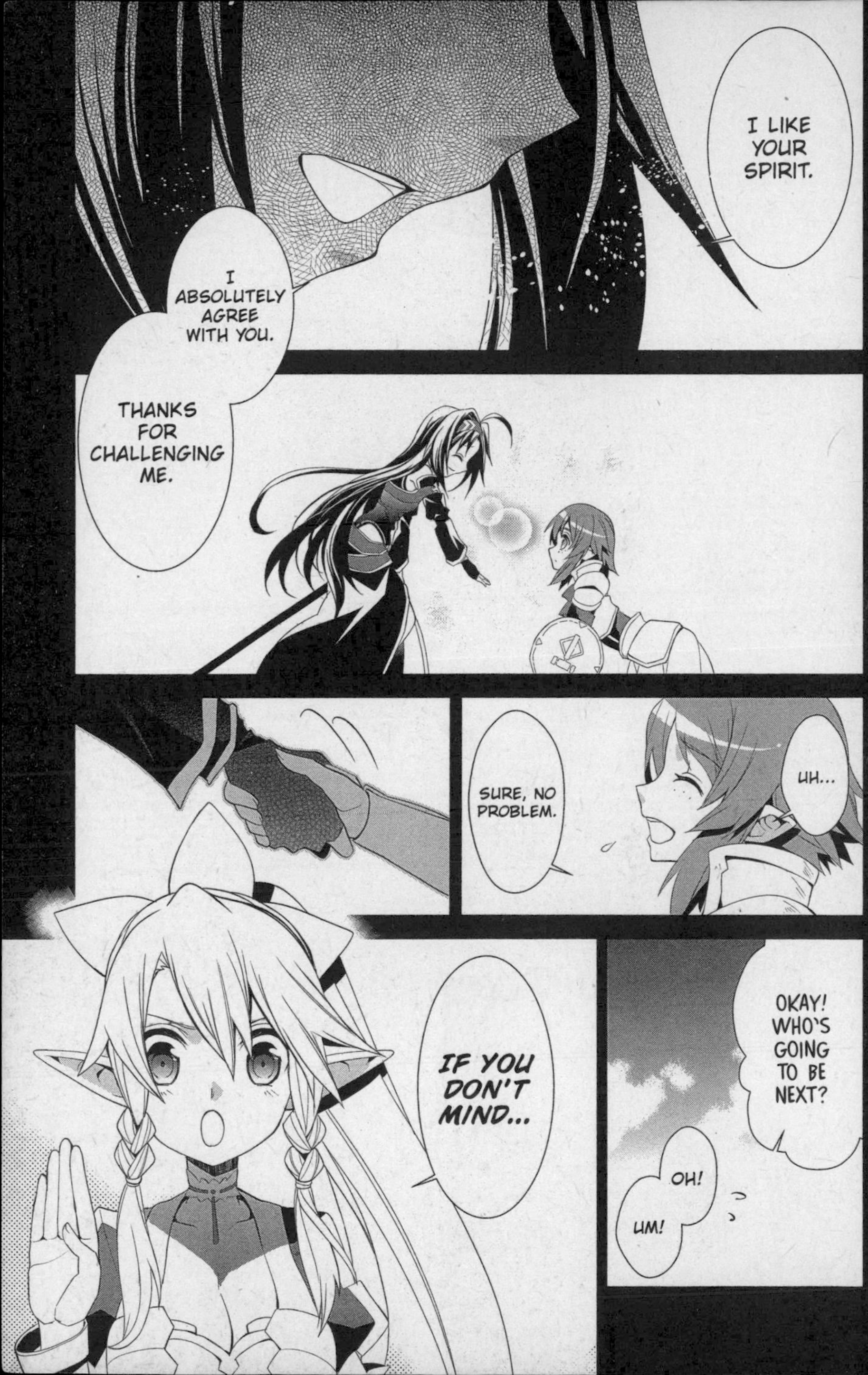
I LIKE YOUR SPIRIT.
I ABSOLUTELY AGREE WITH YOU.
THANKS FOR CHALLENGING ME.
UH...
SURE, NO PROBLEM.
OKAY! WHO'S GOING TO BE NEXT?
OH!
UM!
IF YOU DON'T MIND...

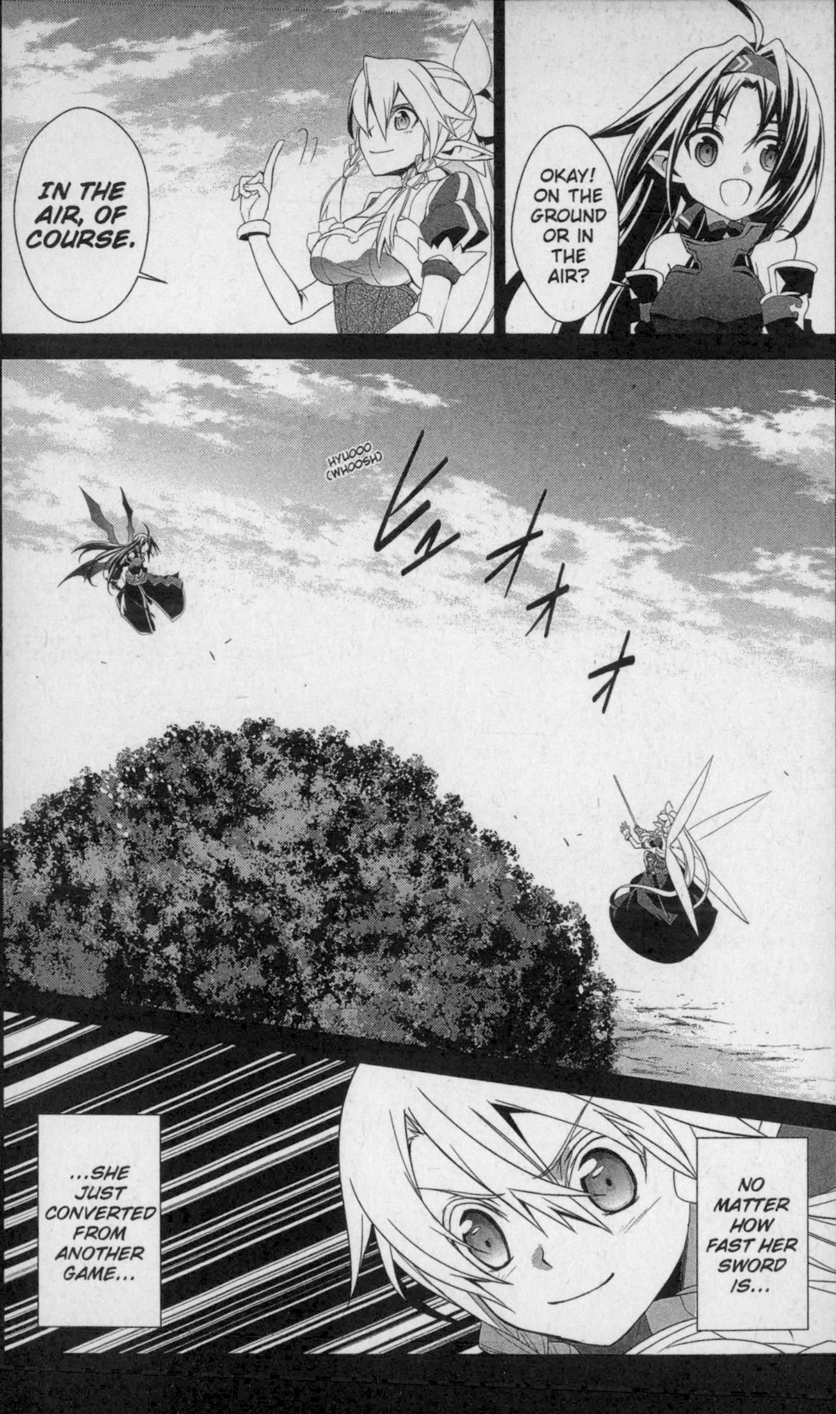
OKAY! ON THE GROUND OR IN THE AIR?
IN THE AIR, OF COURSE.
HYUOOO (WHOOSH)
NO MATTER HOW FAST HER SWORD IS...
...SHE JUST CONVERTED FROM ANOTHER GAME...

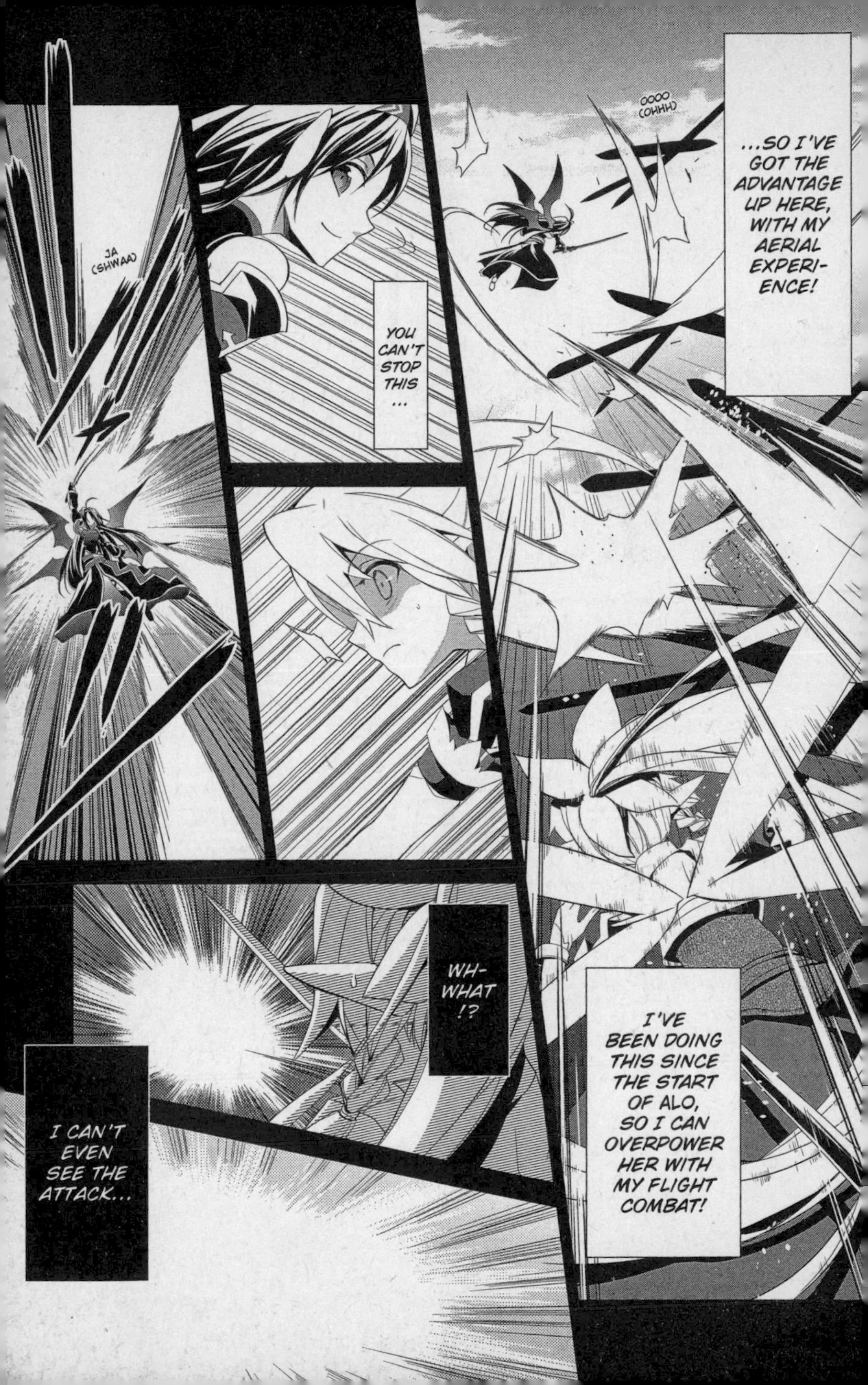
OOOO (OHHH)
...SO I'VE GOT THE ADVANTAGE UP HERE, WITH MY AERIAL EXPERIENCE!
I'VE BEEN DOING THIS SINCE THE START OF ALO, SO I CAN OVERPOWER HER WITH MY FLIGHT COMBAT!
YOU CAN'T STOP THIS...
JA (SHWAA)
WH-WHAT!?
I CAN'T EVEN SEE THE ATTACK...

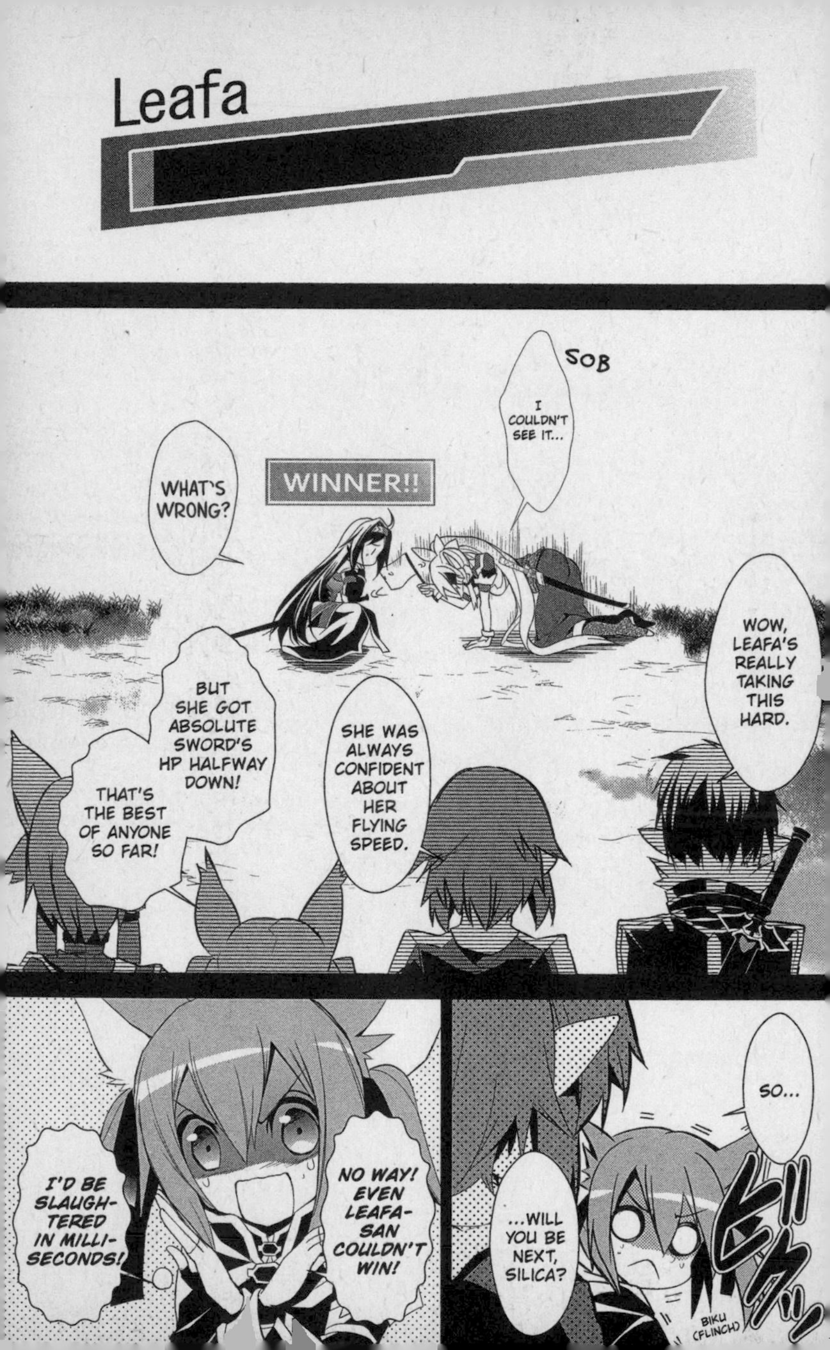
Leafa
SOB
I COULDN'T SEE IT...
WOW, LEAFA'S REALLY TAKING THIS HARD.
WINNER!!
WHAT'S WRONG?
SHE WAS ALWAYS CONFIDENT ABOUT HER FLYING SPEED.
BUT SHE GOT ABSOLUTE SWORD'S HP HALFWAY DOWN!
THAT'S THE BEST OF ANYONE SO FAR!
SO...
...WILL YOU BE NEXT, SILICA?
BIKU (FLINCH)
NO WAY! EVEN LEAFA-SAN COULDN'T WIN!
I'D BE SLAUGHTERED IN MILLISECONDS!

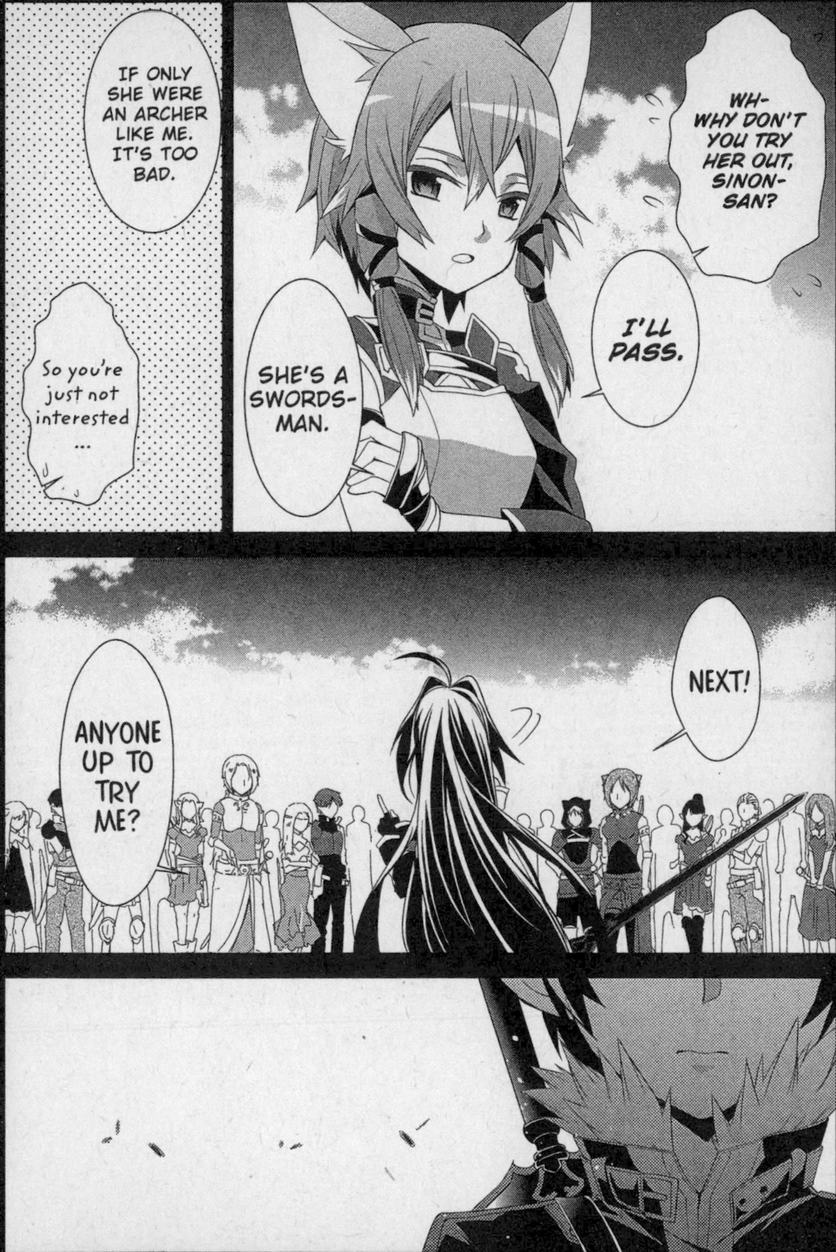
WH- WHY DON'T YOU TRY HER OUT, SINON-SAN?
I'LL PASS.
SHE'S A SWORDSMAN.
IF ONLY SHE WERE AN ARCHER LIKE ME. IT'S TOO BAD.
So you're just not interested ...
NEXT!
ANYONE UP TO TRY ME?

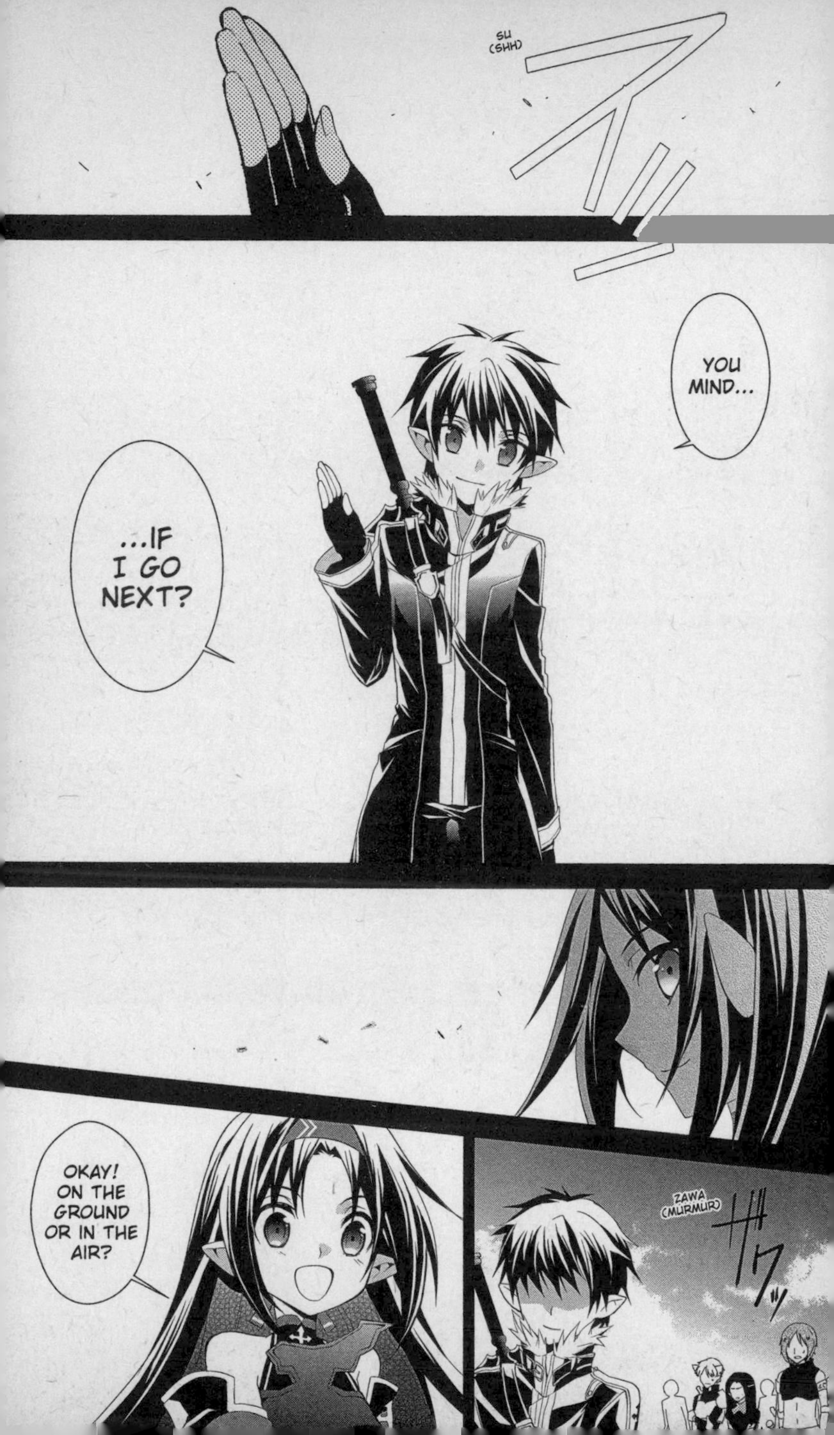
SU (SHH)
YOU MIND...
...IF I GO NEXT?
ZAWA (MURMUR)
OKAY! ON THE GROUND OR IN THE AIR?

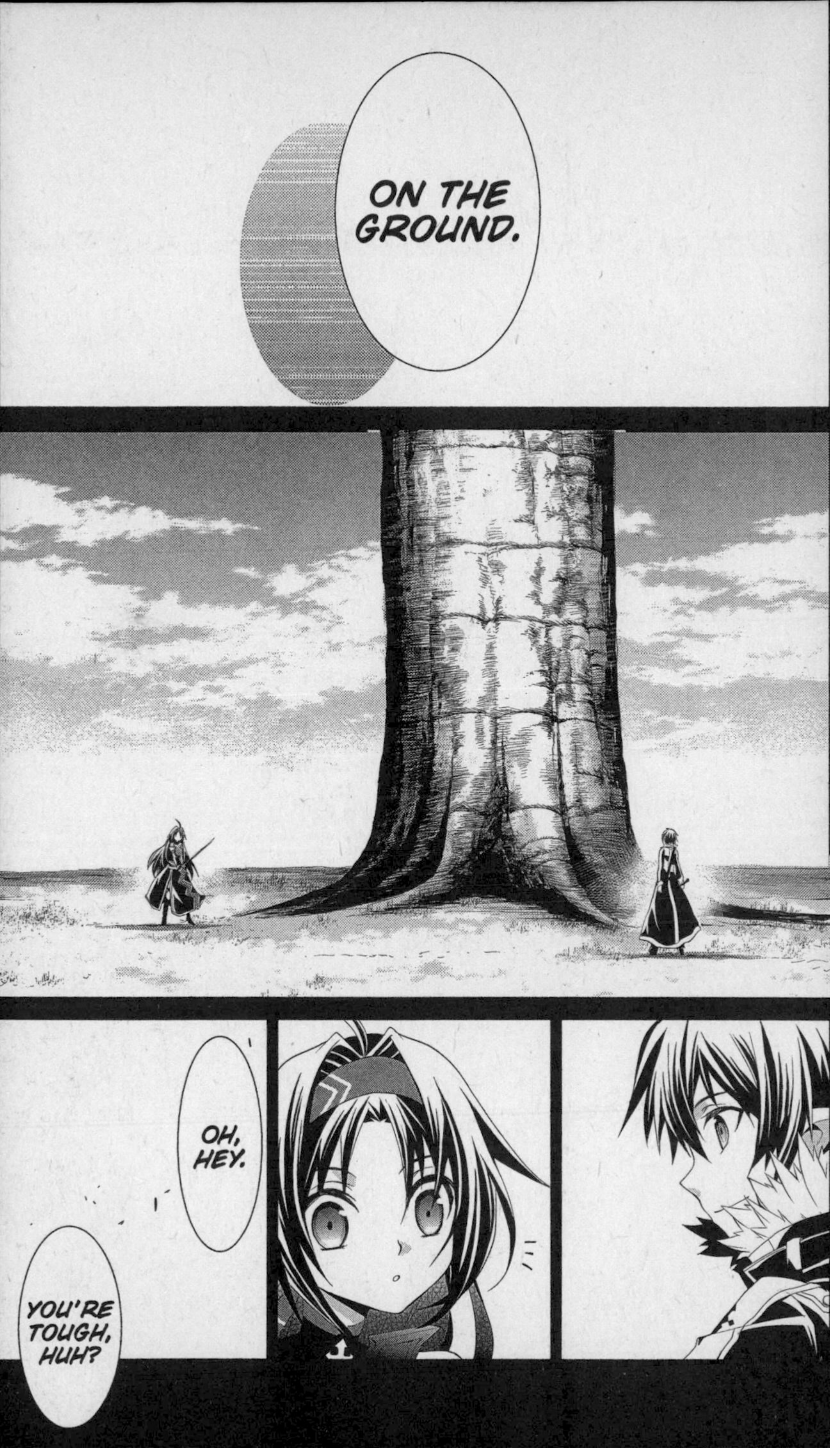
ON THE GROUND.
OH, HEY.
YOU'RE TOUGH, HUH?

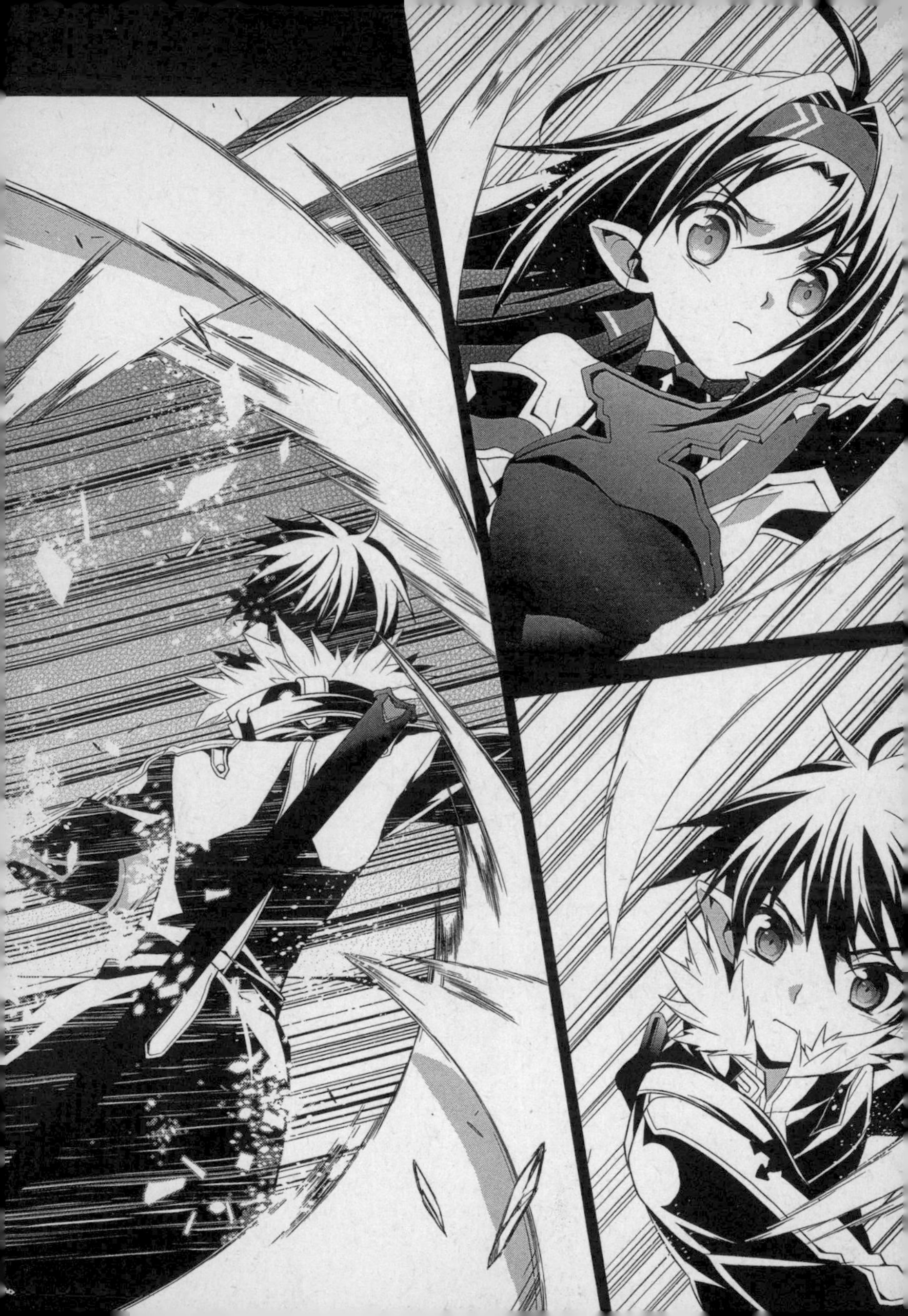

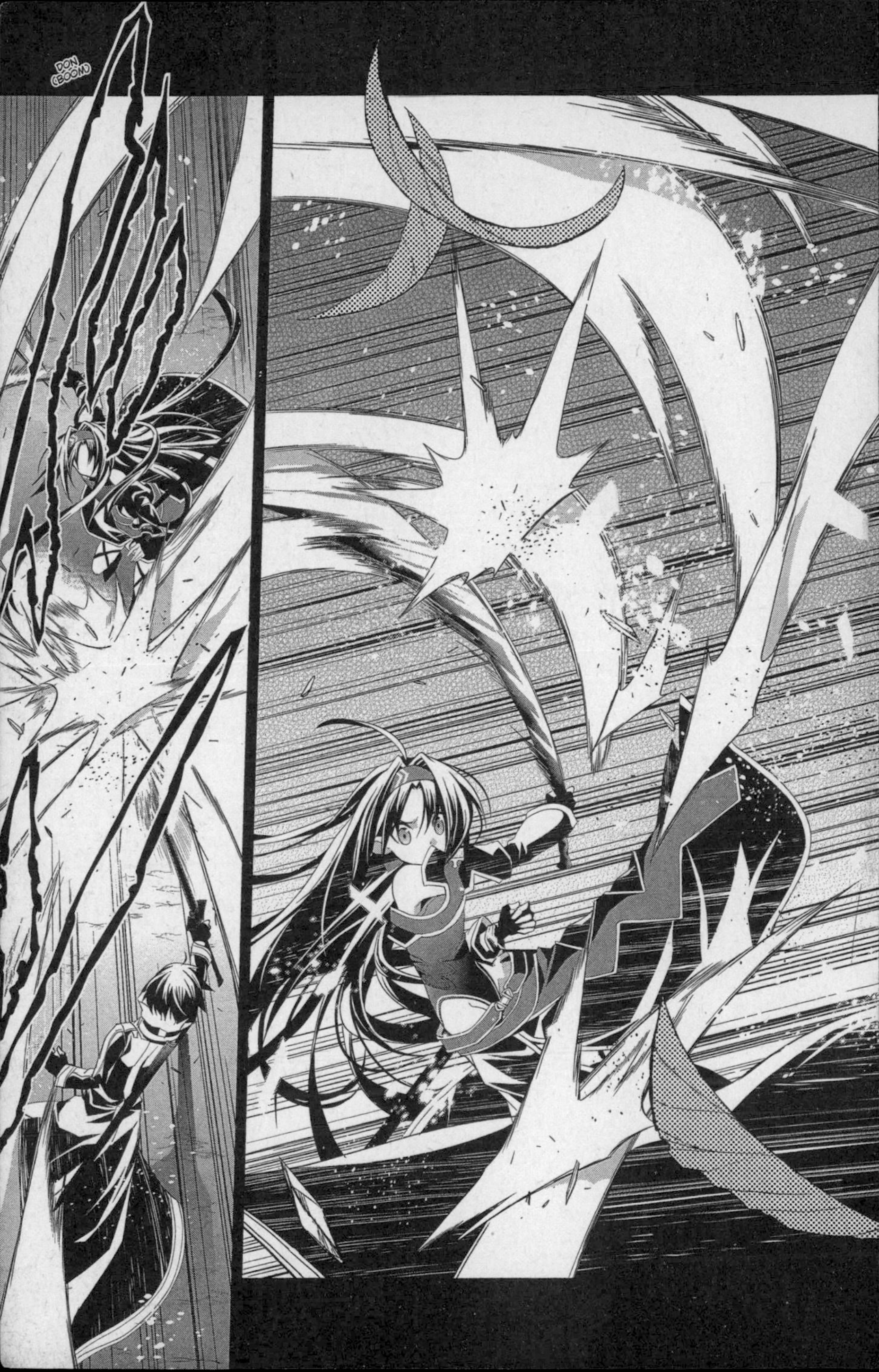
DON
(BOOM)

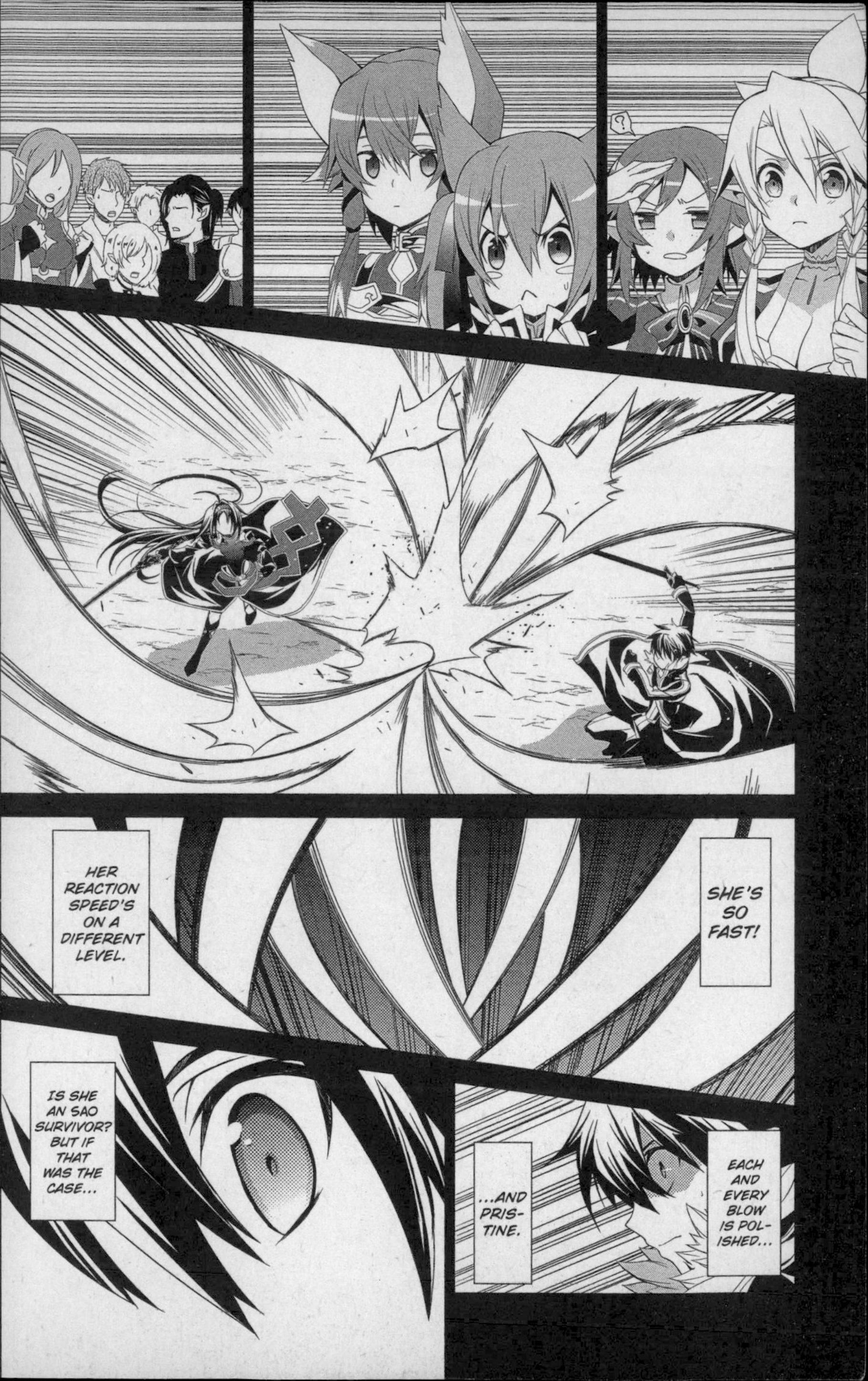
SHE'S SO FAST!
HER REACTION SPEED'S ON A DIFFERENT LEVEL.
EACH AND EVERY BLOW IS POLISHED...
...AND PRISTINE.
IS SHE AN SAO SURVIVOR? BUT IF THAT WAS THE CASE...

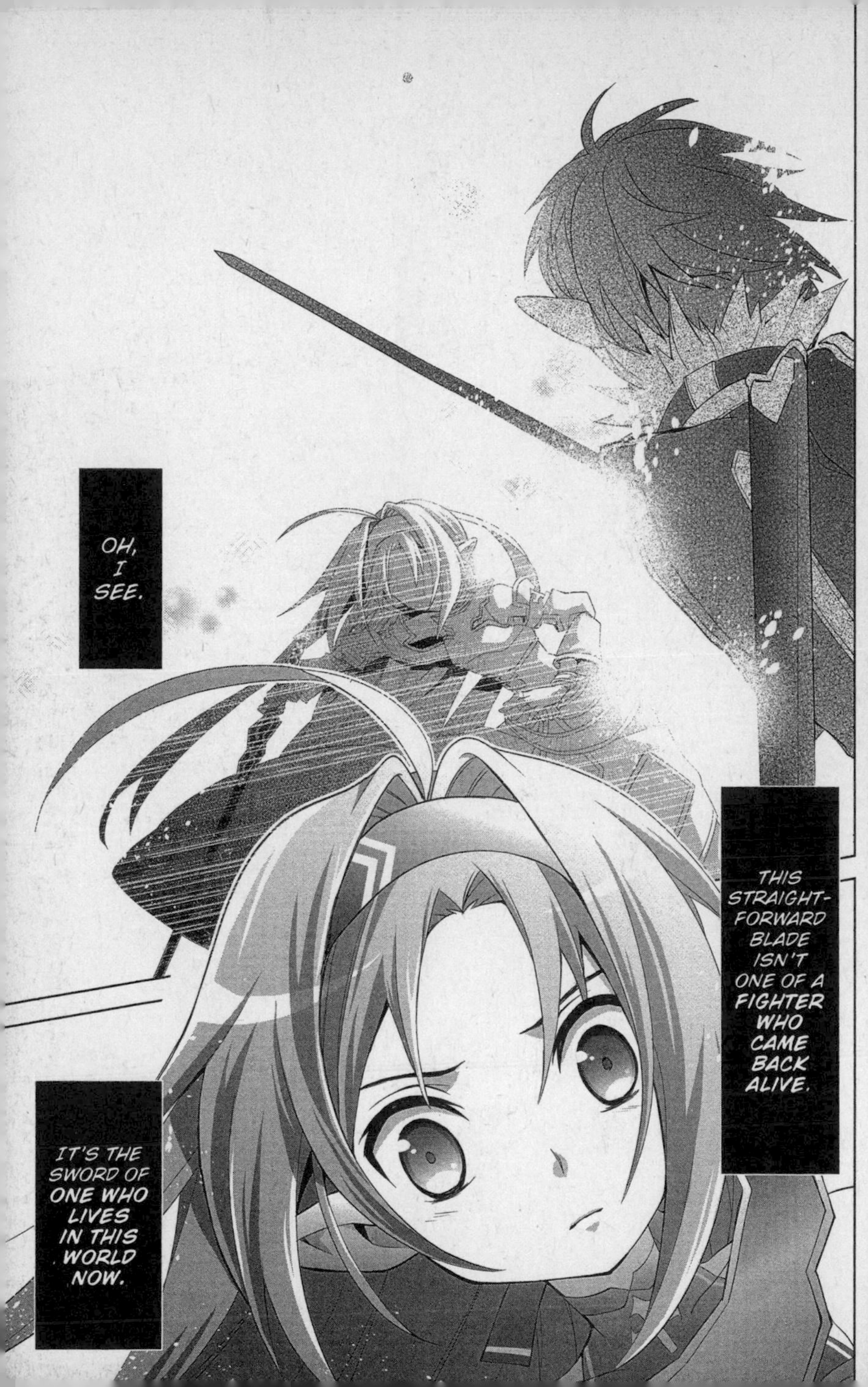
OH, I SEE.
THIS STRAIGHT-FORWARD BLADE ISN'T ONE OF A FIGHTER WHO CAME BACK ALIVE.
IT'S THE SWORD OF ONE WHO LIVES IN THIS WORLD NOW.

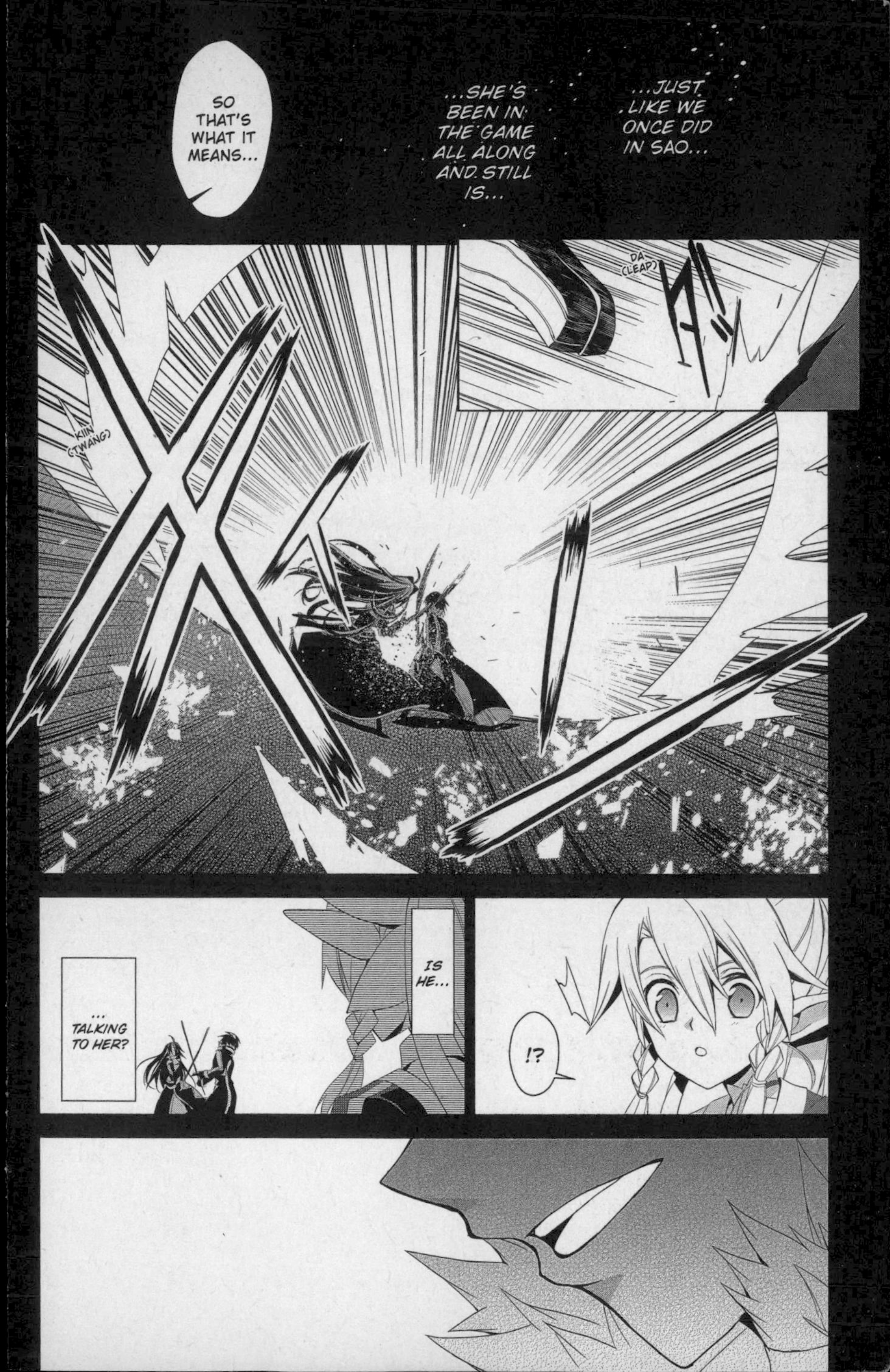
...JUST LIKE WE ONCE DID IN SAO...
...SHE'S BEEN IN THE GAME ALL ALONG AND STILL IS...
SO THAT'S WHAT IT MEANS...
DA (LEAP)
KIIN (TWANG)
!?
IS HE...
...TALKING TO HER?

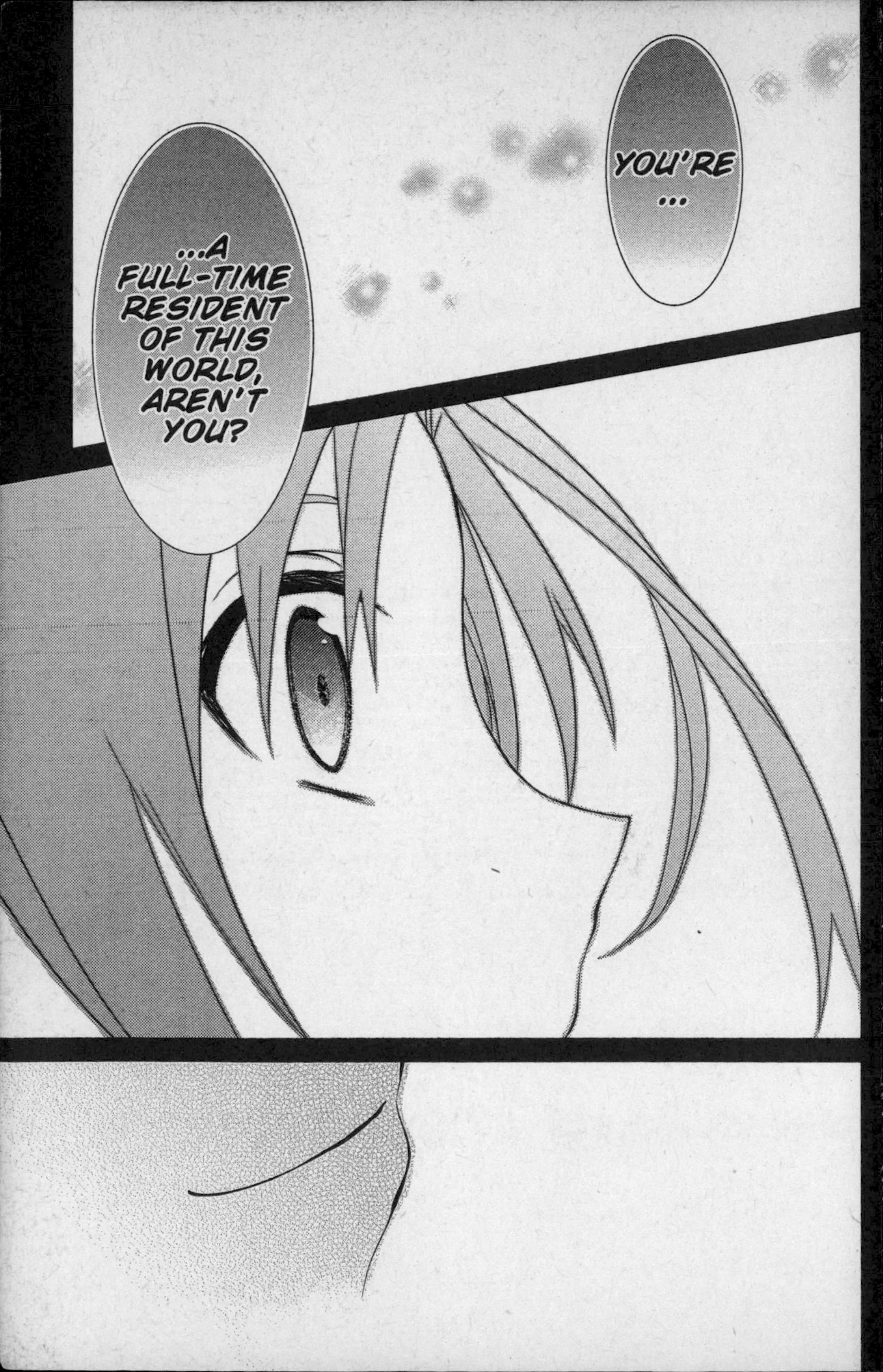
YOU'RE ...
...A FULL-TIME RESIDENT OF THIS WORLD, AREN'T YOU?

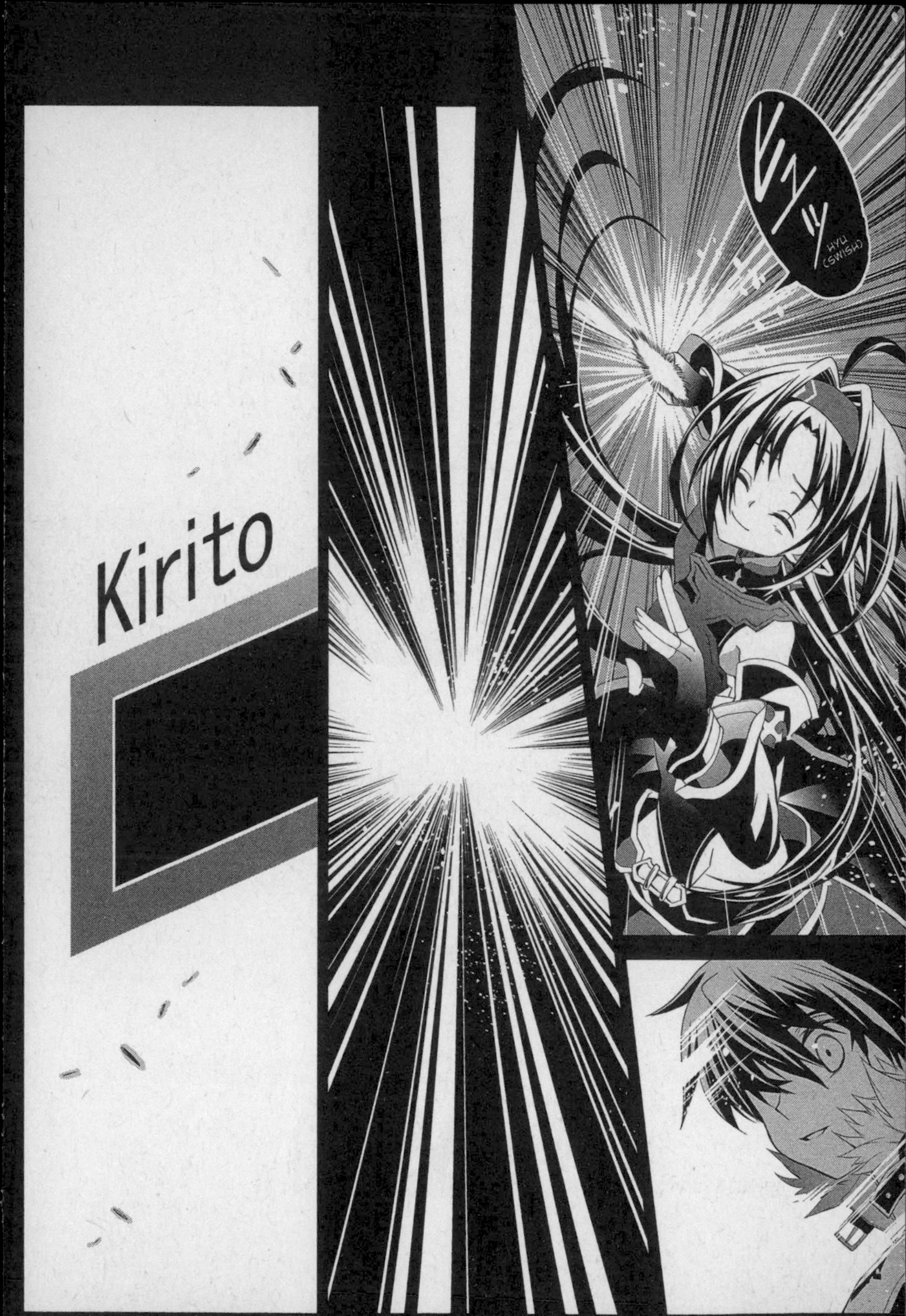
Kirito
HYU (SWISH)

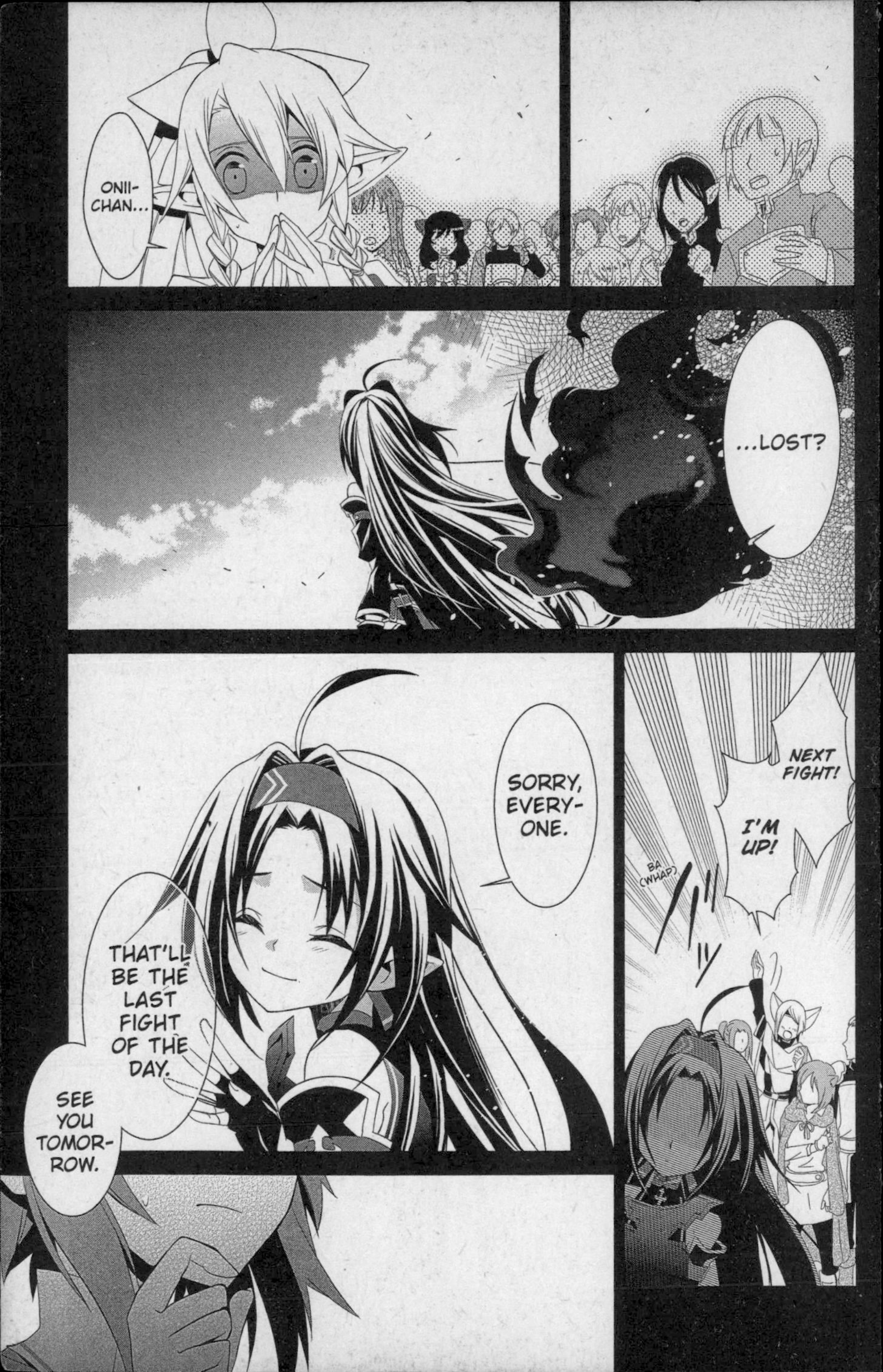
ONII-CHAN...
...LOST?
NEXT FIGHT!
I'M UP!
BA (WHAP)
SORRY, EVERY-ONE.
THAT'LL BE THE LAST FIGHT OF THE DAY.
SEE YOU TOMOR-ROW.

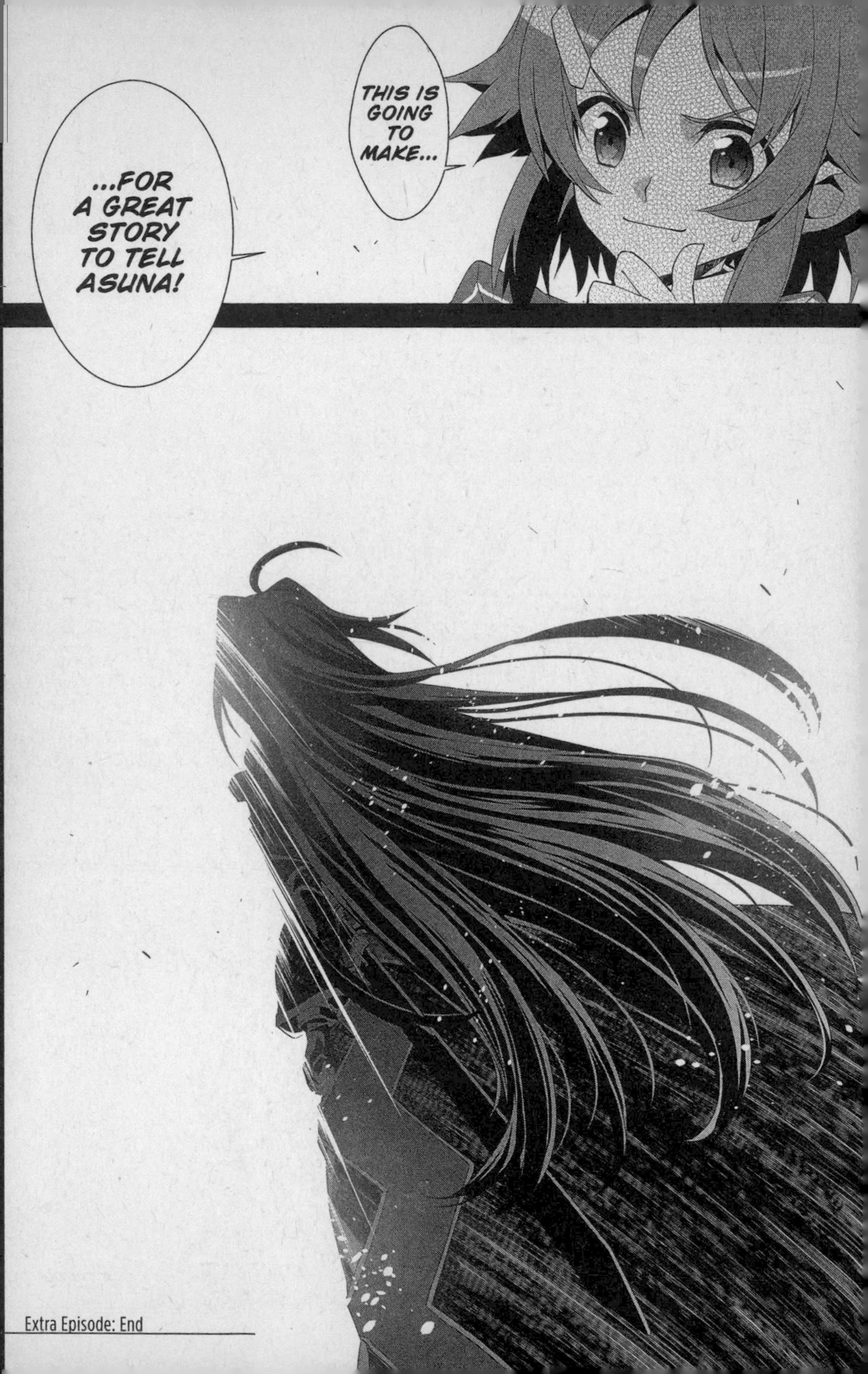
THIS IS GOING TO MAKE...
...FOR A GREAT STORY TO TELL ASUNA!
Extra Episode: End

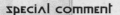

special comment

original story: reki kawahara

CONGRATULATIONS ON THE PUBLICATION OF THE FIRST VOLUME OF *SWORD ART ONLINE: MOTHER'S ROSARY*!

THE *MOTHER'S ROSARY* ARC IS UNIQUE AMONG THE SAO SERIES, BUT THAT'S WHAT MAKES ME SO FOND OF IT. WHEN I HEARD IT WOULD BE TURNED INTO A COMIC, I HOPED FOR AN ARTIST WHO COULD PORTRAY THE STRENGTH AND FRAGILITY OF YUUKI'S CHARACTER...SO WHEN I HEARD THAT TSUBASA HADUKI-SAN WOULD BE RETURNING FROM THE *FAIRY DANCE* ARC, I WAS OVERJOYED. I CAN'T WAIT TO REREAD THE STORY OF ASUNA AND YUUKI WITH HADUKI-SAN'S DELICATE, SENSITIVE TOUCH.

REKI KAWAHARA

001

SWORD ART ONLINE mother's rosary

art: tsubasa haduki
original story: reki kawahara
character design: abec

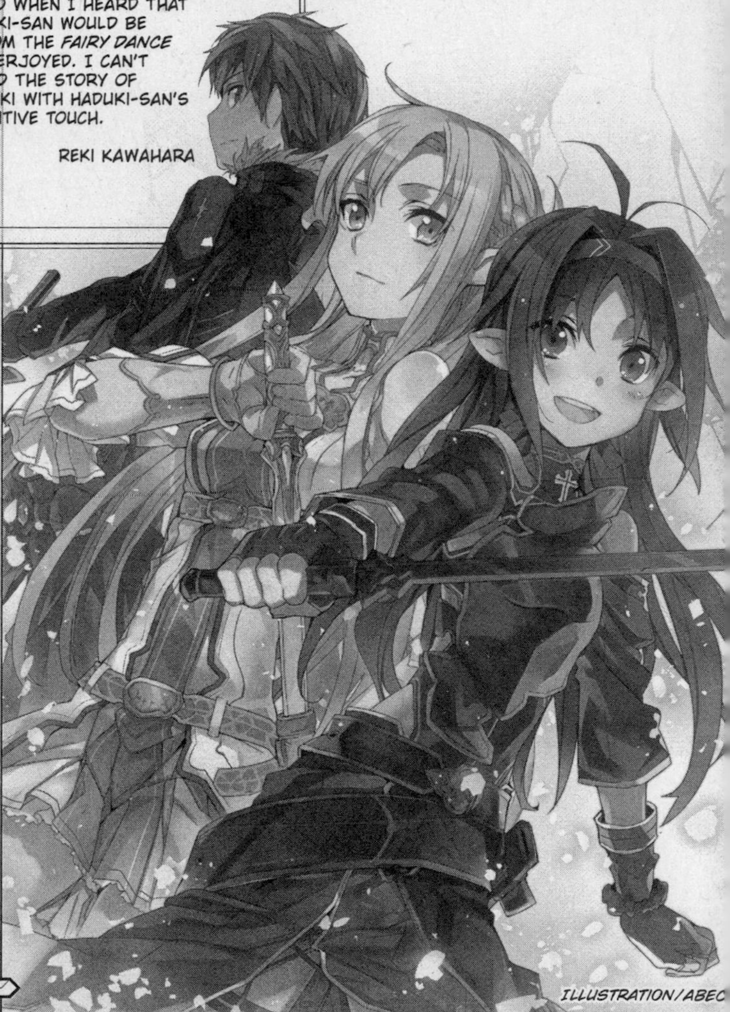

ILLUSTRATION/ABEC

AFTERWORD MANGA

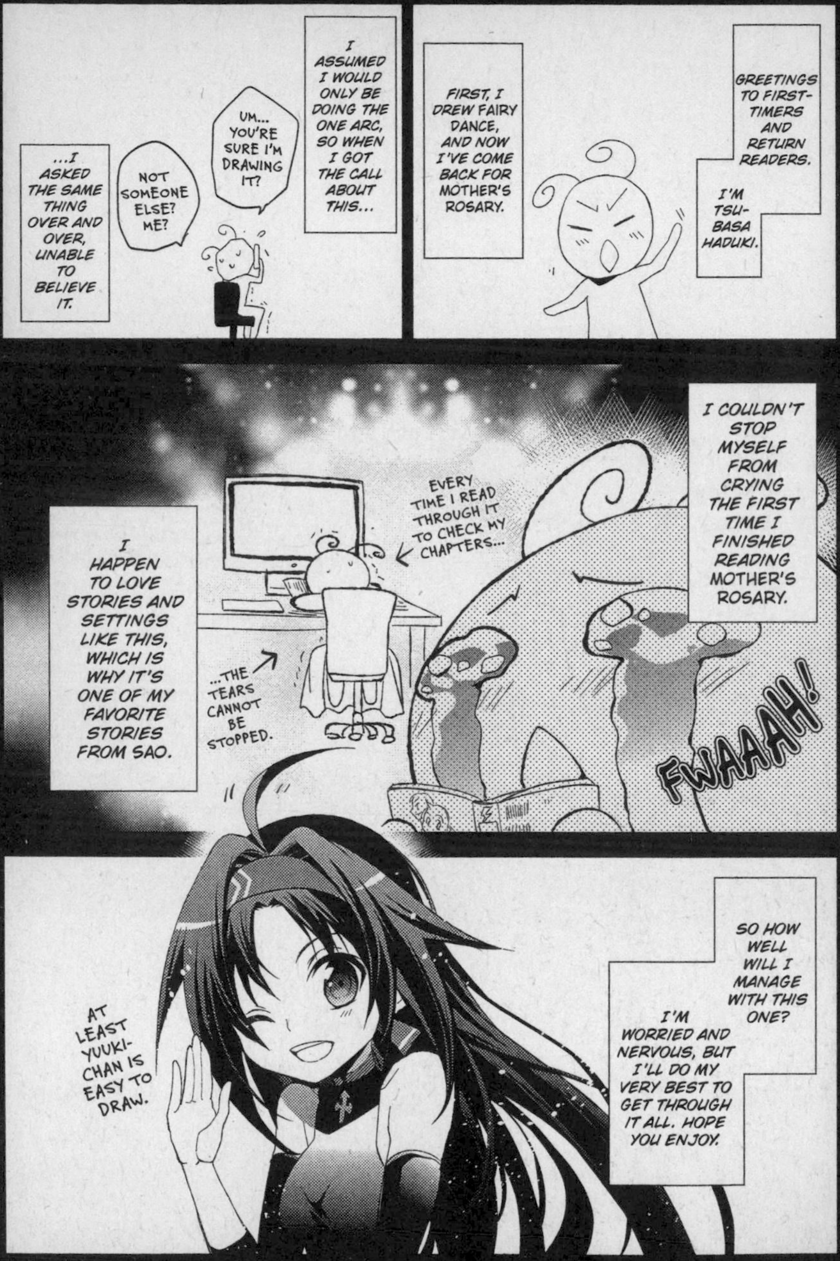
GREETINGS TO FIRST-TIMERS AND RETURN READERS.
I'M TSU-BASA HADUKI.
FIRST, I DREW FAIRY DANCE, AND NOW I'VE COME BACK FOR MOTHER'S ROSARY.
I ASSUMED I WOULD ONLY BE DOING THE ONE ARC, SO WHEN I GOT THE CALL ABOUT THIS...
UM... YOU'RE SURE I'M DRAWING IT?
NOT SOMEONE ELSE? ME?
...I ASKED THE SAME THING OVER AND OVER, UNABLE TO BELIEVE IT.
I COULDN'T STOP MYSELF FROM CRYING THE FIRST TIME I FINISHED READING MOTHER'S ROSARY.
EVERY TIME I READ THROUGH IT TO CHECK MY CHAPTERS...
I HAPPEN TO LOVE STORIES AND SETTINGS LIKE THIS, WHICH IS WHY IT'S ONE OF MY FAVORITE STORIES FROM SAO.
...THE TEARS CANNOT BE STOPPED.
FWAAAH!
SO HOW WELL WILL I MANAGE WITH THIS ONE?
I'M WORRIED AND NERVOUS, BUT I'LL DO MY VERY BEST TO GET THROUGH IT ALL. HOPE YOU ENJOY.
AT LEAST YUUKI-CHAN IS EASY TO DRAW.

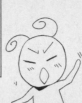

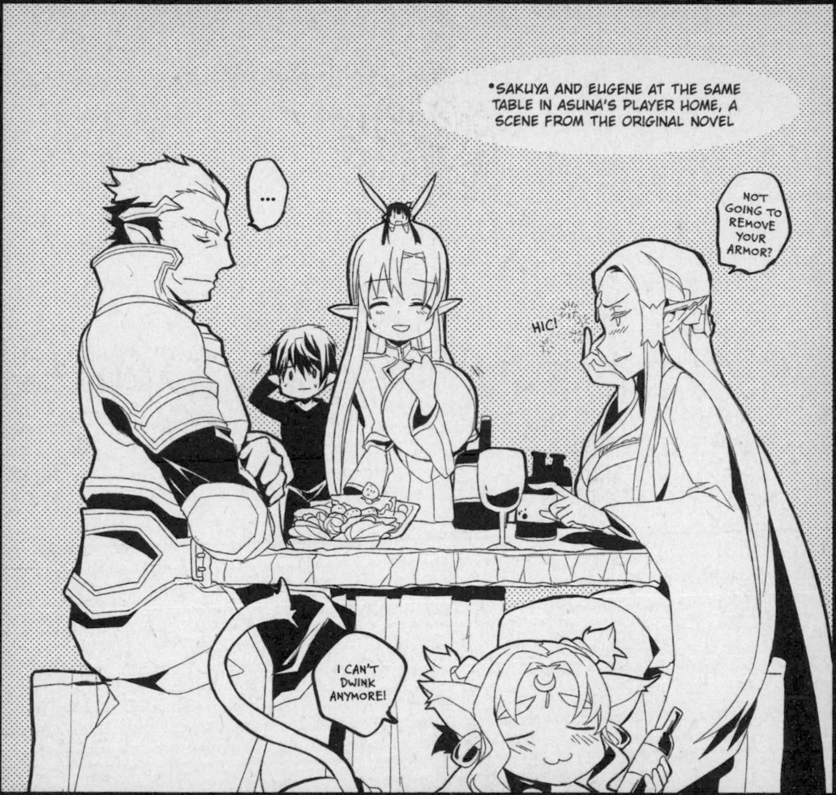
*SAKUYA AND EUGENE AT THE SAME TABLE IN ASUNA'S PLAYER HOME, A SCENE FROM THE ORIGINAL NOVEL
NOT GOING TO REMOVE YOUR ARMOR?
HIC!
...
I CAN'T DWINK ANYMORE!

SPECIAL THANKS

RIONA
CORAL

MITSUHIRO ONODA
SAORI MIYAMOTO
TAKASHI SAKAI
EMIRI NIHEI
NICOE

REKI KAWAHARA
ABEC

KAZUMA MIKI
TOMOYUKI TSUCHIYA

THE STAFF OF THE SWORD ART ONLINE ANIME SERIES

SWORD ART ONLI

ART: TSUBASA HADUKI
ORIGINAL STORY: REKI KAWAHARA
CHARACTER DESIGN: abec

Translation: Stephen Paul
Lettering: Katie Blakeslee & Lys Blakeslee

SWORD ART ONLINE: MOTHER'S ROSARY, Vol. 1
© REKI KAWAHARA/TSUBASA HADUKI 2014
All rights reserved.
Edited by ASCII MEDIA WORKS
First published in Japan in 2014 by KADOKAWA CORPORATION, Tokyo.
English translation rights arranged with KADOKAWA CORPORATION, Tokyo, through Tuttle-Mori Agency, Inc., Tokyo.

English translation © 2016 by Hachette Book Group, Inc.

Yen Press
Hachette Book Group
1290 Avenue of the Americas, New York, NY 10104

www.HachetteBookGroup.com
www.YenPress.com

Yen Press is an imprint of Hachette Book Group, Inc. The Yen Press name and logo are trademarks of Hachette Book Group, Inc.

The publisher is not responsible for websites (or their content) that are not owned by the publisher.

Library of Congress Control Number: 2015956858

First Yen Press Edition: March 2016

ISBN: 978-0-316-27033-5

10 9 8 7 6 5 4 3 2 1

BVG

Printed in the United States of America